D0835803

THE EXPRESS TRAIN *and other* RAILWAY STUDIES

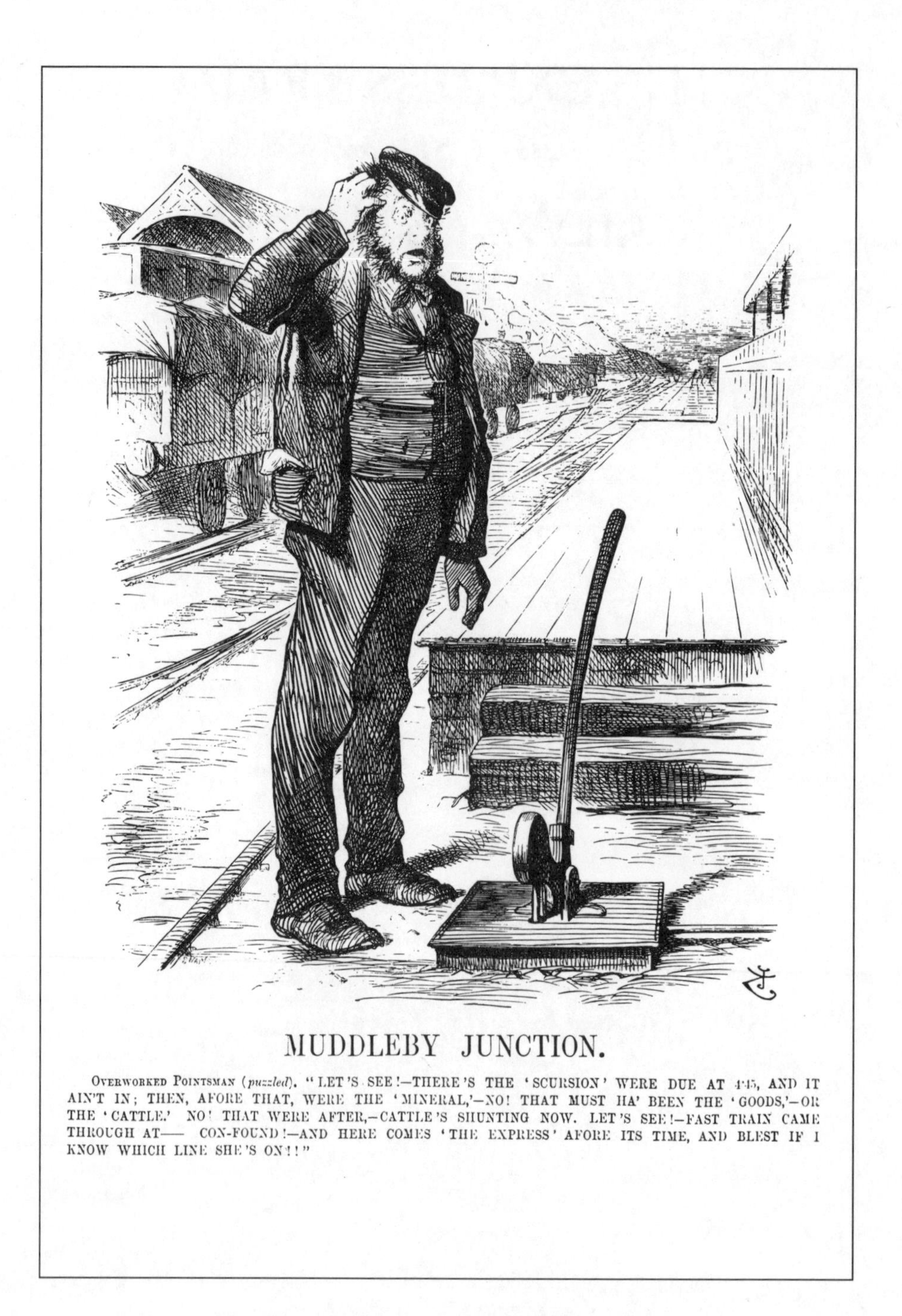

MUDDLEBY JUNCTION.

OVERWORKED POINTSMAN (*puzzled*). "LET'S SEE!—THERE'S THE 'SCURSION' WERE DUE AT 4·45, AND IT AIN'T IN; THEN, AFORE THAT, WERE THE 'MINERAL,'—NO! THAT MUST HA' BEEN THE 'GOODS,'—OR THE 'CATTLE.' NO! THAT WERE AFTER,—CATTLE'S SHUNTING NOW. LET'S SEE!—FAST TRAIN CAME THROUGH AT—— CON-FOUND!—AND HERE COMES 'THE EXPRESS' AFORE ITS TIME, AND BLEST IF I KNOW WHICH LINE SHE'S ON!!"

Tenniel: *Punch*, vol. 63 (1872) p.161. See p145

CONTENTS

TABLES

ABBREVIATIONS USED IN THE NOTES

Acc.	Accident Report.
BE	Sir N. Pevsner and others, *The Buildings of England* (45 vols., 1951–74).
BL	British Library.
Boase	F. Boase, *Modern English Biography* (1965 ed.).
Dow GC	G. Dow, *Great Central* (1959–65).
GR	H. Parris, *Government and the Railways* (1965).
ICE	Institution of Civil Engineers.
JTH	*Journal of Transport History.*
LPA	Local and Personal Acts.
MacDermot	E.T. MacDermot, *History of the Great Western Railway* (1964 ed.).
OED	*Oxford English Dictionary.*
Ottley	G. Ottley, *Bibliography of British Railway History* (1966, with Supplement, 1988).
PGA	Public General Acts.
PL	Public Library.
PP	Parliamentary Papers. Pagination as in BL set.
PRO	Public Record Office, London (Kew).
R	The group "Rail" at the PRO (Kew).
Reg. Hist.	*Regional History of the Railways of Great Britain*, ed. D. Thomas and others (1960–89).
REW	J. Simmons, *The Railway in England and Wales* 1830–1914 (1978).
RM	*Railway Magazine.*
RO	Record Office.
RTC	J. Simmons, *The Railway in Town and Country* (1986).
SRO	Scottish Record Office, Edinburgh.
Tomlinson	W.W. Tomlinson, *North Eastern Railway* (1915).
VCH	*Victoria History of the Counties of England.*
VRY	J. Simmons, *The Victorian Railway* (1991).
Wrottesley GNR	J. Wrottesley, *The Great Northern Railway* (1979–81).

PREFACE

The papers printed here fall into four groups. The first of them is concerned with various types of railway services.

Horse traction was more important on British railways, and survived much longer, than many people suppose. No 1 among these studies begins by looking at an argument of 1821 in which the relative merits of horse and mechanical traction are set out, with the victory going to the horse; and it then offers a brief general survey of the use made of horses for handling trains in Britain thereafter, down to our own time.

No 2 deals with the birth and youth of the express train, developed earlier in Britain, and at first more thoroughly, than it was anywhere else in Europe.

The third study is not concerned exclusively with railways, with what they did in and for itself. It looks at the development of their hotels – which became one of the most important of their numerous ancillary services – in the context of the broad development of hotels in Britain throughout the Victorian age, when they grew from the rambling inns that had been used by the coaches into the big and complicated structures that dominated the industry in London and in most of the large provincial cities by 1914. In that growth the railways played a most important part, providing capital, bringing in guests and taking them away on a scale never imagined before. There is a prime example of the ways in which the railway companies' pursuit of their own business came also to promote the comfort and convenience of the communities they served.

The second set of these studies concentrates on the railways' part in the life of a single county, a small provincial town, and an important group of suburbs.

The county treated in No 4 is Cornwall, the last in England to be connected to the main railway system. It was more strongly individual, one might almost say separate, than any of the other 39, and when at last the link was forged, by the bridging of the Tamar at Saltash, that produced some consequences, for Cornwall and for England, attributable in the later Victorian age to railways alone.

The town of Rugby (No 5) was well established in a quiet way before railways reached it, and it then developed to become an important centre of their business, with lines from nine directions converging on it and a considerable industry for the production and maintenance of railway equipment. All this activity reached its climax, in scale and prosperity, just before the first World War. It then entered on a gradual decline, accelerated in the 1950s and 1960s, when the last of the railway industries departed, and the convergent lines were reduced to three. But the town itself did not decline. It managed to turn to other ways of living instead.

The sixth study is concerned with London suburban business, deliberately fostered by the Great Northern company from the 1860s onwards in order to increase its revenue from passengers, without any careful, realistic reckoning of the consequences that that would entail in the handling of its traffic in passengers and goods as a whole. The difficulties that this policy produced were not resolved, as a result of administrative changes and a full adoption of electric traction, until the 1970s. A railway company is to be seen here exercising its power with a narrow-minded greed, bequeathing the troubles it had stored up to its successors.

The next four studies centre upon the lives and work of individual men. The first (No 7) is of a civil engineer and contractor, first employed on the London & Birmingham Railway under Robert Stephenson, then working with Rastrick and Brunel, and finally launching out on his own account into the construction of railways in southern Italy, to meet there with financial disaster and grave – almost fatal – illness; returning home, prematurely aged, to settle down for the rest of his life as a journalist and to write a book about railways that still has some life in it and thoroughly deserves to be read.

No 8 is based on a diary kept by an Early Victorian fireman, later an engine-driver, on the London & North Western Railway. This is a document of a most uncommon kind. We have very few day-by-day accounts of railway work, written up at the time, and those that survive were almost all written by men who were at the top of their profession, or on the way there. A working man speaks to us here in his own words.

A general manager of the North Eastern Railway comes before us in the next study (No 9). He cannot be said to 'speak to us' at all – except very briefly on one disastrous occasion – for his work was carried on very quietly and in the end, after sixteen years in office, he came to be dismissed in a total silence that seems never to have been broken until now. The immediate occasion of his removal was plainly a series of highly critical reports on four accidents occurring in rapid succession, all of them revealing gross misconduct of the North Eastern's traffic, for which he was ultimately responsible. The inspecting officer who commented on them so incisively figures again in the last study in this book.

No 10 is a study of an artist, well remembered today, though not in connection with railways: John Tenniel, the illustrator of *Alice in Wonderland* and *Through the Looking-Glass*. He worked for 50 years on the staff of *Punch*, and he depicted there with a fierce gusto the crimes, negligence, and follies of railway companies (never, I think, their successes or their good deeds) in a long series of drawings published in the paper between 1852 and 1897.

The last section of the book deals with some of the evidence for our knowledge of railways. No 11 treats their prospectuses, which set out what they meant or hoped to do before their lines were built. These ought to be assigned a place among their founding documents. But they have been dismissed too readily as mere irresponsible babbling, like curtain-raisers designed just to amuse the audience settling down in their seats before the play begins. So much so that no copies of the prospectuses of some companies can now be found. I have indicated what I think may be the value of these papers to students now, and offered some guidance in the business of finding them.

The next pair of papers in this group (Nos 12 and 13) is concerned with timetables, the statements made by the companies of the services they intended to run. The main collection of these until 1961 is to be found in Bradshaw's *Railway Guide* – the most widely famous of all such publications – which was issued monthly for 120 years, assembling the information supplied by all the railway administrations in the British Isles, coming to it in the form of advance proof-sheets of the timetables that each of them put on sale to the public. Bradshaw himself and his *Guide* have been studied several times before, in essays and books, with profit. But I have been looking, at some points, for different things from my predecessors, and I have extended my study with the aim of showing how valuable the *Guide* can be to anyone concerned with British history, whether national or local. I have also paid a little more attention to some elements in the book (the advertisements in it, for instance) than has previously been accorded to them.

Bradshaw's *Guide* was put on sale everywhere, by newsagents and on station bookstalls. But the companies produced timetables of another sort: 'working' or 'service' timetables, which were for the use of their servants only. They were complemented by other printed booklets (sometimes substantial books) issued in the same way, which laid down the general conditions of working the traffic and listed all special arrangements, of additional and cancelled services for example, as they came to be called for. The whole of this literature is of great importance, for it sets out the traffic of each company's system at its fullest extent, of all kinds from mailbags and milk to minerals and men (whilst Bradshaw's *Guide* dealt with passenger services alone) as well as the movements of empty rolling-stock and light engines that were required if all this diverse traffic was to be handled punctually and economically. These timetables are not easy to use or to understand. I hope that what I have written here may assist some people to find their way into and through them, until they come to perceive their historical value.

The last study is of the reports on accidents made by the inspecting officers of the Board of Trade. They have been examined in detail, and sometimes very well, by those who have sought for the causes of the accidents to which they relate; that is, as documents in the history of technology and of its application. But they have much to tell us about other things too: about the lives and work of the men who were involved in accidents, recorded now and then directly in their own words, some of them extraordinarily vivid; about the managements of the companies, the services they expected from their employees and the discipline their rules were intended to impose; here and there about public opinion, the verdicts it passed on the railways' wrongdoing; and constantly about the inspectors themselves. They are more than a chronicle of misdeeds and malpractice, however. They show us care and devotion to duty, not infrequently something of heroism. They deserve I think more recognition than has yet been given to them as a well-informed commentary on the working of railways – in the amplest sense of that phrase.

Most of the studies here relate wholly or primarily to the Victorian age, when the railways were at the height of their power. But some of them continue well into the twentieth century, and come down to our time. Nos 1, 5, 6, and 15 all take at least a look into what followed after 1914.

Seven of these papers have been published before, and they are reproduced here in a revised and extended form. For permission to reprint them I am obliged to the Victorian Studies Centre of the University of Leicester (No 3), the Royal Institution of Cornwall (No 4), the Dugdale Society and the Oxford University Press (No 5), Thomas Telford Ltd (No 7), and the editors of the *Journal of Transport History* (Nos 1 and 5) and *Back Track* (No 8). The other seven studies are printed in this book for the first time.

1
THE HORSE *and the* LOCOMOTIVE

The history of railways has always accorded the greatest prominence to the triumph of the locomotive. Those who put their faith instead in the horse or the stationary steam engine are apt to look ignorant to us now, or obtuse, or both. But in the 1820s the superiority of the locomotive was still open to question. It was not really demonstrated beyond dispute until 1830, when the machine showed what it could do in normal service on the Canterbury & Whitstable and Liverpool & Manchester Railways. And even then there remained some types of service for which the locomotive was not suited, where the horse had the added recommendation that it was cheaper, both in first cost and in maintenance.

This study begins by looking at a debate between the supporters of the horse and the locomotive when a new railway was being planned in 1821–2. The opposed arguments are retailed in the protagonists' own words. It then considers the wisdom of the railway company's decision to prefer, in its own particular circumstances, the horse; and it concludes with a brief survey of the continuing use of horse traction, in many kinds of traffic, even when steam power was firmly established on railways, throughout the nineteenth century and well into the twentieth.

I

The Stratford & Moreton Railway was opened on 5 September 1826, threw out a branch to Shipston-on-Stour ten years later, and was absorbed in 1847 by the Oxford Worcester & Wolverhampton company.[1] During all those years it made no use of mechanical haulage of any kind. That was not because its management and shareholders were unaware of the merits of the steam locomotive. On the contrary, the line had owed its origin to William James, one of that machine's most ardent propagandists, and he was anxious that the new form of traction should be used on it from the start. His case is stated in a report he presented to the shareholders, preserved in the minute-book of their meetings; and by good fortune a second report has survived in another place, setting out the arguments against the locomotive – in this instance, the arguments that prevailed.

William James (1771–1837) is a well-known melancholy figure in early railway history. He was a vigorous and far-sighted projector – the first man to conceive the idea of a railway *system*, covering the whole country and operated by mechanical traction. But he lost a considerable fortune by backing this and other commercial schemes, and he retired to Bodmin to die in poverty, bitterly noting that other people had become rich and famous through developing what he regarded as his own ideas. This is not the place to examine the controversy concerning the relative importance of his work and George Stephenson's,[2] though it is still in need of some further critical analysis. James belonged to a readily recognisable type: an enthusiast and a true originator, but over-sanguine and neglectful in business; a man to inspire others, not an effective practical man himself.

As early as 1808 he had been engaged on a plan for a 'General Railroad Company'. About ten years later he became a large shareholder in the Stratford-upon-Avon Canal, and its deputy-chairman. In 1819–20 he projected a line for a 'Central Junction Railway or Tramroad', running from the canal at Stratford by Moreton-in-the-Marsh, Amersham, and Uxbridge to London, and throwing out branches to Coventry, Cheltenham, and Longcot (on the Wilts & Berks Canal). The first section of this railway, as far as Moreton, was proceeded with at once as a separate concern, and the Stratford & Moreton Railway obtained its powers from Parliament in 1821.[3] The line was apparently laid out in consultation with Telford, though he was never appointed the company's engineer.[4]

From the outset James assumed that locomotives would be used on this railway. The first Act did not refer specifically to them. Section 1 speaks of making 'such roads and ways convenient for hauling or drawing of waggons or other carriages…with men or horses or otherwise'. By section 79 all steam engines used by the railway were required to consume their own smoke; but that provision was applicable to stationary engines just as much as to locomotives. The way was open to the employment of any form of traction, and this naturally caused a good deal of discussion among shareholders, partly on its own account and partly because it affected the design, the material, and the cost of the rails to be ordered for use on the line.

At the first shareholders' meeting, on 13 July 1821, William James presented a report on this subject.[5]

TO THE STRATFORD AND MORETON RAILWAY COMPANY

My Lords and Gentlemen,

Having for the last 25 years given much attention to the subject of railroads and steam engines, I felt it my duty, as Deputy-Chairman of your Managing Committee, to ascertain the recent improvements I had heard of in different parts of the kingdom, that I might provide the Company at their first General Assembly with the necessary information to form a correct determination of the best plan to be adopted, and I have great satisfaction from the result of my observations and inquiries in delivering the following report.

Having seen and considered the railway and forms of rails in Somersetshire, the

Forest of Dean, South Wales, Staffordshire, Shropshire, Lancashire, and Northumberland, and various other counties, I feel bound to state that the patent cast-iron rail of Messrs. Losh and Stevenson [ie George Stephenson] is by far the best *cast-iron* rail I ever saw for strength, compactness, and durability, and by uniting these qualities, for economy and cheapness of construction, which the model delivered to your Engineer will evince. But notwithstanding its excellence I am bound to state that I prefer the malleable to the cast-iron, as a material for the rail, on account of its superior strength, facility and cheapness of construction, security from accidents and the necessity of repairs, and that by welding the pieces together the railway may be laid even for miles together without a joint; the patent malleable iron rail of Mr Burtenshaw [Birkinshaw] manufactured at Bleddington [Bedlington] Ironworks is superior to all I ever saw, and a model of this is delivered to your Engineer. The terms for the use of these respective rails I shall lay before your Managing Committee, for being matters for negotiation I hope I am excused mentioning them in a public assembly.

The employment of locomotive engines on this railway is a subject of vital importance as it respects the prospect of profit to the Company, and of benefit to the public. Of the powers of the Company to permit the use of engines on the railway I have no doubt whatever on the subject, indeed it might with great plausibility be contended that no other mode of draft was ever contemplated. On this subject I confess I kept a steady view during the progress of the Bill through Parliament, and my sentiments upon the excellence of communications by railroad worked by steam engines have been long known to many gentlemen present, as well as my principal plan, conceived and in some degree acted upon above twelve years ago, of a line of communication from Birmingham to the south coast of England, of which this forms the first stage, by railroad. This line of communication, now under consideration, may, with some deviations and expedients perfectly practicable be adapted to the engine with great advantage; of course the capital for the engine trade will not be borne by this Company, but I have authority to say that another company will be found willing to make proposals for a lease of the tolls and powers of this Company, with a view to the employment of locomotive engines thereon.

Under these considerations I am superinduced strongly to advise the Company to adopt the most improved form of rail, for fortunately that rail is equally adapted for draft by steam engines as well as by horses; being confident that when the operation of the mind is not arrested by the novelty of the proposition, the prudence and practicability of steam engine power will be universally admitted. I believe I viewed all the kinds of locomotive engines now in use, but the most perfect one in all its properties is the invention of Mr George Stephenson, and is now in full action in the North of England; a drawing of which I present to the Company's observation. This engine can be delivered *perfect* at Stratford for £440. I beg to state that it will draw on a level railroad 80 tons. On an ascent of ⅛ inch in a yard from 30 to 40 tons. That by the aid of the tugging chain it will work itself up steeper ascents, and going into a fixed frame it will by the aid of the chain draw the carriages its load after it. That in common work it will move 50 miles per day. That when fully employed it will work at less than ¼ the expense of horses; that when it has no work it incurs no expense; that the great objection to railroads, the trespass and plunderings of the people and horses, is by the use of engines prevented; that less expense in the first instance is sustained in forming the earth work, and that the future expense of gravelling and stoning the foot tract is afterwards unnecessary. Upon the whole it may be stated, as a general principle not to be controverted, that the moving articles on railroads by steam engines can be done cheaper, more certain, and twice as expeditiously as by boats on navigable canals, and neither the repairs of locks and banks, the want of water, the summer's heat or the winter's frost, will retard the operation.

I cannot therefore too strongly recommend the Company to adopt that plan of railroad which will enable them to have the full benefit of this great improvement in inland communications, when I shall calculate upon seeing this work a most productive concern to the subscribers and the forerunner of a measure that will produce the greatest advantages to the agricultural, commercial, and mineral interests of the country.

William James

The shareholders referred this report to the committee of management for further consideration. This was a body of eight, including William James himself, presided over by Lord Redesdale (the chairman of the company, who lived at Batsford Park, near Moreton-in-the-Marsh). The committee was evidently not convinced by William James's arguments, for on 4 December it requested two of its members, John Greaves and Thomas Brewin, to visit the north of England and inspect the locomotives in use there 'with the assistance of an able engineer conversant in such business' and to ascertain what advantages, if any, there would be in using wrought instead of cast-iron rails.

It does not seem that Brewin in fact went on this mission; nor do we know what 'able engineer' gave his advice. But Greaves did go, and produced a report on 28 February 1822, which is now at Warwick.[11] Greaves was not an engineer himself. He carried on business at Stratford as a corn, coal, stone, slate, and timber merchant and general carrier and wharfinger. His business premises were on the wharf.[12] He himself lived at Barford, three miles south of Warwick. He held eight £50 shares in the company (reduced to five in 1825), advanced it money, and took an active part in its management until 1829.[13] He was related to William James, and evidently on good terms with him; but his conclusions went clean contrary to James's. His report runs as follows:

In pursuance of the orders of the Committee, I have viewed those railroads in Yorkshire, Durham and Northumberland which are considered to be on the best construction; and I have seen all the locomotive engines which are now at work, and all the various modes of conveying waggons on railroads. I have been introduced to some of the most eminent engineers and proprietors of railroads, who have in the most candid and liberal manner given me their opinion and advice. From these sources of information, aided by the portion of mechanical knowledge I possess, I am enabled to confidently to recommend that the railroad from *Stratford-on-Avon* to *Moreton-in-Marsh* and *Shipston* be constructed on a plan calculated for the use of horses generally, and that the line be formed as *nearly horizontally* as possible, for it is found by extensive experience that a horse of about £15 value, on a well-constructed road, will do the following work, daily, viz.

On a level road he will move fifteen tons twelve miles, and return the same distance with the empty carriages.

On a road rising one-sixteenth of an inch in a yard, he will move eleven tons five cwt. the same distance and return with the empty carriages.

On a road rising three-sixteenths of an inch in a yard he will move seven tons ten cwt. the same distance and return with the empty carriages.

On a road rising half an inch in a yard he will move only three tons fifteen cwt. the same distance and return as above.

Hence it appears how very desirable it is to have the road level, and where an ascent is unavoidable I recommend that an inclined plane be constructed on the summit of which a fixed steam engine be erected to draw up the loads; which will be assisted by the loads which may at the same time be passing in a contrary direction, that is to say the *descending loads* will assist the engine in drawing up the *ascending loads* so that an engine of small power will be sufficient for the trade on this railroad, notwithstanding which I recommend that one of ample power be constructed, for I conceive whatever power we may have to spare may be readily set to drive a corn or other mill, as the situation will be excellent.

Although the patent *malleable*-iron rails of Burtenshaw and Co. are cheapest in the first instance, it is the opinion of some experienced engineers and proprietors of railroads that *cast-iron rails* are upon the whole to be preferred; certainly they are not so liable to oxidate, and are on that account more durable.

If the Committee determine upon having cast-iron rails I recommend that they be four feet long, three inches deep at each end, 4¾ inches deep in the middle, three inches wide at the face, to weigh 36lbs and the chair 3½lbs. This rail and chair is calculated for waggons conveying two tons: which is found to be the most convenient weight on railroads where a general trade is carried on.

If it be asked why I object to the application of *locomotive steam engines* to this line of railroad, my answer is – In the first place, on account of the extraordinary weight of the engines, the rails on which they are used must be twice the weight of those on which animal power alone is used and all the bridges and other works must be proportionally strong; insomuch that so great a capital may be expended in the construction of the works as will render the concern unproductive of interest. Moreover on account of the extraordinary fixture [ie pressure?] of the wheels upon the rails, the latter are continually liable to be displaced, so that the labour of one man is found to be insufficient to keep the rails upon one mile of road in proper place.

In the second place the locomotive engines of Stephenson, which are considered to be upon the best principles, will not ascend a greater acclivity than ½ of an *inch* in a yard, with a load: and I presume our road will not be constructed throughout the whole extent of the line without in some case increasing the angle of ascent beyond that limit.

Thirdly, as it depends on the resistance offered by the iron rails to the surface of the wheels, for the application of power to the purpose of locomotion, it is necessary to create as much friction as possible at the contaction[15] of the wheels with the plates, consequently the friction thus occasioned, together with the movements of the engine itself, and the intendant [ie attendant?] carriage with coals and water for its supply, causes an extravagant waste of power, so that it may be justly questioned (when we bring into the account all the expenses) whether a saving will be gained compared with horse-labour.

Fourthly, the locomotive engines will not move with a load when there is snow upon the rails or in very wet weather.

Fifthly, the appearance of the engine, when in motion, is so strange that it will frighten all the animals in the fields through which it may pass,[16] and will be an insufferable nuisance upon a turnpike road, in confirmation of which I have to state that they are not allowed to cross the Edinburgh road near which they are used.[17]

And lastly, they are constantly liable to explode, as are all *high-pressure* engines. And there is no mode yet invented of constructing locomotive engines upon the *low-pressure* principle. This objection alone, I submit to the Committee, should make us hesitate before we use engines by which so many lives have been lost. And I trust this objection, combined with the others which I have stated (and for the justice of which I am prepared to advance proof if required) will induce the Committee to abandon, for the present, the locomotive engine plan, and construct a railroad upon the plan I have proposed, with as much economy as possible consistently with substantiality, and if, in the progress of science, the locomotive steam engines should be rendered cheap, certain and safe modes of conveyance, the line proposed will be the most convenient for their adoption.

John Greaves

Barford 28th Feby 1822

PS. It may be proper to notice in this report that a patent was obtained on the 14th Decr. last for a method of facilitating the conveyance of carriages along railroads by Mr. Benjn. Thomson [Thompson] of Ayton Colliery.[18] It consists of a number of engines, fixed upon a railroad of [ie at] convenient distances, and the loads are conveyed by the engines from one station to the other by a rope. The railroad whereon I have seen this principle applied is at Ayton in the County of Durham. The road is 7¼ miles long, the engines are some of them one mile, others more than 1/2 mile apart and their action, in the words of the patentee, is reciprocal and interchangeable. This is an ingenious mode of moving waggons and may at any future time be applied to the railway herein recommended. There is also another patent lately enrolled by Mr. Palmer, for a very ingenious railroad and carriage,[19] a working model of which I have seen and it has great merit.

Greaves's report does not seem to have been formally considered either by the committee of management or by the shareholders. But his rejection of the locomotive was evidently endorsed, and on 12 April 1822 it was resolved that no further contracts for the completion of the railway should be entered into until estimates had been received from Mr H.R. Palmer, 'who has invented and obtained a patent for a new form of railroad, strongly recommended by Mr Telford'.[20] Nothing came of this, and the problem was then referred to yet another engineer, J.U. Rastrick of Stourbridge. On 17 September 1822 he reported in favour of wrought-iron rails; and on the question of motive-power he sided with Greaves, on the ground that the levels of the line as planned, under parliamentary sanction, were not suitable for locomotives 'as hitherto constructed'. At the same time he added that the idea should not be given up altogether, in case the locomotive should be so much improved in the future as to make it powerful enough to work over the railway's gradients. This report was accepted by the shareholders; and a year later, on 20 September 1823, Rastrick was appointed the company's engineer.[21] Some of the calculations and sketches he made during his work on the Stratford & Moreton Railway are now in the Goldsmiths' Library of the University of London.[22]

Under Rastrick's direction the railway was laid out for horse-traction only. In 1825 the company obtained a second Act of Parliament,[23] clause 13 of which laid it down that, because the railway passed for six miles parallel and close to the Stratford–Oxford turnpike road, crossing it twice, 'no locomotive or other engine to be worked by the power of steam or by any other power than that of horse or other cattle' should be used along this section of the line. No locomotive was, in fact, ever used on any part of the original tramroad. But the Great Western Railway rebuilt the section from Moreton-in-the-Marsh to Shipston-on-Stour and operated that by locomotives from 1889 onwards.

By the time the line was opened, the company had severed its connection with James. On 12 April 1826 it agreed to pay him £200 (in lieu of £163 11s 10d, which it owed him). The minute-book adds these words: 'The Company, in parting with Mr James, have done so in compliance with the wishes of some of the proprietors and not from any disapprobation of his conduct'.[24]

2

The general superiority of the locomotive over the horse as a motive-power on railways quickly became obvious and unquestionable. But it was not axiomatic, a rule of universal validity; and in the particular instance discussed here the supporters of the horse were surely in the right. James saw the railway as a single small unit in a much larger scheme; and if a main line of communication had been formed by the route he proposed, it would have been as appropriate to use locomotives on the Stratford & Moreton as on the London & Birmingham Railway that was actually under construction less than ten years later. But Greaves and the other shareholders were concerned with their own little company and no more; and as soon as work on it began to be seriously contemplated its financial weakness was exposed. The Stratford Canal was itself no more than a very modest success. Could any substantial return be expected from a railway linking an unprosperous canal with a little town like Moreton, whose population was only 1000? The prudent course was clearly to build the line as cheaply as possible. Moreover, it must be remembered that in 1821–2 the locomotive was still only spasmodically efficient, an unreliable and often dangerous machine. Greaves and Rastrick were rightly cautious, chary of committing the company to an innovation so new and comparatively untried. But both, at the same time, were looking forward to the steady improvement of the locomotive, which would in the future give it the victory over all its rivals. To that victory Rastrick himself made a most substantial contribution. He was an able, intelligent engineer, whose work has never received the full measure of attention it deserves.

Something else needs to be considered here too. We think of George Stephenson as the apostle of the locomotive in its earlier days, and that indeed he was: tirelessly pressing the promoters of the Stockton & Darlington and the Liverpool & Manchester Railways to employ it, as well as many others who sought his advice and assistance. But he was prepared not merely to accept the continuance of horse traction when it was already established, on some short lines up and down the country, but to advocate its adoption on two of the new railways for which he himself became engineer. While the Canterbury & Whitstable Railway (authorised in 1825) was under construction he constantly stated his opinion that it would be worked best by means of horses and gravity. In this case it was the directors of the company who determined, contrary to their distinguished engineer's advice, to employ the power of steam on their railway: locomotives on the more level sections of their line, stationary engines on the long, steep inclines.[25] Again, on the Whitby & Pickering Railway George Stephenson was quite content with horse power. He laid out the line with that arrangement in view, so being able to make its bridges and their works lighter and cheaper than they would have been if they had been designed to carry locomotives; and he agreed that the two steeply-graded sections should be worked not by steam at all but as self-acting inclines. The line was opened in 1835–6 and operated in this way until, after some alterations, locomotives took over in 1847.[26]

3

The use of horses on railways, here and there over long distances, did not cease to be advocated long after the Stockton & Darlington line was opened in 1825. The

Newcastle & Carlisle, 60 miles in length, was intended at first to be worked entirely by horses, and the original Act authorising it in 1829 forbade it to employ locomotives. When the first section of the railway came to be opened in 1835 – the locomotive being by then well established on a number of lines in Lancashire, north-east England, and Scotland – the company decided to ignore that prohibition, and it had brief but serious trouble with one landowner in consequence.[27]

Traction was sometimes mixed. The Stockton & Darlington company at first allowed horses to be used by contractors in working passenger coaches along it, while providing for the haulage of freight trains by its own locomotives; but in 1833 it took the passenger business into its own hands, supplying locomotives for that service too. The operation of passenger and freight trains hauled by horses and by locomotives, on the same pair of tracks, had given rise to obvious difficulties and dangers.[28] It seems nevertheless that a similar mixture of traction was intended to be used on the Leeds & Selby Railway, though in fact that line was worked entirely by locomotives from its opening in 1834.[29] A plan of mixed traction of a quite different sort was put forward by Henry Fairbairn in 1840, when he urged the London & Southampton company to work its passenger trains by means of locomotives in the day-time and its slower freight traffic by horses at night.[30] This proposal was rejected without any serious discussion.

In two branches of the railways' service their employment of horses grew steadily greater during the nineteenth century: for shunting in goods yards, under carefully-framed regulations,[31] and for cartage (here and there for the hauling of their own passenger omnibuses also) through town streets to and from their stations. It was not until after 1900 that the railways' reliance on horses began to be reduced, by their adoption of motorised vehicles. But the eleven largest English companies still had nearly 26,000 horses in their service in 1914, about a quarter of them employed by the London & North Western Railway alone.[32]

However, the British railways continued to use horses a good deal for traction on branch lines; stretches of railway that were similar in essentials to the Stratford & Moreton of the 1820s. For a shorter or longer time, horse-drawn services ran, for instance, on the branches to Brampton and Port Carlisle (Cumberland),[33] Hampton Court,[34] Heywood (Lancashire),[35] Ilkeston,[36] North Greenwich,[37] Tewkesbury,[38] and Weston-super-Mare[39] – not to mention tiny lines to some obscurer places like Errol in Scotland.[40] The branch from St Ives to Huntingdon, which did very little business on its opening with locomotive traction in 1847, was closed two years later, and then re-opened with a horse-drawn passenger service. But that also failed, and from 1852 to 1866 the line became little more than a long siding.[41] The North British Railway at first worked its North Berwick branch (opened in 1850) with locomotives and then, finding the winter traffic very light, turned it over to horses in 1856. That gave rise to a curious legal action, brought unsuccessfully against it by a disgruntled resident of North Berwick.[42]

So horses might be called in to provide a cheaper service than locomotives on a branch line when its prospects did not come up to expectation. But their employment still had its advocates for some time longer, not merely as a remedy for failure but more positively, on new lines to be laid out specially for them: ie with track, earthworks, and bridges much lighter than those required to sustain the weight of locomotives. A pamphlet was published in 1860 to urge the construction of such lines; and the interest it aroused was great enough to call for a second, enlarged edition later in the same year.[43]

That was, however, a flash in the pan. In the later Victorian age services operated by horses grew very uncommon in Britain, outside shunting yards. Mixed traction was adopted again for two periods (1880–5 and 1892–6) in the always curious history of the Swansea & Mumbles Railway.[44] By 1900 only two regular horse-drawn passenger services survived on railways in Great Britain: to Port Carlisle, until that line was closed to passenger traffic in 1914,[45] and to Inchture in Perthshire (withdrawn at the end of 1916).[46] There still remained at least three to be found in Ireland. One of them, at Fintona on the Great Northern Railway in County Tyrone, continued to make its 3/4-mile journey until 1957. This 'tranquil and adequate arrangement' then represented an extraordinary survival;[47] and after it came to an end there seem still to have been two others left, worked in the same way, in County Cork and County Derry.[48] It is hardly less surprising to find that one line worked entirely by horses, running into quarries at Nantlle in North Wales (though carrying slate traffic only, no passengers), survived to be taken over by the British Transport Commission in 1948, after the railways had been nationalised.[49] Some 9,000 horses had been among the assets that the Commission acquired from the four main-line companies.[50] Even then horses were still engaged in shunting in the goods yards at country stations, and their work continued. Such yards themselves were however being closed down by this time, and in 1967 *The Times* thought it worth while to publish a photograph of one of a pair of these horses at the moment when they were taken away from the service, not to be replaced. They were said to be the last of their kind.[51] But then they must surely have been selected as horses of uncommon merit: for their shunting had been done at Newmarket.

NOTES

1 MacDermot, i. 274–5; RM 76 (1935) 113–15; C. Hadfield and J. Norris, *Waterways to Stratford* (2nd ed., 1968), 95–7.

2 See E.M.S.P., *The Two James's and the Two Stephensons* (1961 ed., with L.T.C. Rolt's judicious introduction), and C.F.D. Marshall, *History of British Railways down to the year 1830* (1971 ed.), 181–2.

3 LPA, 1 & 2 Geo. IV, cap. 63.

4 Sir A. Gibb, *The Story of Telford* (1935), 239–40.

5 R673/2 (hereafter referred to as 'minute book', 3–6. The report is a copy of the original, though it is signed by James himself.

6 This rail had been patented by Birkinshaw on 23 October 1820: C.E. Lee, *Evolution of Railways* (2nd ed., 1943), 88–9.

7 This may refer to the plan for a 'General Railroad company' of 1808. James was also engaged on plans for a railway from Dulwich to London, a Thames tunnel, and a turnpike road from Warwick to Buckingham at the same time (E.M.S.P., 22–3).

8 Presumably one of the Killingworth engines, a drawing of which is reproduced on the cover of a pamphlet by William James, published in 1823: C.F.D. Marshall, *History of British Locomotives down to…1831* (1953), 112 and fig. 36.

9 William Hedley had envisaged a locomotive of this kind in 1813 (*ibid.*, 90–1), and it is possible that an auxiliary chain was one of the 'improvements' introduced on the Killingworth engine of May 1821, of which we have few particulars (*ibid.*, 115).

10 Minute-book, 8.

11 Warwickshire RO, CR271, Box 3.

12 W. West, *History…and Directory of Warwickshire* (1830), 542.

13 Minute-book, 35, 101.

14 E.M.S.P., 28–9.

15 A very archaic word. The latest use of it recorded by the OED is of 1682.

16 See questions put to George Stephenson on this subject before the House of Commons committee on the Liverpool & Manchester Railway Bill (1825): *Proceedings*, 196–7.

17 This may refer to the railway from Kenton and Coxlodge to Wallsend, which crossed the Edinburgh road at Gosforth. See Marshall, *History of British Locomotives*, 43–7.

18 Patent No 4602, enrolled 14 December 1821.

19 Patent No 4618, enrolled 22 May 1822.

20 On Palmer see M. Robbins, *Points and Signals* (1967), 36–40.

21 Minute-book, 10, 17, 24.

22 MS. 155/1, 3.

23 LPA, 6 Geo. IV, cap. 168.

24 Minute-book, 55.

25 See company's letter-book (in Canterbury Cathedral Library), 48, 58, 59; R.B. Fellows, *History of the Canterbury & Whitstable Railway* (1930), 87–8.

26 Tomlinson, 269–70, 301–3, 484.

27 J.S. Maclean, *Newcastle & Carlisle Railway* (1948), 22–4. The case for horse traction on this line had been strengthened by the long, steep gradients it required.

28 Tomlinson, 385.

29 See E. Parsons, The *Tourist's Companion* (1835), 72–3; Tomlinson, 256.

30 See his *Letter to the Shareholders of the London & Southampton Railway* (1840).

31 See for instance those of the Great Eastern company in the appendix to its working timetable, November 1910; copy in Leicester University Library (AJ 281).

32 Calculation from the companies' annual reports in R1116/150. On the other hand the total

returned by all the five chief Scottish companies was only 1500; the biggest of them, the North British, possessed none. It looks as if most of the cartage business in Scotland was let out on contract.

33 G. Whittle, *Newcastle & Carlisle Railway* (1979), 156–8. The vehicles used on both these lines were called 'dandies' or 'dandy-carts'. For those terms see Tomlinson, 153, 527. The list of railways worked by horses that is given in the present study offers no more than examples; it makes no claim to be complete.

34 A.A. Jackson, *London's Local Railways* (1978), 97. There is a delicious cartoon of a horse-drawn train on this branch in *Punch*, 16 (1845), 87.

35 J. Marshall, *Lancashire & Yorkshire Railway*, i (1969), 55.

36 PP 1854–5, lxviii. 487.

37 This was a precaution adopted in order to avoid the risk of fire from locomotives passing through the West India Dock, at a time when all ships were still built of wood: J. Pudney, *London's Docks* (1975), 94–5.

38 *Tewkesbury Register*, 2 (1850), 29, 157.

39 MacDermot, i. 72; RM 10 (1902), 144, 148.

40 *The Caledonian Railway* (Stephenson Locomotive Society, 1947), 20. This service seems to have been provided only in 1848–50.

41 *Reg. Hist.*, v. 150–1. See also *Passages from the Diary of an Oxford Lady*, ed. M.J. Gifford (1932), 46.

42 See VRY, 326.

43 C. Burn, *On the Construction of Horse Railways for Branch Lines in England and the Colonies*. See Ottley, 2332.

44 C.E. Lee, *Swansea & Mumbles Railway* (1954 ed.), 23, 25.

45 See A. Earnshaw, 'The Port Carlisle Branch': *Back Track*, 3 (1989), 132–7. There is a bulky file of papers, dating chiefly from 1908–9, concerned with the operation of the Port Carlisle branch by horse-drawn power and considering possible alternative forms of working, with drawings of a proposed carriage to replace the primitive dandy-cart, in SRO, BR/NBR/8/1174.

46 For the service this 'Coach' provided (first- and third-class, backwards and forwards seven times a day) in 1890. See SRO, BR/TT(S)/54,17.

47 E.M. Patterson, *Great Northern Railway of Ireland* (1986 ed.), 37, 117, 132.

48 *Journal of the Irish Railway Record Society*, 5 (1958–60) 86–7.

49 *Reg. Hist.*, xi. 100.

50 Reckoning from the companies' annual reports for 1946 in R1116/93.

51 *The Times*, 21 February 1967.

2
THE ORIGINS AND EARLY DEVELOPMENT *of the* EXPRESS TRAIN

I

The word 'express' has a meaning that reaches back far beyond the railway. Express couriers and messengers are heard of in the sixteenth and seventeenth centuries, men sent out on important business 'expressly' for the purpose. The notion represented here gradually grew common in all classes of society: 'an express is immediately dispatched to the washerwoman's' wrote the young Dickens in 1835.[1]

That is the sense in which the phrase 'express train' was first used. Charles Saunders, secretary of the Great Western Railway, spoke of an 'express train' as a special, not forming part of the regular service, in giving evidence before a parliamentary committee in 1840.[2] He did so with no particular emphasis or explanation, clearly assuming that the MPs he was addressing would know what he meant; and the chairman of the committee used the phrase in the same way. 'An express, *and therefore unexpected* train [my italics] was referred to by William Fothergill Cooke in discussing the application of the electric telegraph to railways in 1842.[3] These trains might be somewhat quicker than ordinary ones because they made no intermediate stops, other than those required for watering their engines; but the speeds at which they were appointed to travel were not exceptionally high.

The idea that similar trains might be put on, not as specials to private order but for public use, began to emerge on the London & Brighton Railway in August 1844. At the instigation of Rowland Hill, the postal reformer, who had joined the board of the company in the previous year, the schedule of two of its principal trains was then altered, reducing the number of stops made between London and Brighton to one, for the engine to take up water at the station called Redhill today, and the time allowed for the entire journey of 50¼ miles was reduced to 1hr 40min down (at an average speed of 30.3mph, including the stop) and 1hr 30min up (ie 33.3mph).[4] These trains were simply called 'fast', however, no reference to 'express trains' appears in Bradshaw until the following year.

In November 1844 the Great Western company came before Parliament in support of plans for building lines connecting it with Rugby, Birmingham, and Wolverhampton. The Board of Trade's report on them firmly opposed any such northward extension of the 7ft gauge, taking occasion also to point out that one of the main advantages claimed to arise from the adoption of that gauge, that it would permit the speed of trains to be much increased, had not been realised; and that the fastest Great Western trains running in normal service were slower than some of those that were travelling on the standard gauge. That statement was true. The journey from London to Bristol by the night mail, the fastest train on the line, took 4hr 20min (27.3mph).[5]

The Great Western was stung by this taunt. It had already given a remarkable exhibition of what it could do, when on 1 May 1844 the line was opened as far as Exeter and the return journey of the special train (an 'express' in the traditional sense of the word) was made in 4hr 40min: 194 miles via Bristol, at 41.6mph. The company's locomotive superintendent, Daniel Gooch, having driven that memorable train both ways himself,[6] was quite confident that the performance could be repeated daily, and on his recommendation the directors now took up what they thought was a challenge thrown down before them. They arranged to run a train, as a part of the normal public service, leaving Paddington every weekday from 10 March 1845, to get to Exeter in five hours, including five stops, at 38.8mph. Satisfied with the results of this acceleration, on 12 May they reduced the time to 4½ hours (43.1mph).[7] The term 'express train' now came to find acceptance in Bradshaw. It was applied there to two on the London & South Western, running between London & Southampton, in May, and to the much faster Exeter trains in June.

The Exeter trains put on in May 1845 were the first to realise the full meaning of the phrase 'express trains' that came to be attached to it later: trains running at high speed over a great distance, and so producing a really significant reduction in the time spent on the journey. Gooch said so in his memoirs: 'This...was the beginning of that important system of express trains which has given so much comfort and accommodation to the public. I may therefore, I think, claim to be the father of express trains'.[8] Those words seem to have been written in 1867, though they were not published until 1892, after Gooch's death. Meanwhile, in 1879, Eliezer Edwards had asserted that Rowland Hill had 'first set the example of "express trains", running past the smaller stations without stopping'.[9] That statement, as it stood, was incorrect, for all the great main lines had been running some trains well before 1844 that called at the principal stations only.[10] Hill died in the same year, and his autobiography was published soon afterwards, in which he made a similar claim himself, in quite modest and guarded language.[11] On this basis the article on him in the *Dictionary of National Biography*, published in 1891, roundly asserted that 'he had the chief merit of introducing the system of express and excursion trains, which were first run on that [ie the Brighton] line'.[12]

The faster trains that Hill proposed and secured were an important innovation, not least in the advertisement they gave to the idea of the quick train for the City man, allowing him to live at Brighton, 50 miles away from his daily work in London. But the Great Western trains maintained a steady speed 10mph higher, over a journey nearly four times as long. That was the kind of express train that came to be accepted as an ideal, gradually realised elsewhere in Britain and across the world.

There were numerous obstacles to be surmounted on the way however, technical, economic, even legal.[13] Express trains encountered a good deal of resistance from managers, directors, and shareholders, as well as support from the bolder kind of passengers. Hill was startled to hear one such passenger say that the fast Brighton train in which they were both travelling was 'a very slow coach', that 'if they can do it in an hour and a half, they can just as well do it in one hour'.[14] 'They' did not in fact manage that, in regular service, until 1898. The idea caught on at once, but a little hesitantly. Here and there it was tried and dropped after no more than a few weeks, on the ground that the express trains were 'not well supported by the public'.[15] However, by the end of 1845 such trains were being run, according to Bradshaw, by all the chief English railways except the Eastern Counties and the Midland. Within two months of the appearance of the Exeter expresses the London & Birmingham put on one of its own, with connections to Liverpool and Manchester. Early in 1846 it came to be remarked that a determined Liverpool merchant could travel up to London by express train, transact four or five hours' business there, and get home again that night.[16] All the same, the Great Western trains ran much faster than any of these others. To Birmingham the overall speed of the express was no more than 37.5mph, to Manchester 35.1, to Liverpool 33.8; and the up trains from Manchester and Liverpool to London were markedly slower.

Express trains of the earlier kind – that is to say specials, put on by private arrangement – continued to run, in response to a variety of demands. In August 1845, for example, the young James Allport (then manager of the Newcastle & Darlington Junction Railway) arranged for a succession of such trains to take him from Sunderland to London and back again, a total distance of 600 miles (via Normanton and Derby), intending by this means to prove that high speed could be attained over long distances on the standard gauge as well as on the broad.[17] In 1847–8 the second W.H. Smith, intent on the rapid distribution of newspapers, chartered trains to convey them from London to Scotland at the highest possible speed.[18] These were convincing demonstrations of the potentiality of the railway. But it had to be recognised that as long as they were fitted with no more than primitive brakes and were controlled by a very imperfect signalling system, these trains run to special order were dangerous. Even where the traffic was regulated by the electric telegraph the danger was still there, spelt out in detail in the report of the inquiries into the accident at Ponders End on the Eastern Counties Railway, occasioned by the running of a special fast train of this kind to a gentleman's private order in 1851.[19]

Here was the most important objection to expresses of all kinds, special or regular. Their running paths had to be plotted so as to accommodate them to the ordinary traffic, which moved very much more slowly. That was far from easy with primitive signalling, based on intervals of time not distance, before the telegraph had been generally installed; and it was not brought into use for the working of trains, even on some first-class main lines, until the 1860s.[20] In 1850 Dionysius Lardner laid down the doctrine that 'in railway traffic, the entire stream of transport ought to proceed as much as possible with an uniform speed, so that one part should be not liable to overtake another'.[21] That was a sound maxim, and it is closely followed by railways today. But few people paid much attention to it then.

Severe strains were imposed by all expresses, running over long distances at high speeds without stopping: on the men in charge of the trains, on the locomotives and carriages, and on the track. Warnings of danger here were heard as soon as the regular trains went into service, for example from the influential journalist John Herapath.[22] The Prime Minister, Peel, wondered if they ought to be entirely prohibited; but he was wise enough to accept Dalhousie's opinion, that it would be best to wait until their development could be watched.[23] If the timid exaggerated these perils and the bolder railway managers were apt to discount their fears, it soon became plain that there were some good grounds for them. Mark Huish, for example, increased the number of express trains on the London & North Western main lines in 1848, in disregard of the warnings of some of the engineering officers. Though he did not accept that they were dangerous, in the following year he allowed that 'the immoderate damage to both the road and the stock outweighs, in positive loss to the company, the additional fare received'.[24] Samuel Smiles, then secretary of the Leeds & Thirsk Railway, said much the same. He contended that it cost twice as much to run a train at 30mph as at 15mph. Expresses were in his view 'much more dangerous', and they 'did not pay'.[25] Let us examine these assertions, in the light of the experience afforded by the working of the earliest British express trains.

2

Lardner agreed with Smiles on the danger these trains presented, setting out his reasons in language designed to be clear to any layman:

'The speed of express trains is both exceptional and extreme. Inasmuch as it is exceptional, they are likely to overtake the slower and regular trains if these be retarded even in the least degree by any accidental cause; and inasmuch as it is extreme, they are more difficult to be stopped in time to prevent a collision in such a contingency. If a collision occurs, the effects are disastrous, in the direct ratio of the relative speed of the trains, one of which overtakes the other. The momentum of the shock, other things being the same, will be proportional to the excess of the speed of the faster over that of the slower train'.[26]

Now Lardner was, to the very core of his being, a theorist: clever and perceptive in tracing causal connections and deriving principles from them – principles that were sometimes salutary medicine for zealous English pragmatists. Moreover, he adduced a good deal of detailed evidence, in order to prove that they were right. But then he paid almost no attention, in this analysis, to the Great Western Railway, and in 1850 he was just too soon to take account of the practice of the Great Northern. Already by 1852 that company was running an express train that was scheduled to make the journey from King's Cross to Peterborough at 43.6mph.[27] These two companies – though they were not at any point competitive with each other – were the leading pioneers of the express train in Britain.

If we look at the Exeter expresses, we find that only two accidents of any consequence befell them in 1845–52. The first occurred three miles east of Slough on 17 June 1845, when the up train was derailed and six or seven passengers were injured, some severely. The causes were held to be a failure in the track and the inclusion of an unsuitably light four-wheeled brake van at the head of the train, with four heavier six-wheeled carriages behind it. Had the track been of 'Mr Brunel's last pattern', the inspecting officer believed that the derailment would not have occurred at all, or that if it had its consequences would have been less serious.[28] The second accident, at Shrivenham on 10 May 1848, was due not to the high speed of the train but to a mistake in shunting, which placed a cattle truck and horse box in its path, so that it was a mishap that would have occurred in any case, even to a train running at a lower speed.[29] In addition to these accidents a third ought perhaps to be mentioned, at Aynho in 1852, although the train involved in it was not a regular express but a special.[30] So the apprehensions of Smiles and Lardner about the safety of express trains were not borne out in practice by the day-to-day experience of the Great Western company. On the other hand they appeared to be in some measure justified by what happened on the Great Northern, where there were at least six serious accidents to expresses in 1852–9. On other railways they were put to less severe tests, for a general slowing-down of such trains occurred at this time, in which the Great Western and its associated companies also participated.

Some anxiety now became evident about the health of those who travelled frequently by these trains – for instance, of those who commuted on them between Brighton and London.[31] But that, after all, was a matter of choice on their part, and such passengers represented only an insignificant fraction of the total number the railways conveyed. One commentator, trying in 1861 to sum up the advantages and drawbacks of travelling by express trains, stated quite firmly that the companies allocated their best engines and rolling stock to them, under the care of their best crews. That was an important point in their favour, but the writer can hardly have reassured all his readers when he went on to say that 'the extraordinary momentum which is attained enables the train to dash through interposing obstacles without communicating scarcely any shock to the passengers, whereas an ordinary train under the same circumstances would experience a concussion, resulting in all probability in the loss of life and limb'.[32]

Smiles's second assertion was that express trains did not pay the companies running them; and the evidence we have does not seem to allow us either to accept or reject it. When these trains were first introduced, it was said at once that a special charge might reasonably be levied for the convenience they afforded. Very shortly after Rowland Hill's accelerated trains were started on the Brighton line, a writer in the *Quarterly Review* was laying it down that on railways there ought to be 'a relation between fares and velocity – between the *value* received and the *price* paid'. After all, he argued truly enough, that had been the long-established custom on the roads. There the price went up from that charged for travelling by stage waggon (the slowest means), by stage coach, by mail coach, and by the hiring of post-horses (the fastest). 'Time was everywhere the ingredient in measuring the price of locomotion; why should it not be so still?'[33]

That doctrine came to be applied very soon. Supplements were charged for travelling by most of the express trains introduced in the 1840s. Some of the rates at which they were set were, at least for a time, remarkably high, especially in Scotland. On the Edinburgh & Glasgow Railway in 1853 first-class passengers paid 25 percent extra for the journey by express train over the whole distance between the two cities, and 33 percent for travelling in that way from Edinburgh to the intermediate station of Linlithgow.[34] But the Caledonian company was more rapacious still. The additional charge for conveyance in the express train running between Glasgow and Carlisle in the same year was at the outrageous rate of 47.6 percent.[35] On the North Eastern Railway in 1854 these supplements added 17½ percent to the ordinary fares (first or second class) between York and Newcastle.[36]

Although at first such charges do not seem to have encountered opposition, travellers in Britain soon came to object to paying them,[37] and they were almost entirely abolished on the main lines between London and the north from 1859 onwards. The innovator here was apparently the Midland company, anxious to attract business to itself by any means from its rivals the London & North Western and the Great Northern.[38] The British competitive system ensured that if one company determined to remove a special charge like this one, others were virtually forced to do the same over routes by which there was competition. On the services between London and Birmingham, which became competitive between the London & North Western and the Great Western in 1852, express fares soon ceased to be levied by both companies.[39] By 1865 they had been discontinued on all the trunk lines north of the Thames except the Great Eastern (which did away with them in 1870)[40] and on the Irish Mail trains of the London & North Western, as between London and Chester.[41]

Outsiders who watched the railways' business with close attention recognised that the companies were here, for whatever reasons, ceasing to levy a supplement that they had been fully entitled to demand. In 1865 William Galt, a reformer who nearly always favoured a reduction of the charges made to railway passengers, quite accepted the argument in favour of these, on its merits. 'There are scarcely a dozen lines in the Kingdom on which express trains run', he wrote; 'their expenses being great, and the number of passengers for a very high speed being necessarily limited, the fares by these trains must always be high'.[42] He published a table of the fares then being charged by all the different companies throughout the British Isles, which showed that on the eight that still maintained express fares by this time, they were imposed at rates varying between 12 percent and 35 percent.[43] On the lines south of the Thames, where these charges were most in evidence, the railway network was dense, the trains' runs were nearly all short, and their passengers included a growing number of commuters, who wished to use them every day. Here the charging of express fares has to be seen, at least in part, as a managers' expedient for regulating the habits of the travelling public. The British railways follow a very similar practice in our own time, though the devices used for the purpose are different; and instead of being levied as separate supplementary charges, they are now hidden within the gross amount of the ordinary fare.

There were two other ways in which the passengers' use of express trains could be regulated. Holders of third-class tickets might be – and, at first they were – refused access to them; and any or all passengers might be forbidden to make use of them for short journeys. The Midland company abandoned the first of those practices for good in 1872, when it suddenly carried into effect a decision that third-class accommodation should be provided on all its trains, expresses included. Though this example was not widely followed straight away, it inevitably came to influence the policy of all the great trunk railways.[44] By 1887 there were only eleven expresses out of London (apart from boat trains) from which third-class passengers were excluded. Eight of them ran on the London Brighton & South Coast Railway. In 1914 the number was down to two on the Brighton line, and there were none anywhere else in Great Britain.

The policy of denying passengers the use of express trains when they were making comparatively short journeys or travelling to minor stations was never practised widely in Britain, though it made its appearance there in one special form. Some companies would stop one or more of their expresses at particular stations – generally, though not always, at the request of first-class passengers only – on prior notice (see p186). But this was a privilege conferred on the rich, not a device for keeping the loads of express trains down by refusing to admit any large groups of passengers to them.

3

These British trains represented a bold and impressive innovation in the 1840s; and it seems surprising to find that some time elapsed before any large effort was made on the mainland of Europe to adopt the same practice. In France, for instance, though on each of the trunk lines there soon came to be one daily train calling only at the principal stations, on the Nord and Orleans railways this was described as no more than a *train direct*, and no such train could be said, by the standards set in England in 1844–5, to travel fast. On the line from Paris to Le Havre there was a daily *train grande vitesse* (high-speed train), but in 1847 it made no more than 24.9mph to Rouen.[45] It seems that the word *express* was first used in France, with reference to a train, in 1849.[46] By 1850 there was an express on the Nord line between Paris and Amiens, running without any advertised stop in three hours (at 27mph); an *express-poste*, or fast mail train, on the Lyons line as far as Châlon-sur-Sâone: a *direct* on the Orleans line. But there were no other similar trains anywhere else in the country.[47]

For some years Britain stood alone in Europe in running express trains, in the form in which we recognise them today; and even when, by the mid-1850s, trains of that sort had been introduced on the Continent none of them ran in regular service at speeds equal to the British expresses. For that there were several reasons. Except in the Low Countries, the chief centres of population lay at a greater distance from one another than in Britain; and even the principal trains had to stop, for their own safety and convenience, at fairly frequent intervals. More important, on the European mainland there were at this time no services that were competitive between one railway and another and encouraged any significant rivalry in speed: whereas in Britain by 1861 express trains ran in hot competition from London to Dover, Exeter, Birmingham, Manchester, Sheffield, and the principal cities in Scotland, and speed was a leading element in these rival services.

A close and well-informed French observer, the engineer Auguste Perdonnet, saw several ways of accounting for these differences, and ways of compensating for them too. 'If the speed of trains in England is greater than it is in France', he wrote, 'the conditions that govern travelling there differ essentially from ours. Time, from a commercial point of view, is reckoned more valuable there, and paid for accordingly. Competition between the railway companies is very great; perhaps indeed excessive. The same reduction of time can be got by reducing the numbers of stops at stations as by increasing the journey speed. The loss of time caused by stopping is also reduced by increasing the engines' boiler pressure'.[48] As the tone of Perdonnet's remarks here makes plain, in the 1850s and 1860s there was a general disposition in France to accept a service rather slower than the one that a Frenchman discovered when he crossed the Channel – or the Atlantic, to the eastern States of North America.

But above all, in Britain these matters were left in the hands of the companies. It was for them alone to decide what services they would run; whereas in every country on the European mainland the State took an important share in their control and management. Civil servants there kept a watch on the railway companies' timetables. It is in the very nature of bureaucracy – in some matters among its virtues – to play safe; to be cautious in accepting new practices and techniques that are claimed to be improvements, until they have demonstrated that they are at once necessary, workable, and wise. The managers of every railway undertaking, in Britain or elsewhere, were expected to pay careful regard to economy of operation. But in France the government guaranteed the shareholders' dividends, so economy was no less a concern of the civil servants (who were always liable to the scrutiny of the politicians), and their approval was required for every change in the train service. In Britain neither Parliament nor the Board of Trade had any similar powers; and however earnestly some of those responsible for the management of the companies might desire to economise, they were continually driven towards making changes, usually involving additional expenditure, by the force of competition – a force that did not begin to appear clearly anywhere in France or Germany much before 1880 and was never at any time powerful in Belgium. The main purpose that originally lay behind the levying of supplementary charges for travelling by express trains, both in Britain and on the Continent, had been to earn an additional revenue that should contribute substantially to the higher cost of running them. Already by 1848, as we have seen, Huish was declaring that in his experience those charges did not bring in enough to compensate for the expense entailed by the provision of the service. His company, the London & North Western, made no move to raise the charges, considering one may suppose that that would serve merely to diminish the use of the trains. Instead, it ceased to extend the services and for a time slowed them down. But that policy could not be maintained as the competitive system grew stronger. From the 1860s onwards no leading British railway manager argued in favour of the levying of express fares on account of the income they produced. The purpose of those supplementary charges, wherever they continued in force in Britain, was to keep down train loads; to regulate traffic, not to augment revenue.

In most countries on the mainland of Europe the revenue from express fares continued to be taken seriously for itself. The charges were not lightly abandoned. Here the State officials and the railway managers seem to have been, for a long time, at one. In France they were given up at last in favour of a different device that was more elaborate, and for many passengers must have been exceedingly tiresome to understand and to carry in their minds. Most express trains there running by day excluded third-class passengers altogether or admitted them only if they were making certain journeys, over substantial minimum distances; so the great majority of those passengers had to travel by night. Anybody whose business called for haste was therefore compelled to travel second-class, at a considerably higher fare. This produced one important result, never noticed by those who made rather simple-minded comparisons between the fares on British and French railways. In Britain, to a steadily-increasing extent from the 1870s onwards, business men travelled third-class, at the cheapest rates; on long French journeys they were often obliged to go second unless they were prepared to put up with travelling overnight in crowded and very slow trains. From Paris to Rennes, for example, as late as 1901 there were two express trains travelling by day that admitted second-class passengers, running at about 34mph; those travelling third, however, were obliged to go by night, with two trains to choose from, one proceeding at 25mph, the other at 20mph.[49] For many Frenchmen the equivalent of their second-class fare was the British third, which was a good deal lower.

The other leading countries of Europe clung to imposing supplementary charges on travellers by express trains, partly as a regulator of traffic but more, it seems, for the revenue they produced. They were still levied in 1914, at low rates, in Germany and Italy; but on the Austrian railways they remained obstinately high – the highest rate of all (40 percent) being exacted from third-class passengers travelling 1000km, a little further than from London to Inverness.[50]

4

Some of the broader consequences of the British railways' policy in the provision of express trains were already beginning to be observed in the 1880s, and critically analysed. There were those who argued that it had been carried much too far; that the force of competition induced the companies to run more trains than were really called for, many of them, as a result, being lightly loaded; and that they travelled much faster than was necessary. This practice was said to be due to public demand, although very little proof of that assertion was ever adduced. If so, then the public was demanding a service set above the standard of what the railway companies (and therefore of what the country, in the long run) could sensibly afford. This analysis led to gloomy conclusions, not altogether ill founded, about the railways' financial future.[51]

Yet the British express trains also called forth strong admiration – outside the island as well as inside it.[52] The most thoughtful and eloquent praise of them came from Ernest Foxwell, in a pair of short essays published in 1884. Though his language may appear to us today, here and there, a little naively optimistic, his enthusiasm is often suggestive. Here is a man who set out to place express trains in the context of the life of his country, as he had seen it developing before his eyes.[53]

He was mainly concerned to illustrate the stimulus to thinking and to rapid action that express trains had engendered:

'It is the invigoration put into men's energies by the *quick conversion of intention* into *deed* which is the most valuable effect of expresses...

'High speed enables men to do more work and do it better, to come across a wider choice of facts and form surer decisions for dealing with them... Distance becomes possibility...where a coalition is required of distant individuals; because enthusiasm cannot always go by post, but by express it flies like a Promethean spark, to fuse isolated thoughts into an ardent project'.

As he goes on to put it later: 'express speed is – in its social effects – almost equivalent to the acquisition of a new sense'.

But the benefits arising from these trains were not, Foxwell argued, to be seen only in the conduct of business. As soon as they set themselves to carry passengers, railways had begun to weaken the stultifying effects of parochialism. Express trains had carried that process a great deal further. They were 'through-currents of life, which arouse localism from its habit of aloofness and stir up a disposition for contact, for intelligent "society"'.[55]

He regarded these trains also as presenting an example of high perfected achievement ('an express is the death of mediocrity, or mediocrity will be the death of it')[56]

– and at the end of his first essay he let himself go, in a rousing panegyric set off by the Flying Scotsman:

'Those who remember this express at York in the icy winter of 1879–80, when the few travellers who were not thawing themselves at the waiting-room fires used to stamp up and down a sawdusted platform under a darkened roof, while day after day the train came gliding in from Grantham with "couplings" like wool, icicles pendant from the carriage eaves, and an air of punctual unconcern, or those who have known some of our other equally striking trains – these will hardly mind if friendship does let them drift into exaggeration when speaking of expresses. Whoever admired any living thing without describing it in terms a little extreme?'[57]

5

This study takes leave of British express trains in the 1880s when, as contemporary observers were agreed, they stood out clearly ahead of all others, whether in Europe or in America. They had maintained that superiority ever since their first introduction some 40 years earlier. They maintained it still in Europe – not in America – for 40 years more, though to a steadily lessening extent (see p189). In the 1920s and 1930s that supremacy appeared to pass away. But one thing still characterised British express trains, as it had long done, marking them off from their equivalents elsewhere in Europe. All of them – the Cornish Riviera Express, the Irish Mail, the Flying Scotsman – carried third-class passengers. Neither the Blue Train nor the Rheingold nor the Orient Express did that. Anybody who chose could leave King's Cross at 10 o'clock on the Flying Scotsman for Edinburgh, paying the lowest standard fare, without any supplement.[58] In that sense the British express train was still, by comparison with its costly equivalents on the mainland of Europe, a quiet, firm assertion of what may surely be considered a sensible kind of democracy.

NOTES

1 'Early Coaches': *Sketches by Boz* (Oxford Illustrated ed.), 132.

2 PP 1841, viii. 177.

3 See OED, 'Express', a.4.

4 For these trains see traffic committee, 2 and 16 August (R386/21), and the directors' statement to the shareholders (R386/2).

5 MacDermot, i. 113–14, 335, 340.

6 Sir D. Gooch, *Memoirs and Diary*, ed. R.B. Wilson (1972), 44–5. The down run was made by another special train, in only five minutes more, on the following 30 October: J. Keast, *The King of Mid-Cornwall* (1982), 150.

7 MacDermot, i. 340.

8 Gooch, *Memoirs*, 45.

9 E. Edwards, *Sir Rowland Hill* (1879), 98.

10 The first trunk railway in Europe, the Grand Junction, had from its outset run 'first-class trains' calling at only five of the 22 stations between Birmingham and Warrington: *Grand Junction...Railway Companion* (pub. J. Cornish, 1837), 5–6.

11 G.B. Hill, *Life of Sir Rowland Hill* (1879), i. 98.

12 The writer was his nephew, George Birkbeck Hill. This claim was quite unjustified where excursion trains were concerned, for they had been running elsewhere in Britain long before Hill paid any attention to them. See VRY, 272–3.

13 An argument about what constituted an 'express train' came before the Court of Chancery in 1845. The original concession for working the refreshment rooms at Swindon, made by the Great Western company to the firm of J. & C. Rigby, had provided that all trains should stop there 'for refreshment of passengers for a reasonable period of about ten minutes'. When these terms were agreed upon in 1841 no trains like the Exeter expresses had been thought of, and the court (surely with good reason) held that this provision applied to them; the excepted category being only that of privately-chartered expresses, of the original kind. Although the Railway Commissioners thought that a legal definition of 'express trains' was desirable (PP 1847, xxvi. 318), none was ever laid down in Britain. The Great Western company was therefore obliged to stop its expresses at Swindon for ten minutes, along with all other passsenger trains, until 1895, when it bought out the lessees at the high price of £100,000. See MacDermot, i. 75–6, 340; ii. 213.

14 Hill, *Life of Sir Rowland Hill*, ii. 21.

15 See note in Bradshaw's *Guide*, August 1845, 4.

16 T. Baines, *History of Liverpool* (1852), 673.

17 F.S. Williams, *Our Iron Roads* (1888 ed.), 332.

18 C. Wilson, *First with the News* (1985), 96–7.

19 See PP 1852, xlviii. 142.

20 The Great Western decided to work its line between Paddington and Didcot by telegraph in 1865 (acc. Keynsham, 7 June: PP 1865, xl. 204). The telegraph was not yet in use for this purpose on the northern section of the Great Northern main line in 1867 (acc. Tuxford, 23 March; PP 1867, lxii. 211).

21 D. Lardner, *Railway Economy* (1850), 200.

22 He attacked them repeatedly in the seventh volume of his *Railway and Commercial Journal* (1845).

23 SRO, GD45/7/15, No. 30.

24 T.R. Gourvish, *Mark Huish and the London & North Western Railway* (1972), 152.

25 S. Smiles, *Railway Property: its Condition and Prospects* (2nd ed. 1851), 51.

26 Lardner, 339–40.

27 Wrottesley GNR, i. 83.

28 Acc. Great Western, Slough, 17 June 1845: PP 1846, xxxix. 152.

29 Acc. Great Western, Shrivenham, 10 May 1848: PP 1849, xxvii. 381.

30 MacDermot, i. 168–9.

31 See for example *The Influence of Railway Travelling on Public Health* (*The Lancet*, 1862), 53.

32 *The Railway Traveller's Handy Book*, ed. J. Simmons (1972), 42, 44.

33 *Quarterly Review*, 74 (1844) 263.

34 SRO, BR/TT(S)/59/1.

35 SRO, BR/TT(S)/54/64.

36 Tomlinson, 546. Exceptionally, the supplements charged on this railway were regulated by statute. The Act sanctioning the formation of the North Eastern company, by the amalgamation of four separate companies into one, laid it down (LPA 17 & 18 Vict., cap. 211, sect. 36) that the supplements of this kind were not to exceed 1d a mile first-class or ½d a mile second-class. The rates actually charged, however, were a good deal below these maxima.

37 I have come across no important agitation against them, and I do not know of anyone who has tried to account for this British attitude of mind.

38 Gourvish, *Huish*, 199.

39 James Grierson's evidence to the Royal Commission on Railways: PP 1867, xxxviii (1). 649.

40 C.J. Allen, *Great Eastern Railway* (2nd ed., 1956), 56.

41 PP 1867, xxxviii (1). 818.

42 W. Galt, *Railway Reform* (1865), 95.

43 *Ibid.*, 77.

44 C.E. Lee, *Passenger Class Distinctions* (1946), 43; MacDermot, ii. 246, 249.

45 *Livret-Chaix*, July 1847.

46 *Le Petit Robert*.

47 *Livret-Chaix*, November 1850.

48 A. Perdonnet, *Traité Elémentaire des chemins de fer* (3rd ed., 1865), iv. 66–7.

49 *Bradshaw's Continental Guide*, January 1901, 80.

50 For the rates see *ibid.*, August 1914, 461 (Germany), 269 (Italy), 237B (Austria).

51 These arguments are set out clearly by J.S. Jeans in his *Railway Problems* (1884), 267–8, 370–3.

52 See VRY, 313.

53 E.E. Foxwell, *English Express Trains: Two Papers* (1884). This Ernest Foxwell (1851–1922) was the brother of H.S. Foxwell, Professor of Political Ecomony in the University of London, with whom he has sometimes been confused in railway literature.

54 *Ibid.*, 5, 27.

55 *Ibid.*, 13.

56 *Ibid.*, 10.

57 *Ibid.*, 57.

58 The London & North Eastern Railway was bold enough to re-introduce into Britain supplementary charges for travelling by express train on the three new high-speed trains it put on between London, Edinburgh, Newcastle, and west Yorkshire in 1935–9. They too conveyed third-class passengers as well as first. All the supplements were set at very low rates, between 3.9 percent and 10.2 percent of the ordinary single fares.

3

RAILWAYS *and* HOTELS IN BRITAIN, 1839–1914

The large hotel, offering accommodation alike to passing travellers and to visitors making a longer stay, designed and built for its purpose (not adapted from a town house or a group of several adjoining houses thrown together), and equipped with all the latest machinery that might promote the comfort and convenience of its guests: that kind of hotel is a creation of the nineteenth century and emerges first in France, in Britain, and in North America. The emergence was slow and gradual to begin with, but the number of these houses multiplied and their scale grew notably bigger in Britain in 1839–76, chiefly as a consequence of the growth of railway systems. The modern hotel does not owe its invention to the railway. But the railway opened out quite new opportunities before projectors, investors, and alert managers, offering them chances of earning a revenue much more substantial, and steadier all the year round, than that which had been enjoyed by most of the coaching inns that had served travellers in the past.

The railways set examples in the development of hotels that were imitated, and sometimes improved on, by those who went into the business of putting them up. Their hotels knitted them more closely into the social and economic texture of the towns in which they were established – here and there of rural districts too. The benefits were mutual, and a good many people recognised that.

All the most important work of pioneering the development of large hotels in the British Isles was undertaken before 1914. This paper sets out to examine their origins, the growth in the nature and scale of their business and in the range of what they came to undertake, treating the railways' hotels throughout as one section – especially important – of what grew to become the very extensive hotel industry of the whole United Kingdom.

I

In the Early Victorian age, Mona Wilson remarked, 'the inn, one of our national glories, deteriorated into the hotel, a national disgrace'.[1] That comment may serve here as a text, without being accepted as just, because it focuses attention sharply on two things, which are both true: that in most towns and some villages the hotel displaced the inn at that time, and that there were differences of character, of quality and tone, between inns and hotels.

The French word *hôtel* first became established in England, in this sense, late in the eighteenth century. It appeared in Ash's *Dictionary* in 1775.[2] John Byng used it in his travel diaries without any special remark: at Worcester in 1784 he called the Hop Pole both a 'noisy, dear inn' and a 'great noisy hotel'.[3] When the New Inn at Leeds changed hands shortly after that and was refurbished, it became first Cowling's Hotel and Tavern and presently just The Hotel or – here perhaps it was hedging its bets – the Hotel Inn.[4] At Tewkesbury the Star went one better still to become a 'Hotel Inn and Tavern'. In all these cases the word 'hotel' indicated nothing more than a certain degree of pretension.[5]

Except in London, where in the late eighteenth century a number of private houses – usually two or three together in a terrace – came to be joined up and furnished as quarters for rich visitors. These were never called inns – applied to them, the word would have been ridiculous; they went at once for the French word 'hotels', distinguished not by adjectives like New or Royal but by the proprietor's name. So the young Byron, up from Cambridge in 1807–8, moved from Gordon's Hotel to Dorant's in Albemarle Street and then to Reddish's;[6] and when in 1816 James Edward Mivart purchased four houses in Brook Street, he opened them up as Mivart's Hotel. His house became illustrious under his successor, whose name still attaches to it now: Claridge's.

These hotels were the most expensive places to stay in London, and socially very much the most select. The well-to-do visitor who did not go there normally looked to the great inns, at one of which, if he arrived by stage-coach, he would be delivered. Most of these were not in the same quarter of London but further east, in Holborn, the City, and Southwark. None of them was ever modernised, or as far as one can see improved in any important way, during the half-century when the coaching business was most resplendently prosperous.[7] The money cascaded into each of these houses, and their proprietors merely pocketed it. We know exactly how they appeared from the account of the White Hart in Southwark at the beginning of the tenth chapter of *Pickwick Papers*: no sketch but as sharp as an etching by Rembrandt.

What was it really like to stay in one of these inns, in London or the provinces? The answers to that question have ranged from rhapsodical enthusiasm to vehement curses. Let us return for a moment to Byng. He was not an easy man to please, it is true; but his wishes were reasonable. He wanted a dry bed, for instance, and he cared about his horse; he was not rich, and liked value for money; he could praise as heartily as he condemned. Here he is in 1781, after a bad dinner at the Bear at Woodstock:

'The imposition in travelling is abominable; the innkeepers are insolent, the hostelers are sulky, the chambermaids are pert, and the waiters are impertinent; the meat is tough, the wine is foul, the beer is hard, the sheets are wet, the linen is dirty, and the knives are never cleaned'.[8]

On the other hand Byng appreciated the Ram's Head at Disley, travelling south from Stockport – 'Take it for all, in all, I ne'er may look into such inn again', he wrote on his bill;[9] and he always delighted to return to the Haycock at Wansford (in Northamptonshire) – 'a nice inn; everything clean, and in order; a napkin with a wash-hand glass at meals; the beds and stabling excellent'.[10]

The business of inns grew rapidly in the late Georgian age, as coach and carriage travelling reached its apogee in speed and comfort, calling for much extension to provide more bedrooms and stables. Here and there on the principal coach routes some entirely new buildings appeared, the Stamford Hotel for instance, the George at Grantham, and the Waterloo at Edinburgh. The Royal Hotel at Plymouth, erected in 1811–19, was perhaps the most important of them all,[11] quickly followed by three at Brighton, the Royal York, the Albion, and the Bedford, opened in 1823–9: large houses for their day, each making up 100 beds or more.[12] Then, in 1838, came the Queen's at Cheltenham; planned and built by Robert William and Charles Jearrad at an enormous cost, traditionally reported to have been £50,000. The Queen's still remains, intact: one of the handsomest hotels today anywhere in Britain.[13]

This fine building closes one story and opens another. In Cheltenham itself it was the last monument of the town's development as a watering-place: the next prominent buildings were all churches and schools.[14] Architecturally, it belonged to the Regency, and to the Georgian age behind that. But, conspicuous on its free-standing site, at the centre of a substantial town, it was a powerful demonstration of all that an ambitious hotel might become and (to any bold promoter) what he might hope to make out of it. The Queen's deserves to be remembered as the first Victorian hotel; looking backwards in its architecture and forwards in its commanding size and situation.

That hotel was erected at an ambitious health resort. The great industrial and commercial cities were not quick to seize the potential value of new hotels. In 1839 there were said to be fifteen 'principal inns and hotels' in Manchester, six of them described as 'coaching houses'. Beyond adopting the new name 'hotel', as nine of the fifteen had done, they had made little apparent effort at modernisation. (All the same, we may say that Manchester was better off in this matter than Lyons, which we may take as its equivalent city in France. 'There is no *really* good inn here', said Murray in 1843;[15] 'the dirt and insects horrible'.) The provision in Manchester soon came to be felt inadequate, and in 1845 the Queen's Hotel was erected, a quarter of a mile from the terminus of the new railway from Birmingham and London. This was a most satisfactory building, designed by the admirable Edward Walters, and it kept its leading position in the social and commercial life of the city, even after many other new hotels had been built there.[16] Alas, it made way for the march of progress some thirty years ago. In the history of the hotels discussed here it had an exceptionally long life, and a successful one almost to the end.

2

Railways now came to play a vital part in the development of British hotels down to about 1875, especially for one reason.[17] The stage and mail coaches had, of necessity, been based upon inns, accommodating their horses and their passengers, and the inns were all at or near the centres of their towns. Railways, on the other hand, scarcely ever came near those centres. Unlike the coach proprietors, the companies had to buy the land on which their vehicles ran, and land was at its costliest there; the pollution that railways brought with them, moreover, made them unwelcome. So they stopped, or passed by, on the outskirts. But their passengers often had need of the facilities the old inns had supplied; and that led before long to the building of new ones near the stations. They sprang up quickly at some important junctions, at Crewe, Swindon, and Peterborough, at Birmingham, Derby, Normanton, and York; here and there at ports, where railways and ships met, for example at Hull, Folkestone, and Dover. Above all, after a slow start, they grew important in London.

The first venture of a railway company into the hotel business was made at Euston. The station was opened in 1837, and a year later the railway arranged to erect a pair of buildings at the entrance, flanking the great Doric portico (and at once ruining its main effect), to be fitted up for the reception of visitors in two different ways. The western one, called the Victoria, offered sleeping accommodation and an unlicensed coffee-house only. The other, the Adelaide, was intended to serve 'more as a respectable club-house than as an ordinary hotel', and it was let on lease to two caterers: Joseph Déthier, a Belgian, and Zenoni Vantini, who is said to have come from Corsica. The Victoria was opened late in September 1839; the Adelaide early in 1840.[18]

Quite why travellers passing through Euston station should require a 'club-house' may not be immediately evident. But club-houses had just then become the rage in London. The Athenaeum, the Travellers', the Carlton, and the Reform had all been opened recently in Pall Mall, and the directors must have thought that provision of this kind, so described, would help to bring in custom. The whole undertaking succeeded well in financial terms. It was promoted and built not by the railway itself but by a nominally independent company. A total of £55,173 was spent on the two buildings, their attendant stabling, and the equipment of the Victoria – so they seem to have cost more than the Queen's at Cheltenham; but that capital before long was earning a steady dividend of six percent.[19]

Taking these two units together – they were really one, under one ownership and ultimate control – they form the first of all railway hotels,[20] the parent of a numerous progeny across the world. When Euston station was built it stood on its own, well away from any established place of refreshment, inn or hotel. The railway was at the outset still in competition with the coaches. To attract passengers away from them it must offer facilities as good as theirs, or better. That was the purpose of the hotel at Euston.

Yet though it was unquestionably successful it found no imitators in London for some time. Why? Partly because the railways' victory over the coaches was so swift that by the 1840s they no longer had to fear much serious competition. Partly too because others were prepared to set up hotels near their stations, at no expense to the railways. And moreover, railway companies had soon to grow careful about incurring expenditure outside their main business of providing trains. That practice was frequently called into question in Parliament and by their shareholders. So nothing was done in this way by any company in London in the 1840s. In 1854, however, two railways provided hotels at their terminal stations, opened within five weeks of each other: the Great Northern at King's Cross and the Great Western at Paddington.

The Great Northern, a tall curved building of marked dignity, stood – still stands, I am glad to say, though its future is now in doubt – at the side of the station. It was undertaken by the company itself and apparently aroused no criticism. The cost of putting it up was said to have been about £35,000.[21] The other hotel was bigger. A new Paddington station was then being built. The Great Western Railway was extending its system northwards to Birmingham and beyond, in the hope that it would abstract some of the traffic from the route leaving London from Euston. The Euston hotel was recognised as an element in the older route's established success; so Paddington must have one too.[22] What emerged, largely under the influence of Brunel, was a building that was a portent in the capital city of England.

The station itself lay in a cutting, well below ground level; as such, necessarily inconspicuous. Brunel and the younger Hardwick, the architect chosen by the company, seized the opportunity to make the hotel a big structure, proclaiming the railway's presence both by its height and by its bulk – it towered over all the neighbouring houses, indeed over the railway itself – and also by its style. It was, Pevsner tells us, 'one of the earliest buildings, if not the earliest building in England with marked influence from the French Renaissance and Baroque'.[23] No British hostelry, whether inn or hotel, had ever been designed to impose itself in this fashion before. Like its rival at Euston this one was established by a separate company (with Brunel as its first chairman), and it was an immediate financial success. A committee probing the railway's finances in a highly critical report in 1856 allowed that the hotel was already making six percent on a capital expenditure of £59,500 and that it had 'proved an inducement to the public to select this line for travelling to London'.[24]

Some modern writers have been unkind to the Great Western Hotel as a building. Goodhart-Rendel characterised it, in no friendly spirit, as a 'railway advertisement'. Hitchcock spoke of it with contemptuous dislike: 'dreary', 'tawdry', 'pretentious', 'clumsy' – the rude adjectives tripped off his pen.[25] It is Summerson's calm verdict, the historian's, that is most to our present purpose. 'The large hotel was the creation of the railways', he remarked, 'and Paddington was the first'.[26]

Whatever might be thought of their appearance, these railway hotels displayed the comfort, the modern facilities, that a well-designed hotel could now offer. 'The less you have to do with hotels [in London], the better': the advice came from a countryman in 1851, the novelist R.S. Surtees – with one exception, not in favour of an old coaching inn but of the hotel at Euston, though even there with the warning that it was dear.[27] The opening of the new railway hotels was followed by volleys of complaint about the rest. Another novelist, Albert Smith, wrote a sprightly booklet on them entitled *The English Hotel Nuisance* in 1855. His assault on English hotels there is comprehensive. It implies that even the most august of them, in Mayfair, were very dismal; and as for the rest, in London or elsewhere, they made up a 'fortress system of discomfort and dreariness which is the terror of tourists in England'.

'Let us go to the Lakes [he says], or the Trossachs, or Killarney... There are the same harpies fluttering about the building: the same grim expensive coffee-room: the same equally grim and more expensive formally-furnished private apartments: the same unchanging bill of fare that condemns the hapless tourist to fried soles, broiled fowls, and chops and steaks day after day; with the almost compulsory pint of sherry or bottle of port "for the good of the house"'.[28]

The waiters Smith divided into two classes, 'the Haughty and the Mouldy'.[29] The old coaching inns were dingy and decaying; he thought that 'every inn ought to be entirely burnt down every ten years'.[30] What he wished for was new hotels on the good Continental pattern, where a fixed tariff guarded the traveller against English extortion, where a bedroom was furnished so as to be comfortable to sit in, thus releasing him from the gloom and expense of a 'private room' for the purpose; in short, where the seedy pomposities of the past had been swept away, to meet instead the customers' real wants.

This vigorous onslaught was not just a squib written by a lively visitor to a bad inn. *The Times* had already published a leading article in the same sense.[31] A Metropolitan Hotel Company was launched for the construction of a group of hotels, the success of the one at Paddington being pointed out, in order to lure investors into subscribing.[32] Though this project did not succeed, the idea had been well aired and action soon followed, with the opening of the Westminster Palace Hotel at the top of Victoria Street and of the Langham in Portland Place in 1860–2. Neither of these had any connection with a railway company at all. They set their sights on other customers than casual passing travellers. The Westminster Palace, from its very position, had a strong political character. It accommodated Members of Parliament during the session. Nearly half its rooms were occupied by the newly-established Council of India.[33] In 1866–7 the terms of the British North America Act, establishing the federal government of Canada, were hammered out there between the Canadian delegates and the Colonial Office.[34] The Langham was in the principal diplomatic quarter and equipped itself with an Ambassador's Audience Room.

Three more station hotels appeared at the same time: the Grosvenor at Victoria (not built by the Brighton railway nor in association with it, however), those at Charing Cross and Cannon Street, both due to subsidiary companies of the South Eastern Railway. The Cannon Street Hotel became a favoured place for company meetings. Here were hotels slipping quietly into the political and economic life of London. Into the general social life of England too. The novelists now began to use them as the settings for episodes in their stories. Trollope placed a whole important chapter of *The Belton Estate* in the Great Northern Hotel in 1865; the attempted theft of the Eustace diamonds occurred in what is clearly the County Hotel at Carlisle.[35]

3

Since hotels had now no longer to be situated, like the old inns, at places convenient for stage-coaches, the newly-built houses were free to establish themselves wherever that might be judged desirable – even in the West End of London. High ground-rents might be a deterrent there, but in the later Victorian age nevertheless new hotels were being built in Mayfair and near the edges of the Parks. They were laid out on plans quite different from those of their ancient predecessors, not facing inwards on to courtyards but four-square and solid, with no more than a glazed well to light a central staircase – in the smaller hotels not even that. Purpose-built, to meet the needs of the time, they exemplified coherence, simplicity, and cleanliness.

The provision that the larger of these new hotels offered to their guests was different in a number of ways from what had been usual in Britain before. Here it is, set out clearly at the time:[36] 'grand hotels...built expressly for the purpose, in the fashion of those in America and the Hotel du Louvre at Paris...have been established at the termini of the chief railways...and in other quarters of London. They have fixed tariffs of prices[37] and coffee-rooms for ladies as well as for gentlemen'.

For a long time past the whole world of inns and hotels, still more of eating-rooms, in London had been a man's world. That had not always been so. 'Any tavern will admit a well-dressed man and woman' said Dr Johnson (referring particularly to London) in 1781.[38] But since then Victorian prurience had taken over. It was not until the 1860s, and then chiefly owing to these hotels, that the established Early Victorian custom began to change. A guide-book of the time listed 50 eating-places in London, widely different in character and price. One of them, and one only, was described then as 'a house in which ladies may dine with comfort'; one more had a separate ladies' dining-room. The other 48 were wholly or mainly the preserve of men – or perhaps of women with whom ladies would not wish to associate.[39] Though the whole of the accommodation in the new hotels may not have been open to ladies (provision had to be made, for one thing, for smokers, who were chiefly men), ladies were no longer served in them only in the purdah of private sitting-rooms; they could eat comfortably in the public rooms of the hotels too. Here was a substantial contribution to the social emancipation of women – in its broadest and most practical sense, not simply as a cant phrase – in the Mid-Victorian age.[40]

For the rest, these hotels boasted all the latest equipment. The Westminster Palace was provided with lifts in 1860, a prompt adoption of an American device, taken up only three years after Elisha Graves Otis had installed his first production model in a New York store.[41] Later grand hotels played their part in further experimentation with this machinery, more and more necessary as they came to be built on more and more stories. The apparatus was complicated and not always reliable – we know that to our own cost still. In 1887 the Imperial Hotel at Torquay advertised that a 'first-class passenger lift' had lately been installed there, but it also felt it necessary to proclaim that the lift was 'working admirably'.[42]

4

The grand hotel made a striking appearance in the 1860s outside London also. It was a good time for financing such developments as joint-stock companies, on the rising tide before it turned in 1866. The first, as perhaps we might expect, was at Brighton. The Grand Hotel there was opened in 1864, nine stories high (served by lifts too), with 150 bedrooms: those facing the sea furnished with balconies, their bronzed and gilded ironwork rippling in curves across the *façade*.[43] The hotel decisively broke the whole coherent line of the Brighton front. In the same way as the Great Western Hotel at Paddington, but in a much more important architectural context, it dominated its surroundings – domineered over them.

Before long this grand hotel on the south coast was entirely eclipsed by another in the north: as a building the most spectacular hotel erected anywhere in Britain (London included) in the Victorian age. The Cliff, or Cliff Bridge Hotel – it was only later called the Grand – at Scarborough was commissioned in 1863 and opened four years later. The architect was Cuthbert Brodrick, famous in Yorkshire for his Town Hall and Corn Exchange at Leeds. He had a superb site: no built-up sea-front to take account of, as he would surely have had to do at Brighton, but on a cliff straight above the shore; and upwards the sky was his limit. He exploited all these advantages to their full extent, to produce what Hitchcock (having cast an eye quickly over other similar erections across the world, from Hungary to Colorado) described as 'internationally the most notable example of the type'.[44]

The building was said to have 1,000 rooms in all, 300 of them bedrooms. Yet it is worth noting that in the eight close-packed pages that J.W. Walker devoted to Scarborough in the last edition of *Murray's Handbook for Yorkshire* in 1904 – filled out to become one of the most copious and excellent of all Victorian guidebooks – he never refers once to the Grand Hotel. He pretends that it is not there. It would be hard to find a more striking example of a Victorian antiquary's dislike of the world of his own time.

What did the mighty building finally cost? The estimate of £120,000 given when its plans were first published in 1862[45] must surely have been much exceeded. Brodrick himself retired from practice as an architect about the time it was finished, moved to France to paint, and died in Jersey in 1905.

Hotels of this character now multiplied, though nowhere else on such a huge scale. For some of them it was not enough to be Grand Hotels; they had in the 1860s to be Imperial (the reference was French), as at Torquay and Blackpool. The Grand at Blackpool originated as the Imperial Hydropathic Establishment when it was opened in 1868. The vogue for hydropathy had been growing in England since the 1840s and had already led to the erection of special hotels at Malvern, at Ilkley and Ben Rhydding in Yorkshire, and at Matlock. As it caught on it called for a whole new branch of hotel design and construction, especially in Scotland. But let us look now at two more orthodox hotels that went up in this decade at the seaside.

Ilfracombe, in North Devon, lay on a wild, romantic, inhospitable coast, frequented for some time past by summer visitors. They had to toil there over steep hills by road from the nearest railway, opened to Barnstaple (ten miles off) in 1854. Ever since then an extension to Ilfracombe had been talked of, but it had not been built. The visitors went on arriving all the same, and in 1867 a large hotel was opened to provide for them. In relation to the place it was very large indeed, out of harmony with all around it in size and materials and design, exemplifying what Pevsner, in speaking of it, very well characterised as 'the somewhat grim styles of High Victorian pleasure architecture'.[46] There was still no railway, however, until 1874.

The other hotel, on the coast north of Scarborough, presents a pattern-book of one of the ways in which this business could be most efficiently managed. It formed an integral part of a project planned in collaboration between a landowner, developers, and a railway company. In 1858 the Stockton & Darlington Railway secured powers to extend its line from Redcar to the fishing hamlet of Saltburn. The Pease family were already set to exploit the ironstone near by, and Henry Pease perceived the capabilities of Saltburn as a seaside resort. He and the railway company came to terms with Lord Zetland, the landowner. By the time the line was opened in 1861 a small town was being laid out, to a carefully-considered plan, which provided for an hotel in a prime position high up on the cliffs. It was designed by William Peachey, with Alfred Waterhouse of Manchester as consultant, and Lord Zetland agreed to allow it to bear his title.

The hotel was less ambitious than most of those that have just been spoken of here, containing only 50 bedrooms when it was opened in 1863, though more were added later. It had one interesting feature, not found in any other hotel in Britain. A short extension from the railway ran into the back of the hotel itself so that guests could move straight on to trains and off them, under cover, and provisions could be delivered unobtrusively. The whole enterprise had been well thought out, and it succeeded.[47] The little town that lay around it grew modestly. The hotel remained under railway ownership until 1975.

These two hotels were built primarily for the pleasure trade. There were others, however, now springing up at seaports, designed to cater for steamship passengers and for general business too. One was the Duke of Cornwall at Plymouth, still in use today. Another was built at Harwich in association with the Great Eastern Railway, which began to run its own steamers to the Netherlands in 1863. It was designed by Thomas Allom, much better known as a draughtsman than as an architect. He produced an elegantly-finished drawing of it, which showed the man of taste applying himself to the visual capabilities of the hotel, not on a virgin site but as part of an old-established town.

Financially, the success of these hotels built during the 1860s varied a good deal. Those undertaken in conjunction with railways seem to have done quite well, as a rule. They enjoyed a steady trade from the stations, from travellers and from those who were meeting visitors or seeing them off, and much of that trade went on all the year round. The railways could quietly steer custom towards them too, from their trains. But with the pleasure hotels on the coast it was different; they were much subject to the fluctuations of general prosperity.[48] The shareholders in the companies that built them expected quick returns, and some of them began to feel they had chosen an unwise investment.[49] Other people were inclined to think that the hotels had been wrongly conceived. An intelligent leader in the *Builder* in 1870 suggested that, for seaside hotels, the mammoth building was an entire mistake; that they should be 'pleasure villages, not palaces... Like villages they should grow as the requirements of visitors demanded'. The living quarters ought to be dispersed in separate units, let either as apartments or as complete houses for families, with a central building for common services; much like some of the chalet hotels we have today.[50] But this idea did not catch on. The large pile, towering high, remained the standard, the ideal of ambitious projectors.

Another huge monument of this type was now slowing emerging above ground in London: the Midland Grand at St Pancras, opened in 1873–6, the climax of railway hotel-building in Britain. We know what that cost: £438,000, more than seven times as much as the Great Western at Paddington, which went up only 20 years before. And even this was for a building reduced in size, with some things omitted that Gilbert Scott had designed for it and some cheaper materials adopted here and there – deal for oak, Ancaster stone in place of Ketton.[51] The result was a powerful new monument in north London, however superciliously it might be spoken of by some critics.[52] It proved a good hotel and kept its footing for over 50 years.[53] But in London it was the last of its race. Although three more railway hotels were still to be built at terminal stations there, at Holborn Viaduct, Liverpool Street, and Marylebone, none of those could be said to emulate St Pancras in scale or image.

5

There was now a pause in the building of big hotels. In the course of the 1870s, however, three men began to give the business a new direction.

The first two of them were partners, Felix Spiers and Christopher Pond. They had met in Australia and established cafés in Melbourne, taking also a railway refreshment contract there. Early in the 1860s they moved to London, contracting similarly with the new underground railways. They set up the Silver Grill – their first independent restaurant – under the railway arches of Ludgate in 1866.

Restaurants lie outside consideration here except in so far as they influenced hotels. Even the hotels' critics allowed that some of them were satisfactory in London. A number of those they commended are still happily with us: Rule's and

Simpson's, for example. The railway hotels, as we have seen, provided both food and drink, not solely to their own guests but to all comers; largely from necessity, arising from the special nature of their business. Spiers and Pond, by now experienced caterers, perceived the capabilities of linking restaurants with other kinds of provision for the enjoyment and comfort of Londoners. They began with their Criterion at Piccadilly Circus, which united a group of restaurants with a theatre,[54] and then did the same at the Gaiety in the Strand. Next they took the lease of the new hotel at Holborn Viaduct station, which they opened in 1877. Pond died, aged 45, in 1881 (leaving the very impressive personal fortune of £215,000), but his partner continued and acquired new hotels, having no financial connection with railways, such as Bailey's in Gloucester Road in 1890.

Another new projector of hotels in the Late Victorian age was Frederick Gordon. He was a solicitor by profession, but his father was a decorator and his brother-in-law owned a well-established City restaurant, Pimm's. Gordon's first substantial venture was a dining-room occupying the historic Crosby Hall in Bishopsgate: perhaps the earliest example in this country of turning a distinguished ancient building, which was no longer used for its original purpose, into a restaurant. It was opened in 1868 and continued there until 1907. Next Gordon formed a company and went on to build the ambitious Holborn Casino (later Restaurant), a suite of dining-rooms of different sizes. He then turned his mind to hotels. In 1881 his company opened the Grand on the corner of Trafalgar Square and Northumberland Avenue; two years later the First Avenue Hotel (one notices the American inflection in its name) in High Holborn; two years after that a second hotel in Northumberland Avenue, the Metropole, followed in 1887 by yet a third in the same street, offloaded cheap by the developer Jabez Balfour. In the 1890s the interests of the same company began to extend outside London, with the establishment of other Metropoles, at Brighton and Folkestone, at Cannes and Monte Carlo.

We are now moving into the world of hotel tycoons. The name of one of them may surprise us today, for it is chiefly remembered in a quite different connection. Richard D'Oyly Carte established himself in business first as a theatrical agent. He then moved inside the theatre to become an impresario, putting on the new light operas of Gilbert and Sullivan, each in turn, as they were written from 1875 onwards. In collaboration with these two men he presently erected the Savoy Theatre for this purpose, in the Strand; and he went on to build, entirely on his own account, an adjoining hotel at the back of the theatre, facing on to the river, opened in 1889.

The Savoy made itself known quickly as an hotel of a very high class. It had all the latest comforts: an adequate number of bathrooms; electric light – Carte's theatre had claimed to be the first public building in the world lighted wholly by electricity. And its restaurant soon attained distinction also. Some of its arrangements were evidently not right at the outset, and Carte called in two new men to reform what seemed to be wrong. Their names have passed into history: César Ritz, who was Swiss by birth, and the Frenchman Auguste Escoffier. They did all that Carte can have desired, and much more. The Savoy attracted discriminating clients: rich Americans of course – all hotel-owners now set their sights on them – but others too of the most various kinds. We ought always to remember that Monet stayed there three times in 1899–1901 and that it was looking down from its windows that he sketched and painted the Thames. The Savoy also made its way into fiction. Arnold Bennett used it as the setting of *The Grand Babylon Hotel*, published in 1901; not from any familiarity with it – he was by no means rich enough yet to enter it on his own account – but after being taken to tea there once and observing, with his habitual sharpness, everything he saw.[55]

Carte had reason to be satisfied with his investment. He went on to buy two other hotels of the highest rank, Claridge's and the Berkeley, and rebuilt both of them. Then in 1904 he extended the Savoy to run through to the Strand. Naturally he had rivals. The Cecil was opened in 1896, almost next door to the Savoy.[56] This was another enterprise originated by Jabez Balfour, though not completed until after he had begun his sentence of fourteen years' penal servitude for the publication of false accounts. Ritz and Escoffier moved to the new Carlton in the Haymarket in 1899. Then in 1906 came the Ritz in Piccadilly, often thought of with the other Ritzes in Paris, Madrid, and New York as the summit of hotel luxury.

All these hotels were of the most expensive kind. But change was now coming at every level in the business. Less wealthy visitors were asking for better accommodation too. Something was done to meet them in London at the big hotels in Russell Square and at the Strand Palace, just across the street from the Savoy. (How piquant to think that this temple of secular pleasure arose in 1907 on the site of the most famous centre of revivalist meetings in England, Exeter Hall!) The Strand Palace brings us to another firm of promoters, J. Lyons & Co. They had established their teashops all over London and were now moving into the management of hotels also.

6

Reflections of these metropolitan developments were to be seen outside London. Some of the new railway hotels now erected there were very large: the obese Midland at Manchester, for example, the more suave reconstructed Adelphi at Liverpool. The two biggest Scottish railway companies strove with each other in Edinburgh, providing enormous hotels one at each end of Princes Street, opened in 1902 and 1903.[57] Purpose-built hotels multiplied, sometimes in obvious competition with those of the railways: the Metropole at Leeds lay between two railway hotels, the County at Newcastle right opposite the Central station, which already had its own hotel attached to it. Most large towns got hotels of this sort, some now for the first time. Leicester for example had made shift with the one old coaching inn that survived there, the Bell, and two or three other quite modest establishments until the Grand was opened in 1898. Still Baedeker felt it right to comment in 1910: 'in many of the large commercial and industrial centres the requirements of the "uncommercial traveller" are very inadequately met'.[58]

There were also some new developments peculiar to the provinces. One of them goes back well into the nineteenth century. The Great Western Railway opened a branch to St Ives in Cornwall in 1877, at the same time taking a lease of an eighteenth-century country house, Tregenna Castle, lying just outside the town, to make it into an hotel. This was a bold move, for which there were hardly any precedents, but it succeeded. The company bought the property outright in 1895 and maintained the hotel thereafter.[59] Something similar appeared later in Scotland, with a rather different purpose. Three hotels were built by railway companies away from large towns altogether, served by new branch lines, standing on the sea, with good golf-links: at Cruden Bay (Aberdeenshire), Dornoch in Sutherland, and Turnberry (Ayrshire), opened in 1896–1906. The Cruden Bay Hotel, though commended on its merits, was not successful because its season was uneconomically short.[60] The Turnberry hotel prospered greatly, however, and found an imitator in another at Gleneagles in Perthshire, opened in 1926. So the notion of the country-house hotel, with or without golf-links or a good fishing river, was beginning to take on. Here were some of the pathfinders.

This survey must end with a reference to one more plan, which was to form the basis – quite outside the thinking of its originators – of what has become in our time a large international enterprise. The fourth Earl Grey, whose public energies were given chiefly to the British Empire, was also interested in the reform and improvement of public houses. He was mainly responsible for evolving a scheme to establish trusts, county by county, for the running of rural inns and hotels; not big and expensive but small ones adapted to the needs of people with limited incomes, particularly of cyclists and walkers. This was not intended to be any large commercial undertaking. It involved no erection of ambitious new buildings. Its principal work lay in the purchase and adaptation of old inns, many of them declining into seediness owing to the development of railways and modern hotels. The movement got under way in Hertfordshire in 1903. Seven years later the Hertfordshire, Essex, and Middlesex Trusts were combined to form the Home Counties Public House Trust Ltd. In 1919 that again changed its name to Trust Houses Ltd. Presently it became Trusthouse Forte, with a chain of about 250 hotels in Great Britain, and others all over the world. It was not until 1991 that this huge combine turned its back entirely on its origins and earlier history, to re-name itself Forte alone.

7

At the beginning of the Victorian age the hotel was displacing the inn. Here, at its end, were some inns being brought back into use, refurbished; to be appreciated and enjoyed not only by cyclists and walkers but soon by the very much more powerful band of motorists. Let us now take a general view of what the Victorian hotel was, and of what it became.

It was a device evolved to meet the needs of a far greater body of travellers than had moved about in the past, more demanding in some ways, in other ways careless or indifferent. English inns had long been reckoned dear, even when they had had to incur no significant capital expenditure. The new hotels – new buildings, newly equipped – looked to their customers to recoup them for their outlay. They remained expensive, as Baedeker, from his international standpoint, constantly asserted;[61] they are still, as we know, a great deal dearer than hotels of the same sort on the mainland of Europe today. Did the Victorians get good value for the high charges they paid? In some ways they certainly did. Their new hotels were clean. They incorporated the latest sanitary arrangements. Those things added much to the capital cost of construction. But they were welcomed by many Victorian travellers, disturbed in mind, if they thought of going to France, to learn from Murray as late as 1892 that in the provincial hotels there 'some of the most important essentials to *sanitary comfort* and *personal decency*...are utterly disregarded, and evince a state of degradation not to be expected in a civilised country'.[62] It would have been impossible for any fair observer to generalise like that in speaking of hotels in Britain.

Some of the reforms called for in the 1850s had come to be adopted. There was less of the bargaining that most Englishmen disliked; the number of concealed charges was reduced. The old need for hiring private sitting-rooms disappeared owing to the provision of communal rooms, which in the reign of Edward VII came to be absurdly called 'lounges'.[63]

On the other hand, as the new system of charging came in one great opportunity was missed: the opportunity of reconsidering the relationship of sleeping with eating accommodation. The *hôtel garni*, affording bedrooms and a light breakfast only, without any dining-room, was hardly adopted in Britain at all. For that there were some good reasons: the scarcity of cafés and restaurants, as they were understood on the Continent; the insistence of most middle-class Englishmen on having a cooked breakfast, which required the hotel-keeper to maintain and staff a kitchen. In London it was clearly understood that the visitor who slept at an hotel ate there also. In 1879 the younger Charles Dickens was explicit on this point: 'Foreign visitors will do well to bear in mind that the Continental custom of taking all, or the great majority of meals out of the hotel does not obtain in England, and that a London hotel-keeper, under such circumstances, will consider himself ill-used'.[64] The guest might therefore be called a prisoner of his hotel, and that had two bad consequences: it invited the hotel to be careless and offhand, providing whatever food it chose, to be taken or left; and it discouraged the opening of good restaurants.

So it comes about that while the great changes initiated in London from 1839 onwards brought about a considerable improvement in living accommodation, they did little or nothing towards securing any improvement in food. That statement calls for two qualifications. After 1890 some of the best hotels did establish restaurants of their own that were internationally acclaimed; and, as we have seen, the hotels certainly eased and improved the conditions of eating. In that important matter the more expensive set an example that soon came to be imitated.

My own conclusion – from what people said at the time, from traditions long established and lasting into the years of my personal observation, from photographs and from looking at the surviving appointments of the kinds of hotel I have been speaking of – must be that in this matter the English mistook the shadow for the substance. They could be readily persuaded by changes in furnishing or *décor* to overlook the pretentious dreariness of the food they were eating. And that Victorian habit of thought remains established in this country today, more firmly than ever.

Then *were* the old inns 'a national glory' and the Victorian hotels that ousted them a 'national disgrace'? Should we agree with E.C. Bentley, writing just before 1914, that 'mechanical travel has abolished the inn, or all that was best in it'?[65] I have found little evidence that English inns were especially excellent (in the opinion of those best entitled to judge, through familiarity with the inns encountered in other countries), and a good deal to suggest that at Queen Victoria's accession the large majority of the more important inns throughout the country cried aloud for overhaul, repair, and rebuilding. The development of the railways greatly increased the demand for travellers' accommodation. Most of the old inns in London then succumbed;[66] the most historic of them all, the Tabard in Southwark, in 1876. Though they were mourned by antiquaries, they had long been deserted by travellers. The hotels that took their place were much more efficient, a branch of Victorian technical progress. Some of them were brash; some, in their self-confidence, brutal. It was the building of the Langham Hotel that began the degradation of Portland Place, one of the most spacious and handsome streets in London. The Empire at Bath, opened in 1901, was a scarcely-credible atrocity, which would have been condemned by any town-planning officer today after he had scrutinised the application for five minutes. But few of them were quite as coarsely arrogant as that.

In general these hotels made their contribution to the Victorians' comfort and pleasure, and to the reception of well-to-do visitors from abroad. They also played their part in the industrial and commercial life of the country. Collectively, they formed a very substantial investment. That is impossible to set out in detail. Chains of hotels, on a national scale under the control of single companies, were still only emerging in Britain before 1914. There is however one very large group of them for which we have some figures, not as precise or as elegant in accounting terms as we could wish, but still in a broad way reliable: the aggregate accounts of all the 92 hotels owned by railway companies in 1913, stretching across the whole of Great Britain, from Sutherland to Cornwall and Kent. The railways then declared that they had spent just over £8 million on them, including those in Ireland: an average of £84,000 on each of them, large and small.[67] As far as can be judged, the net receipts from all their business represented nearly seven percent of the total investment in them.[68] Their capital and running costs had always been high, and the local rates they paid were not negligible; but this was a revenue good enough to make it worth while for the companies to maintain them, as a steadily useful service to travellers.

In the later Victorian age an increasing number of hotel guests were choosing to make extended stays there. Some, if they could afford it, were then coming to reside in them permanently. That was a tribute to their quietness, the calm and reliable service they afforded. Who could ever have thought of spending an hour longer than necessary in the Great White Horse at Ipswich, as Dickens had portrayed it in 1836?[69]

8

Like a great many other things, in Britain and in most European countries, hotels changed their character after the first World War: above all through the development of motor transport on the roads, which freed their visitors from all dependence on a train service and made movement within a town somewhat more flexible. As a result of the grouping in 1923 the London Midland & Scottish and London & North Eastern Railways came to own chains of hotels much larger than those that had belonged to any of their constituent companies, numbering 37 and 24 respectively. They kept their reputation as sound, quiet establishments, valued by a good many of their regular users. Two notable ones were added: the Manor House, Moretonhampstead (Devon), as a country-house hotel, and the Midland at Heysham on Morecambe Bay, completed in 1933 to the designs of Oliver Hill; one of the few large commercial buildings of any sort that were erected between the wars in Britain and seem likely to be remembered as works of any true architectural distinction.

In 1948, after nationalisation, the British Transport Commission acquired 44 hotels from the railway companies (together with ten that were still closed then on account of war damage). Though some of them continued profitable – in good years at least – the chain did not do well enough to justify its retention, and the government ordered them all to be sold off in 1982.

That was a decision taken entirely on financial grounds, when the economic condition of the country was very different from that at the time when most of these hotels had been built. It cannot be accepted, in any sense, as a sound retrospective judgement on the value of building them.

NOTES

1 *Early Victorian England*, ed. G.M. Young (1934), ii. 295.

2 'Hostel' is there defined as 'an inn, an hotel'.

3 *The Torrington Diaries*, ed. C.B. Andrews (1934–8), i. 188.

4 T. Bradley, *The Old Coaching Days in Yorkshire* (1889), 158–9.

5 For the emergence of hotels as buildings see chap. 11 of Sir N. Pevsner's *History of Building Types* (1976).

6. *Letters and Journals*, ed. L.A. Marchand, i (1973), 126, 134, 169.

7 I think the only one that was extensively reconstructed was the Golden Cross, further west at Charing Cross, in 1832.

8 *Torrington Diaries*, i. 53.

9 *Ibid.*, ii. 181–5.

10 *Ibid.*, ii. 211, 213, 408.

11 See Pevsner, *Building Types*, 173–4.

12 E.W. Gilbert, *Brighton* (1954), 102.

13 H. Colvin, *Biographical Dictionary of British Architects* (1978), 456; J.M. Wilson, *Imperial Gazetteer of England and Wales* (?1869), i. 409; D. Verey, *BE Gloucestershire, the Vale and the Forest of Dean* (2nd ed., 1976), 133, 140.

14 G. Hart, *History of Cheltenham* (1965), 209.

15 *Handbook for France* (1843), 365.

16 It remained at the head of Murray's list in 1880, commended as 'good' (*Handbook for Lancashire*, 1880 ed., 12); in 1910 Baedeker gave it a star and put it second only to the huge new Midland Hotel (*Great Britain*, 7th ed., 1910, 356); it was still 'first class' in the *Blue Guide to England* of 1950 (413).

17 I have discussed the connection between railways and hotels in general in the *Journal of Contemporary History*, 19 (1984), 201–7.

18 R384/98: minutes of the committee of the London & Birmingham Railway Hotel Company, esp. 24 July 1838, 25 and 26 Jan., 25 Aug. 1839; first general meeting of proprietors, 1 Sept. 1840.

19 London & Birmingham Hotel Company minutes, 1 Sept. 1840, 31 Jan. 1844.

20 Gordon Biddle (*Victorian Stations*, 1973, 139) has claimed this title for the Crewe Arms at Crewe, which was certainly in existence by 1838, when it was referred to in Osborne's *Guide to the Grand Junction Railway*, 255; not built by the railway, however.

21 It was originally proposed to the company by Déthier (formerly of Euston) and the contractor who was building the station, John Jay, but they quarrelled and the company went ahead on its own: R236/70, pp. 225–8, 236–9, 276; 236/16, pp. 85–6, 202, 242. See also Wrottesley, *GNR*, i (1979), 81; no authority given.

22 R250/4, pp. 248, 259.

23 *The Buildings of England: London except the Cities of London and Westminster* (1952), 304.

24 *Report of a Special Committee on Great Western Affairs* (1856), 13.

25 H.S. Goodhart-Rendel, *English Architecture since the Regency* (1953), 104; H.-R. Hitchcock, *Early Victorian Architecture in Britain* (1954), 212–13.

26 *The Victorian City*, ed. H.J. Dyos and M. Wolff (1973), 324.

27 *Town and Country Papers*, ed. E.D. Cuming (1929), 237.

28 *The English Hotel Nuisance* (2nd ed., 1858), 10.

29 *Ibid.*, 38.

30 *Ibid.*, 24.

31 *The Times*, 3 Nov. 1855.

32 Prospectus in BL, 1881 b. 23.

33 P. Cunningham, *London as it is* (c. 1865 ed.), xxxviii.

34 This was duly recalled 50 years later in the *Blue Guide to London* (1918), 75.

35 *The Belton Estate*, chap. 24; *The Eustace Diamonds*, chaps. 45, 46. Though the Carlisle hotel is not named, it was evidently close to the station, which the County Hotel (later called the Cumbrian Thistle) adjoins.

36 Cunningham, xxxviii.

37 That practice had already been in force, however, twenty years before at the Pavilion Hotel, Folkestone, under a foreign manager and no doubt to meet the wishes of foreign visitors: see advertisement in *New Illustrated Handbook to Folkestone* (pub. H. Stock, 1848).

38 *Boswell's Life of Johnson*, ed. G.B. Hill and L.F. Powell (1934–50), iv. 75.

39 Cunningham, xlii (the Albany), xli (the London).

40 See Francis Sheppard's comment: *London 1808–70* (1971), 354.

41 *History of Technology*, ed. C. Singer and others, v (1958), 478.

42 *Bradshaw's Guide*, August 1887, 584.

43 Gilbert, *Brighton*, 161.

44 H.-R. Hitchcock, *Architecture: Nineteenth and Twentieth Centuries* (1971 ed.), 232–3.

45 *Building News*, 9 (1862) 16.

46 *BE North Devon* (1952), 107.

47 The minute-books of the hotel are in R 667/100–4.

48 See for instance Zetland Hotel minutes, 10 Sept. 1877: R667/103.

49 Letter in *Builder*, 27 (1869) 550.

50 *Ibid.*, 28 (1870) 1012.

51 J. Simmons, *St Pancras Station* (1968), 61, 53–4.

52 *Ibid.*, 91–4.

53 *Ibid.*, 81.

54 D. Olsen, *The Growth of Victorian London* (1979 ed.), 108–9; C. Dickens, *Dickens's Dictionary of London* (1879), 82.

55 A. Bennett, *Journal 1929* (1930), 131.

56 For a sample set of photographs of the interiors of the Savoy and the Cecil see P. Boniface, *Hotels and Restaurants* (1981), plates 47–51.

57 Interesting details of the construction and management of the North British hotel at Edinburgh are given in O. Carter, *Illustrated History of British Railway Hotels* (1990), 89–90; for comment on this hotel and its rival the Caledonian, as buildings, see *Buildings of Scotland: Edinburgh*, 267–8, 285.

58 *Great Britain* (7th ed., 1910), xxv.

59 There are extensive papers relating to this hotel in R253/24–6; 266/45, 109; 267/45.

60 Sir M. Barclay-Harvey, *Great North of Scotland Railway* (2nd ed., 1949), 113.

61 *Great Britain* (7th ed., 1910), xxv.

62 *Murray's Handbook for France* (18th ed., 1892, 23).

63 OED Supplement, example of 1908. The term is freely used in advertisements in *Bradshaw's Railway Guide* for April 1910, 1049, 1065, 1100, 1105, 1139.

64 *Dictionary of London*, 116.

65 *Trent's Last Case* (1913), 147.

66 See H. Hobhouse, *Lost London* (1976 ed.), 194–8. Henry James evokes one of them beautifully in his early story 'A Passionate Pilgrim' (1871), arising out of his stay in London in 1869: *Complete Tales*, ed. L. Edel (1962–4), ii. 227–8, 236–7.

67 PP 1914–16, lx. 719, 721, 794.

68 R266/109: Great Western Railway statistics, 1913–20, sect. 7, p. 27. The total capital expenditure shown here is about £½ million higher than that given in the parliamentary return just cited.

69 *Pickwick Papers*, chap. 22.

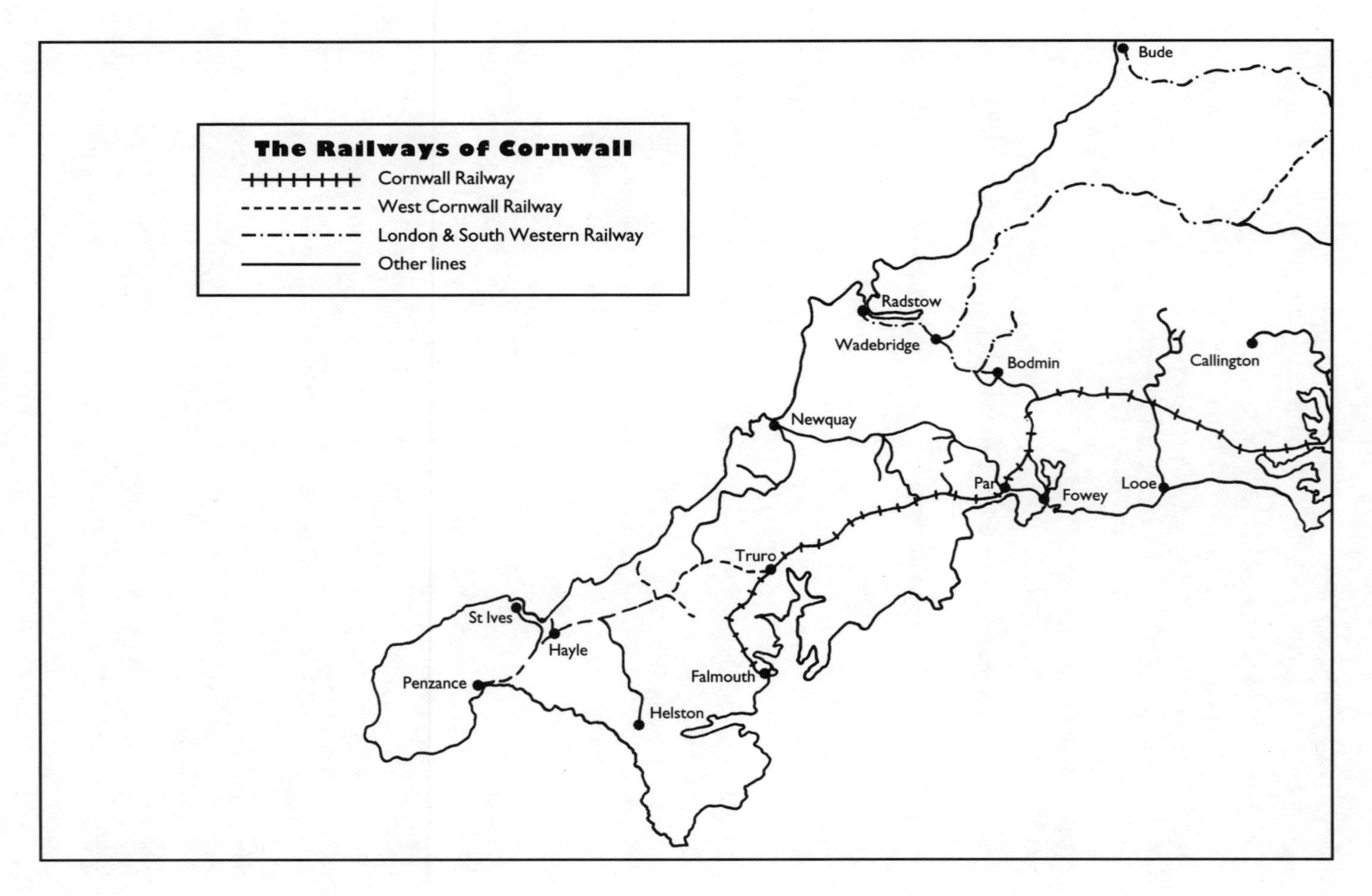
The Railways of Cornwall
Cornwall Railway
West Cornwall Railway
London & South Western Railway
Other lines
Bude
Radstow
Wadebridge
Bodmin
Callington
Newquay
Par
Fowey
Looe
Truro
St Ives
Hayle
Falmouth
Penzance
Helston

4
THE RAILWAY *in* VICTORIAN CORNWALL

I

Although a great deal has been written about the history of railways in England, most of it has been concerned with their building and operation, above all with their mechanical equipment; not much with the consequences arising from their work. We are now copiously informed about what the railways were, and to a smaller extent about the ways in which they were run. We cannot claim to know very much about what they did. How far can they be said to have aided the societies they were built to serve?

For that ignorance there are some good reasons. It is easy enough to assert that the opening of a railway produced an economic or social change – the development of a new trade or a growth in population. But that may be impossible to demonstrate precisely. The evidence is unsatisfactory, discontinuous or absent just when we need it most. Where Cornwall is concerned, for example, we have no long-extended series of figures for the traffic handled at any single station before 1914.[1] Nor do we know with certainty what employment the railways afforded there, except at rare moments. The census returns are of very limited value in this matter. So, with these deficiencies of information, what are we to say about the business the railways transacted at any town or village they touched, or about the work they offered?

The same difficulties confront the student of railways, if he is looking not so much for events as for their consequences, in most parts of Great Britain. Their construction and some of its effects have been investigated in four English counties[2] as well as in eight provincial cities[3] and in London, where attention has been paid very profitably to the long-term consequences arising from it[4]. Here this inquiry is extended into Cornwal, where the study enjoys some advantages and one special importance.

The first advantage comes from the county's peninsular position, which makes it the easiest in England to examine in isolation[5]; the second that it had its own separate railway companies, the Cornwall and the West Cornwall, which between them provided the main trunk line from Plymouth to Penzance and Falmouth. As long as they continued to be separate, they kept their own records, which can now be studied – in so far as they have survived – in the Public Record Office at Kew[6].

Cornwall was the last English county to be connected to the main railway system, as late as 1859. As it happened, the connection was made just at the time when its mining industries were moving towards disaster. When the railway arrived it offered some help to an economy damaged perhaps more seriously than that of any other English county in the Mid-Victorian age save Lancashire during the Cotton Famine and a few others in the agricultural troubles that became acute and lasting in the 1870s. The railway offered that help. How valuable was it? Might it have done more? Could the help have been made available by some other means, in a better way?

Railways had been laid down quite early to serve the Cornish mines, both as part of their internal equipment and as a means of conveying their copper and tin to the ports: Portreath and Hayle on the north coast, Devoran on an arm of the Fal. But the lines on the surface of the ground were not promoted or managed by the mine-owners, as they generally were in Northumberland and Durham; they were independent undertakings.[7] Since all the minerals were sent away by sea, there was little demand from the mining industry for any improved communication eastwards. That demand, when it came, arose from interests connected with Falmouth, as a mail packet station now threatened with the loss of that business through the building of railways to other ports nearer London. The threat was rapidly realised. The plans for a trunk railway down from London failed altogether in the 1830s and matured very slowly thereafter. Falmouth did not get its railway until 1863, when its packets had long since been transferred to Southampton.

The first piece of trunk railway in the county, the West Cornwall, was completed from Truro to Penzance in 1852,[8] a modest and economical affair with 'wooden viaducts, plain stations, and low prices'.[9] By that time there was a continuous line from London to Plymouth, and the task of linking Plymouth with Truro had been begun by the Cornwall Railway.

There had always been two possible routes of approach to Cornwall from the east. Both had their supporters in the county, who fought the battle energetically from 1835 to 1846.[10] The 'central' line, to be built on the standard gauge, went by Okehampton and Bodmin Moor to Truro and Falmouth. This had the advantage of a shorter distance and a somewhat easier terrain, but it traversed an almost empty country from Okehampton to Truro. Its rival the broad-gauge 'southern' line ran from Plymouth parallel with the sea, serving all the chief towns or passing near them. Like most such coastal lines – like the East Suffolk and the Whitby Redcar & Middlesbrough – it had to see-saw up and down, bridging the valleys made by rivers at their broadest not far from their mouths. And at the Plymouth end there was the formidable difficulty of crossing the Tamar to be faced. Had Falmouth retained its packets and had West Cornwall included some large towns, the central line might have justified itself. As it was, Parliament decided in 1846 – no doubt rightly – in favour of the coast line, the Cornwall Railway. This had been surveyed first by W.S. Moorsom and then more carefully by Brunel. The line that emerged, and is still in use, has sometimes been criticised since. Its operation has always been inconvenient from its curves and gradients, and here and there the alignment itself could certainly have been bettered, as the building of the present wholly new section from Saltash to St Germans in 1908 demonstrated. But the railway's defects were not mainly attributable to any faults in engineering. They arose from the route chosen by the promoters and the rigid economy that their shortage of capital imposed. So far from being an engineering failure, the line was a demonstration of Brunel's resourcefulness in meeting his difficulties: the 42 timber viaducts, with an aggregate length of nearly five miles;[11] the crowning triumph, the Royal Albert Bridge over the Tamar at Saltash, a structure unlike any other except Brunel's smaller study for it at Chepstow.[12]

The Cornwall Railway was financially assisted by the established main lines with which it was to connect at Plymouth. The company did not succeed at this stage in attracting much investment from outside, from the usual sources in London or Lancashire. By a peculiarity rare in any other mining or manufacturing district of England or Wales, the capital was raised hardly at all from the wealthy industrialists of the locality. With two notable exceptions they stood aside from it, as a costly enterprise that would not benefit them. Instead, the money seems to have come predominantly from landowners, from mercantile interests like those of the Foxes at Falmouth, and from small local investors. A fair number of landowners were persuaded to accept part of the payment for their land in shares.[13]

The negotiations for property were laborious. Some of that work was undertaken by Brunel himself.[14] We can watch him in detailed discussion with the second Lord Vivian, whose Glynn estate had to be intersected by the railway east of Lostwithiel. The line could not take an inconspicuous path beside the Fowey River at the bottom of its deep valley, for that would have required at the eastern end either an impossibly abrupt climb or a long and expensive tunnel. It had to run up instead on a broad ledge cut in the rock face at a steep incline seven miles long, crossing eight high viaducts.

The Cornwall Railway had great financial difficulties to contend with, but Lord Vivian's were hardly less. His father and he had both overspent themselves in trying to set their estate on its feet. He could reasonably demand a good price for the land the railway wanted. It proposed not only to run close to his house, in full view of it, but also to cut a great swath through his trees. The thousands that would remain would be in constant danger from fire, from locomotives pounding up the incline and emitting streams of cinders. In his battle with the railway our sympathies may well be evenly divided.

Unfortunately he took a dislike to Brunel. 'The gentleman is a shifty personage', he wrote after meeting him, 'without any high sense of fair dealing.'[15] Mistrust played a part in his subsequent obstinacy. He demanded to be shown very precise details of the line the railway intended to take. 'Without such plans and sections', he wrote to his solicitor, William Longbourne, '...I apprehend that I should be entirely in the power of the company, who might pass through Glynn regardless of the amount of incidental injury they were doing.'[16] That anxiety was justifiable: yet Lord Vivian's necessities pressed him on his side towards a swift bargain. Four days later he wrote again: 'I absolutely and entirely concur in your recommendation of making the best terms we can, but above *all* of making terms, and getting money paid down by which to ease the estate of its difficulties'.[17] Time now pressed the railway company as hard as Lord Vivian, for it had let its contract and needed quick possession of the land. A fortnight later Brunel reached terms with Longbourne. He spelt them out in his own handwriting:

'I will repeat my offer clearly. It is that in consideration of the agreement as to the line through Glynn being altered in the manner following and in consideration of the claim which Lord Vivian has made in respect of the Newham branch[18] the sum of £20,000 shall be paid, which sum to include every pecuniary compensation whatever and the £9,000 for the purchase money of the land as provided for in the existing agreement. That the line shall be altered by bringing it nearer to the turnpike road and carrying it in open cutting and embankment on the surface according to the ground, in the manner which has been suggested, and according to a plan and section to be agreed upon'.[19]

Here the sparring ended. No doubt Longbourne had warned Lord Vivian of the risks involved in taking the matter further, to arbitration or to a jury. This struggle deserves remembrance for its cut and thrust; it was a direct, personal clash of landowner and engineer.

Seventeen years went by between the passing of the company's Act and the completion of its line to Falmouth: a longer time than any railway of comparable importance required elsewhere in England. Work was stopped entirely for three years for lack of money. More than 60 percent of the shares were forfeited because the calls on them were not paid. In 1855 the company was obliged to lease itself to the South Devon, Bristol & Exeter, and Great Western companies jointly in order to secure their guarantee of interest on £375,000 of its debentures. Two years later these 'Associated Companies' gave it additional help; and the line could not open until they had allowed a further issue of £40,000 in preference shares to be made, for the purchase of rolling stock.

What Cornwall did not supply in money it made up for, in large measure, by tenacity. For most of the period of construction the company was presided over by two chairmen: the only two Cornishmen with large industrial property who appreciated the importance of the work for the public interests of the county as a whole. The first was J.T. Treffry, of Place at Fowey, who was already engaged in developing railways to work the produce of his estates when he was called to the chair, first of the provisional committee for the trunk line in 1844–6 and then of the board of the Cornwall Railway. It was one of that railway's misfortunes that he was already ill, and he died early in 1850.[20] He was then succeeded by Michael Williams, who also died in office, in June 1858, when the railway was nearly finished. W.H. Bond served as secretary to the promoters and to the company through all its trials from 1841 to 1865.[21]

The railway owed a special debt to some of the Cornish landowners, headed by the first and second Earls of Falmouth. They patiently chaired meetings in support of the early projects,[22] and a number of them subscribed liberally towards the cost of the surveys. As the struggle grew more severe they gave way to the professional and mercantile men, who battled through all discouragements to success.[23] Once the railway was open the responsibility for its working rested chiefly with the Associated Companies, which had six representatives on the committee of management against the Cornwall's four.

The completion of the line, after so long a struggle, was a proper subject for rejoicing. The Prince Consort travelled down to open the great bridge, named after him, on 2 May 1859.[24] That night there was a big ball at Plymouth. Next day came demonstrations at most of the towns that the line served.[25] On the day after that the railway was opened for public traffic as far as Truro and so by the West Cornwall line to Penzance. The section from Truro to Falmouth followed on 24 August 1863.

The traffic did not prove to be large. Only about 1500 passengers a day were being booked over the whole 60 miles of line from Plymouth to Falmouth during the 1860s. Goods business did better, rising uninterruptedly – though also at a slow pace – from 1860 to 1873. The total receipts doubled over the first thirteen years.

But the conveyance of passengers and goods was not the only sort of communication the railway produced. It gave Cornwall a postal service of a quite new standard. A Night Mail was established from London, and a North Mail making connections at Bristol; two trains that, in changing forms, continued to run for many years. Anybody who could read and write and had a penny to spend on a stamp could now send a letter to London from Penzance on Monday afternoon and expect a reply on Wednesday. What more could he ask than that? It may well be that this was the most important contribution made by the Cornwall Railway to its county in its early days – more important than conveying passengers and goods. And another service, entirely new, appeared at the same time. The telegraph was laid down beside the railway. It was adopted as an instrument for working the line, but it was also available to the public for their own business at some of the stations.[26] As soon as the through route had been completed, the town council of Penzance resolved that its clock should be set to Greenwich time.[27] Penzance was one of the last towns in England to adopt this practice; the arrival of the telegraph alone had made it possible. The railway, the Saltash bridge, the Night Mail, the telegraph and Greenwich time – they all proclaimed the full union of Cornwall with the rest of England.

2

Although the traffic on the railway continued to grow (see the table on p73), it was not until 1882 that it began to show the smallest profit, and that was never enough to allow any dividend to be paid on the company's Ordinary shares. No sensible person could have supposed, at least after 1850, that the railway would be a rewarding investment. Later, when the price of the shares remained very low, some speculators bought them cheap; but they did not make much by that. The capital was held mainly by those who looked to the indirect benefits the railway might bring: that is by the Associated Companies, which thought of a developing traffic in the long run; and by local people, who saw it as a necessary instrument for the economic life of the county, especially for its towns and its agriculture.[28]

They were justified there more amply – more tragically too – than they could ever have guessed. The production of copper had gone on increasing until 1856. But the ore was becoming exhausted, save at depths where it was uneconomic to work it, and Britain no longer dominated the world supply. By the 1860s her share of the total had fallen to one-eighth. In the disruption of the money market in 1866 many of the mining enterprises were ruined. In six years (1864–70) the number of mines producing copper in Cornwall fell from 174 to 80.[29] They did not necessarily close. For some of them remedies were at hand, at least for a time: they were able to turn to the mining of tin and the production of arsenic instead. But those were only palliatives. In the 1870s tin-mining began to go the same way, overtaken by large new supplies from Malaya and elsewhere.

The social consequences of these great changes appeared quickly. Although Cornish miners had always led a harsh life, they were experts and knew no other trade. Some were able to turn from working copper to tin, some were absorbed into the china-clay industry. There were no other comparable employments for them in Cornwall. But they were in demand, as acknowledged specialists, everywhere. The contractors building railways in the Mid-Victorian age recruited a few of them, where tunnelling was required.[30] Many more went to the mine-works overseas: to the United States,[31] to Africa and Australia. This emigration become marked in the 1860s, when Cornwall was the only English county in which the population fell. In the 1870s it declined much further, by 8½ percent, and it continued to go down through the rest of the Victorian age.[32]

In these conditions it became essential for Cornwall to diversify its occupations, to find new business. There was little manufacturing industry: some foundries in the west – one of them, Harvey's of Hayle, nationally important[33] – but none of them large. No substantial development could be looked for there. Nor was it likely that any new manufactures would be attracted into the county. It was too remote; it had no coal of its own. The china-clay industry continued to expand; irregularly however, for it was ill organised and recurrent crises arose from over-production. It was not a large employer. In 1881, at a time of adversity, no more than 1600 men were engaged in it.[34]

The railway provided new hope, as an employer and as a creator of fresh business. None of the companies in Cornwall maintained any large engineering establishments there, though the Cornwall Railway had repair shops at Lostwithiel and the West Cornwall at Carn Brea. In June 1856 a total of 1163 men were engaged on the construction of the Cornwall Railway, and 350 more were employed by the four small companies whose lines were already working.[35] Four years later, when the main line was open, its staff amounted to 316, the others' to 429.[36] In December 1873 the numbers were as follows:[37]

Bodmin & Wadebridge	30
Cornwall	466
East Cornwall Minerals	28
Liskeard & Caradon	47
Redruth & Chacewater	70
West Cornwall	258
Total	899

That is, however, an understatement in respect of the Cornwall and West Cornwall companies.[38] Making some allowance on this account, and also for the addition of the Cornwall Minerals Railway, opened six months later, we can say that the total number of jobs afforded by the railways in Cornwall in 1874 was about 1,000. No subsequent returns of the kind help us here: for by the time they came to be made the Cornwall and West Cornwall Railways' staffs had been subsumed in the Great Western's. If we turn to the census figures instead, which are difficult to use because of their uncertain classification, it appears that at least 690 people were employed by railways in 1891. By 1911 the number was stated in the census returns to be 1858, but it may well in truth have approached 2500.[39] These are no large totals. But it must be remembered that the railways' employment – in sharp contrast to everything in copper, tin, and china-clay – was stable. Even in very hard times their business had to be carried on, in safety, and they made no significant reductions in staff. What work the railways did afford was therefore more continuous and permanent than any that had been offered in Cornwall before, except in agriculture and domestic service.

The development of the railways' traffic was not rapid. The main external communications of Cornwall in the past had been by sea:[40] along the south coast, or from Hayle to Bristol. The new railway had two great advantages here, in speed and in reliability during storms and fog. The speed was low: little more than twenty mph (including stops) for most passenger trains, for goods much less. Moreover there was at first a tiresome break of gauge between the Cornwall Railway (broad) and the West Cornwall (standard), involving a change at Truro for passengers and the transhipment of all goods. This was remedied by the laying-down of a third rail on the West Cornwall line in 1866–7, permitting through carriages to be run from London to Penzance.

3

Almost as soon as the Cornwall Railway opened, two developments appeared that portended change.

In the first half of 1861 the railway carried 1,063 tons of fish, 1,787 of potatoes, and 867 of broccoli and other vegetables. The corresponding figures for 1862 showed an increase of about 30 percent in fish and potato traffic, and the quantity of vegetables carried increased to 2,268 tons.[41] Hitherto the potato trade had gone by sea, and a good deal continued to do so. But the broccoli and the early potatoes (now coming to be appreciated as a delicacy; the 'new potato' is one of the best Victorian additions to the English cuisine) needed rapid conveyance if they were to reach their markets in their best condition. Here the railway could offer something much better than the steamers. The growers had to pay heavily for it. In 1872 the rates from West Cornwall stations to Paddington were 80s a ton by passenger train, collection and delivery extra: 47s 6d by goods train, delivery included. By the late eighties these rates had been halved.[42] That was due to the increasing traffic.[43] In 1880–1, a good season, the West Cornwall potato crop had grown to 11,000 tons. But the expansion of the trade owed something also to competition. The steamers still played a part in the business. The Midland Railway took up a substantial share of the traffic at Bristol (for Birmingham and the north of England), brought there from Cornwall by sea.[44]

The railways carried other perishables too, with profit to themselves and the county. Soon after 1880 the trade in narcissus and other early spring flowers began from the Scilly Islands. It quickly grew. The flowers were brought across to Penzance twice a week and sent up by the mail train overnight, to be at Covent Garden by 5am.[45] No other mode of transport could then have looked at a schedule like that. Similarly with milk. London eventually reached out for its daily supply right down to Penzance.[46]

The fish traffic also became extensive, though it oscillated sharply from good seasons to bad. In 1876 the Cornwall Railway conveyed 3,941 tons; in 1878, a year of disaster, 2,105.[47] The London & South Western company, having nosed its way down to Plymouth in 1876, was interested in getting some of the trade brought into that port by sea and carrying it thence up to London itself, or northwards by arrangement with the Midland. A steamer with South Western officials paid a visit to Mevagissey for the purpose.[48] They evidently thought the prospect unpromising. In 1884, when a Mevagissey Railway and Harbour Improvement scheme was set on foot, the South Western board refused to meet a deputation to discuss it.[49]

The other main development that sprang from the opening of the Cornwall Railway was in the holiday trade. Before 1859 a visit to Cornwall was an adventure: 'you will find in any miscellaneous company many more Englishmen who have visited Paris than Truro.'[50] There was special point in the title Wilkie Collins chose for his book, *Rambles beyond Railways*, in 1851; and in the new edition that was published ten years later, after the railway had arrived, he deliberately retained it.[51] The adventurous flavour is well communicated in the first edition of Murray's *Handbook for Devon and Cornwall* (1850); tours into Cornwall recommended in it started from railheads at Taunton or Plymouth.

With the opening of the railway in 1859 all this began to change quickly. Next year Thomas Cook – an entrepreneur of genius, his antennae always alert for new opportunities – descended on Cornwall to prospect the ground and prepare his first excursion there. It was announced for 20 June, a ten-days' trip in a special train from Bristol, to take in Land's End, St Michael's Mount, and a voyage up the Tamar, all under Cook's personal guidance. This succeeding, it was followed later that summer by another, the bookings for it starting as far north as Kelso and Berwick.[52] The opening of Cornwall to popular, organised tourism had begun.

Hitherto no Cornish town could claim to be a recognised English watering-place. The guidebooks said nothing on that matter, beyond commending the mild climate of Mount's Bay.[53] There were some visitors, but they were few and the accommodation provided for them was accordingly simple. All this changed in the 1860s. At Penzance, where general business was already growing steadily,[54] there was much new bustle. The Queen's and Mount's Bay Hotels appeared. Alexandra Road was opened by the Princess of Wales in 1865, and the impressive Public Buildings went up, costing £13,000.[55] It was observed that two shops bought in 1836 for £220 were sold to the railway company for the enlargement of the station in 1874 for £2,700.[56] The Falmouth Hotel was built, close to the station and the docks there, for £9,000. The foundation stone was laid a fortnight before the railway arrived in 1863, and it was opened two years later.[57]

Here, in the growing holiday traffic, must be seen the main explanation of the rising number of passengers on the Cornwall Railway in the 1860s and 1870s, at a time when the resident population of the county itself was declining. The growth was a very gradual business, not attributable to the railway alone: coach services continued in Cornwall very late,[58] and coastal steamers went on carrying passengers from London to Falmouth and Penzance. But there was no doubt that the influx of visitors increased very much after the arrival of the main line and the branch railways. We can see the process clearly, taking different forms, at St Ives and Newquay.

In the 1860s St Ives had a population of 7,000 and a flourishing pilchard fishery. A branch was authorised to it in 1864, but it was not opened until 1877. During that interval the town had fallen on hard times. The trade with the neighbouring tin mines decreased, and the pilchards went elsewhere. It had few visitors, and those who did come found the air 'tainted with the effluvia of the cellars'. After 1877 the place was tidied up, set itself to invite them, and soon appreciated that they offered a regular livelihood. The Great Western company contributed handsomely to this end by taking a lease of Tregenna Castle, adjoining the town, and opening it as an hotel in 1878.[59]

Newquay owes its first substantial development to J.T. Treffry, who bought the manorial rights there in 1838, rebuilt the pier, improved the harbour, and laid down a railway to it from the china-clay district on the moors above in 1844–9.[60] This eventually became part of the Cornwall Minerals Railway, which began carrying passengers to and from the south coast at Fowey in 1876. Newquay was by then recognised as 'quite a favourite summer resort'.[61] It was at first select, containing 'some handsome villas of a superior class, belonging to gentlemen of the county'.[62] But after 1879, when the Cornwall Minerals Railway had been taken over by the Great Western and a convenient connection with the main line had been put in at Par, the place grew more popular. The village swelled into a little town; by 1901 it had a resident population of 3,000. Its industrial character had by then gone, the china-clay being handled at Par and Fowey on the south coast. With its magnificent sandy beaches, the way was open for it to become the most frequented resort in Cornwall.[63]

Much the same thing happened, on a smaller scale, in the other little towns to which branches were built from the trunk line – all largely for the same purpose of developing the holiday business: to Looe (1879);[64] to Fowey,[65] which skilfully managed both to receive visitors and to develop as an industrial port;[66] to Helston (1887);[67] and to Perranporth (1903–5).

So, by all these means, the railways helped the economy of Cornwall to withstand the heavy blows dealt at it in the 1860s and 1870s. On the other hand they failed to help, or actually injured, a good many people there in the process. The fishing trade, for example, was not damaged only by the changing habits of the fish. By creating new markets for the higher-priced fish up the country the railways may be said to have discouraged the catching of the cheaper sorts, which had formed the staple diet of many of the Cornish poor.[68] Here, as elsewhere, there were bitter complaints of the railways' rates, for the conveyance of both fish and vegetables.[69] The complaints were sharpened in Cornwall because the Great Western company exercised a monopoly there, and that was rendered more glaring by the slow and inconvenient service it provided. Protests, of one sort and another, were endless. The chairman of the Port of Falmouth Chamber of Commerce voiced 'the very strong and universal complaints from all parts of the United Kingdom of the impossibility under present arrangements of reaching any point in this county westward of Liskeard from London, and also from the eastern as well as the Midland counties, at a reasonable hour on the day of starting'. At the same time the town council of Penzance asked for a quicker train west of Exeter. It was supported by the superintendent of the West Cornwall line; but the withering retort came back from his superior officer that this would require the running of an extra train from Plymouth to Penzance – 92 *miles!!*'(doubly underlined).[70] That was that. The principal express trains (one only each way) carried no third-class passengers. When Lostwithiel complained in 1883 that these trains no longer called there, it was simply told that first and second-class traffic was insufficient to justify stopping them. This class distinction was already obsolete by then in most other parts of England (see p185). The Mayor spoke rudely of the Great Western at a public meeting; and James Grierson, the company's general manager, resented his remarks.[71]

4

There was nothing peculiar to Cornwall in such exchanges. But they took on a rougher edge there partly from the county's bewildering economic difficulties, partly because it depended, as few other English or Welsh counties did, on the services of one trunk line, and partly because that line was poor, and poorly equipped. The timber viaducts, which had always alarmed many travellers,[72] were becoming a reproach. The replacement of them, by embankments or by new structures of masonry and metal, had begun in 1871, and a third of them east of Truro had gone by 1882. But progress was slow, and it then caused a dispute between the Cornwall and the Great Western companies, taken to arbitration with unsatisfactory results.[73] The line was single the whole way from Devonport to Falmouth, and that, combined with its steep gradients, severely limited the amount of traffic it could take. To many people – not only in Cornwall, but all over the West Country – the continuance of the Great Western's broad gauge seemed the hallmark of ancient monopoly, behind the times and unimproving.[74]

Some Cornishmen came to believe that their only hope lay in breaking that monopoly. In the 1840s the London & South Western Railway had supported the Central Cornwall project, as a continuation of its own system on the standard gauge, and though that had been defeated it had driven a line down to Exeter in 1860 and reached Plymouth, via Okehampton, in 1876. It still had ambitions in Cornwall, and a curious pledge of them in its control of the little Bodmin & Wadebridge Railway, acquired in 1846 by a purchase that had never been legalised.[75] It was natural that those who were discontented, for whatever reason, with the Cornwall Railway and its master the Great Western should look in this direction; natural too that the South Western should be willing to entertain their approaches smilingly. But when it came to taking action, it showed remarkable ineptitude. The company's historian rightly characterises its policy here as 'dabbling'.[76] It would neither go into Cornwall whole-heartedly nor stay out.

Three main opportunities presented themselves to it in the 1870s and 1880s. One was to support the building of a long line westwards from Okehampton by way of Launceston (which had secured a broad-gauge railway only after a struggle in 1865)[77] to join up with the Bodmin & Wadebridge. The other two arose in a large tract of East Cornwall hardly yet served at all by railways: for a branch across the Tamar towards Calstock and Callington, where there were mines still at work, or for one to link up with the failing Liskeard & Caradon line by an extension southwards from Launceston.[78] The South Western backed the North Cornwall Railway, authorised in 1882 to spring from its line at Okehampton and run through Launceston, Camelford, and Wadebridge to Padstow. This railway, like the trunk line in the south, took seventeen years to complete, the South Western blowing hot and cold towards it all the time.[79] It was at last finished in 1899; a branch had reached Bude in the previous year. An effort then appeared to make something of Padstow, with a well-equipped fish dock and a substantial hotel. But the fish trade there did not in the end amount to much.[80] The railway captured the traffic in slate from Delabole, carrying it down to Wadebridge and Padstow for shipment and so putting Port Gaverne out of work.[81] For the rest its passenger and goods traffic always remained scanty. Though nobody who ever travelled by the North Cornwall line, through that clean and spacious landscape, could have the heart to regret that it was built, it was a palpable loser: a monument of the late-Victorian competitive spirit almost as striking as the Great Central company's extension from Sheffield to London.

By the time it was opened the broad gauge was no more; swept away throughout the West Country in May 1892. The Great Western (which now owned the Cornwall Railway outright) was coming to be imbued with a spirit of fresh enterprise. It built a new line, twelve miles long, from Chacewater to Perranporth and Newquay. That was completed in 1905, and in the same year the company secured powers to build another piece of railway, to link the Bodmin branch to the old Newquay line at Roche with an intermediate station at Lanivet; affording an easier passage for trains going to Newquay, Truro, and West Cornwall than the old route, with its awkward curves and gradients, through Lostwithiel, Par, and St Austell.[82] Though this line was not in the end built, its promotion showed the Great Western company's concern to improve its services in Cornwall.

The old complaints were now stilled. Whatever they might have thought of the company in the past, people in Cornwall had to recognise that they were well served now, and still better with each year that went by. In 1887 the fastest train between London and Penzance took $9^1/_4$ hours ($11^3/_4$ hours for third-class passengers). By 1904 the time had come down to seven hours, for all passengers alike. In 1914 it was $6^1/_4$.

It happens that we can observe something of the growth of Penzance's railway business from 1890 to 1910 through a fortunate survival of a record of the takings from passengers booked there month by month.[84] Here they are, in summary:

TABLE I

PASSENGER BOOKINGS AT PENZANCE, 1890–1910

	Average per year	Increase % on previous period
1890–6	£14,866	
1897–1903	16,621	11.8
1904–10	23,433	41.0

These figures are of limited value. To judge the growth of the holiday traffic we should like to know the numbers of passengers *arriving*. Here we are given only the amount spent by those who left, whether on day trips or on long journeys. Still, the returns show one thing clearly. For most of the 1890s the business fluctuated, no doubt partly according to the weather. It took off in 1898 and increased, with one trifling exception, every year thereafter. The biggest increase in any one year (by 68.4 percent) was in 1904, and that was evidently due – the monthly figures put it beyond doubt – to the introduction of the new seven-hour train from London that the Great Western company presently called the 'Cornish Riviera Express'. The concept of 'the Cornish Riviera' proved a brilliant stroke of publicity. The phrase was first used (by the railway company at any rate) as the title of a little book designed to advertise the attractions of the district and the railway services it enjoyed, published early in 1904. A quarter of a million copies of that are said to have been sold in a single year.[85] Perhaps the greatest value of the expression was that it emphasised the attractions of Cornwall in the winter (in those days the Riviera of the Mediterranean was known to English people primarily as a winter resort), so helping to bring in visitors all the year round. Introduced for the summer season only, in 1906 the train began to run throughout the year.[85] The station at Penzance was already by 1903 the busiest and most lucrative on the system in Cornwall. Table 2 shows that, by comparison with others that were busy and lucrative too.

The railway benefited some Cornish towns at the expense of their rivals. Truro and Bodmin had both claimed the honour of being the county town. There was no need to adjudicate between them: Truro was accepted as the chief town of the western division of the county, Bodmin of the eastern. Eventually, however, the question had to be determined. When a separate diocese was established for Cornwall in 1876, its seat was placed at Truro. Then came the creation of the County Council in 1889. Where should it meet, and – more important – where should its permanent administration be placed? Again the debate was settled in favour of Truro. Both these decisions must have been influenced (they were probably determined) by the comparison between the two towns' railway facilities; vital at this time before motor transport had been developed. Bodmin lay off the main railway system, linked to it by a little branch only in 1887. Truro was the most important junction in Cornwall, where the lines forked for Penzance and Falmouth. For the great majority of those who had business with the Bishop or with the county administrators – clergy, agitated ratepayers, or the Lord Lieutenant – the railway provided much better facilities at Truro than at Bodmin. It was surely the railway that made Truro the administrative capital of Cornwall.[86]

It helped to do something more than that. The Three Towns, the conurbation of Plymouth, Devonport, and Stonehouse united into one in 1914, had always been closely connected with Cornwall, by coastal ships and ferries. Before the railway was opened there were six coach services a day coming in from Cornwall and steam packets on five days a week, as well as carriers' services from as far afield as Truro and Stratton.[87] The railway brought no startling increase in this service. It provided five week-day trains to Plymouth; 30 years later there were still only six. But then it must be remembered that each train could accommodate at least ten times as many passengers as a stage-coach.

Fresh opportunities were afforded at once by the railway, and the alert were quick to take them. It was no accident that a new daily paper, the *Western Morning News*, should have made its appearance at the beginning of 1860, which aimed from the

TABLE 2

TRAFFIC AT TEN CORNISH STATIONS, 1903 AND 1913

1903

	passenger receipts a £	Goods receipts £	Total receipts £	Staff	Paybill expenses £
Camborne	10464	16119	26583	19	1178
Falmouth	16381	13262	29643	20	315
Fowey	4350	58333	62683	21	7742b
Liskeard	8625	9881	18506	17	082
Newquay	8018	8296	16314	18	1066
Penzance	52324	46448	98772	52c	5279c
Redruth	10812	20298	31110	23	1129
St Austell	12514	32466	46780	25	1448
St Ives	13541	20887	34428	20	814
Truro	20864	19075	39939	66	4213

1913

	passenger receipts a £	Goods receipts £	Total receipts £	Staff	Paybill expenses £
Camborne	12120	23535	35655	21	1515
Falmouth	19460	27532	46992	19	1499
Fowey	5398	86858	92256	22	12503b
Liskeard	9887	15572	25459	22	1684
Newquay	13705	12451	26156	21	1456
Penzance d	24700	40552	65252	73	7423
Redruth	16117	28556	44673	29	1918
St Austell	18249	27970	46219	21	1590
St Ives	10267	7907	18174	11	953
Truro	24525	28454	52979	63	5178

a Including parcels and miscellaneous.
b Including cost of casual labour employed in the china-clay traffic.
c Excluding staff at the goods station (figures not available).
d A puzzling reduction, unexplained.
Source: R266/45 (Plymouth Traffic Division, no. 4)

start at serving Cornwall as well as Devon; or that the *Plymouth & Devonport Weekly Journal* should have converted itself that summer into a *Western Daily Mercury*, with the same purpose in mind. Since Cornwall could not support a daily newspaper of its own, it depended largely on these two from Plymouth, though its own weeklies the *West Briton* and *Royal Cornwall Gazette* maintained themselves sturdily at Truro.

By the end of the century the conurbation counted more than 12 times as many people as Camborne, the most populous town in Cornwall. Its industries, and especially the naval dockyards, could usually offer work. That was what many Cornishmen badly needed; they made their way there in substantial numbers, and settled. In 1911 nearly twelve percent of the population of Plymouth and Devonport had been born in Cornwall.[88] Moreover, Saltash and its district, on the Cornish side of the Tamar, became in some measure suburbs of Plymouth. Season tickets were being offered across the railway bridge as early as 1874.[89] With the aid of steam railcars and push-and-pull trains, nearly forty services came to be provided on every weekday in each direction by 1910. The suburban business was not large compared with that in the big northern towns, but what there was of it the railways had almost wholly created.

By 1914 Plymouth had come to be something like a regional capital, the headquarters of a good many businesses with names beginning 'Devon and Cornwall'. It furnished services, facilities, and occasional amusements that Cornwall could hardly have secured on its own; and the railway link made that provision better worth undertaking.

5

Looking back over the story, we can see that the railway played a very considerable part in the life of Victorian Cornwall. It had at first been a simple tool in the hands of the mining industry; a necessary tool, but nothing more. The construction of the chief trunk line represented a pertinacity that rose to a quiet kind of heroism. The passengers it came to serve were quite different from those that had been contemplated by its first promoters. If the management was not quick to seize new opportunities (it had no funds for any bold experiments), it faced the baffling consequences of the collapse of the mining industry. The steady growth of its traffic, particularly in goods, is some indication of its success. Had it been a wealthier enterprise and its line easier to work – had Cornwall itself been a wealthier community – the success might have come sooner and have been greater when it arrived.

The decline of Cornish copper and tin production was primarily due to causes beyond the industry's own control. The discovery of vast new resources overseas might have come at any time. Their exploitation and working owed little to railways that was of real importance and could even have been managed, though rather clumsily, without steamships. Had that exploitation occurred while Cornwall was still as much isolated from the rest of England as it was before 1859, it is difficult to see what alternative livelihood any of its people would have been able to find. In ordinary agriculture – in maincrop production – the Cornish growers could not compete with the bigger men further east. The unique asset they enjoyed was their climate, which allowed them to produce well in advance of the rest of England. To get the best out of that privilege they required the speediest and most regular transport that was possible to take their goods to the richest English markets. This the railway afforded, not only to them but also to the milk-producers and to the flower-growers of the Scilly Islands.

Though the mechanised railways never did a great deal for metalliferous mining in Cornwall, they helped the production of china-clay most materially. Its growing business depended largely on the ports of Par and Fowey, which both passed into the ownership of the Great Western Railway. At Fowey the traffic expanded successfully to the point where it produced serious congestion, and that became a considerable problem after 1918.

As for the holiday trade, we can say with certainty that nothing but the railway could have engendered it in the form it came to take, or handled it as it grew larger. If it had been a luxury trade primarily for the well-to-do, with the addition of some adventurous folk coming by cheap coastal steamers, the roads and the small harbours might have continued to be adequate with only a little backing from railways for a good deal longer, as they did in north-western Scotland. But the Cornish Riviera never became, after the fashion of its Mediterranean prototype, a preserve of the rich. From the 1870s we can observe Cornwall developing as a place for family holidays, even for those who could afford to go there only by the slow third-class trains from London.[90] It could offer a wide range of pleasures to many different kinds of people. The railway allowed them to discover, and to choose; its business was to encourage them. It did so with a steady persistence, and optimism to the end. The London & South Western company showed that in the completion, long delayed though it was, of its lines to Bude and Padstow. The Great Western proclaimed it confidently in its shrewd development of motor-bus services radiating out from the stations at Helston and Penzance,[91] no less than in the splendid new express train it introduced from London in 1904.

In 1914 Cornwall remained, as it had been in 1859, the remotest part of England. But in the course of half a century railways had changed the meaning of remoteness itself.

TABLE 3

THE CORNWALL RAILWAY
PASSENGERS CARRIED, RECEIPTS, AND EXPENDITURE, 1859–88

1 Year	2 Passengers carried	3 Total receipts £	4 Working expenses £	5 Col 4 as % of Col 3	6 Preferential charges a £	7 Total expenses £	8 Deficit/profit (Cols 3 & 7) £
1859*b*	378240	36869	19095	56.3	12888	31983	+ 4886
1860	528887	63071	36882	58.5	44195	81077	– 18006
1861	506204	68236	39290	57.6	44751	84041	– 15805
1862	503172	69903	38746	55.4	44466	83212	– 13309
1863	554147	76186	42211	55.4	42020	84231	– 8045
1864	620528	91075	51381	56.4	57737	109118	– 18043
1865	631653	94371	51530	54.6	58251	109781	– 15410
1866	591626	92894	47465	51.1	61675	109140	– 16246
1867	563956	93909	42488	45.2	65108	107596	– 13687
1868	578753	98957	47027	47.5	65343	112370	– 13413
1869	579286	98176	47624	48.5	64648	112272	– 14096
1870	602859	101297	50710	50.0	65105	115815	– 14518
1871	620810	105088	53896	51.3	66131	120027	– 14939
1872	649472	118494	58129	49.1	63016	121145	– 2651
1873	694859	133694	80440*c*	60.2	64730	145170	– 11476
1874	705823	134310	80583	60.0	64112	144695	– 10385
1875	719782	128565	79733	62.0	65126	144859	– 16294
1876	713613	129015	75342	58.4	64427	139769	– 10754
1877	733661	129383	71599	55.3	64163	135762	– 6379
1878	755767	127764	70140	54.9	64550	134690	– 6926
1879	740984	127769	69815	54.6	65310	135125	– 7356
1880	778245	136660	76040	55.6	65320	141360	– 4700
1881	795416	140626	75234	53.5	65864	140918	– 292
1882	848820	147175	80038	54.4	66013	146051	+ 1124
1883	871656	150641	80590	53.5	65128	145718	+ 4923
1884	873376	152133	77633	51.0	65961	143594	+ 8539
1885	861061	149812	73989	49.4	66402	140391	+ 9421
1886	872801	149020	70555	47.3	66766	137321	+ 11699
1887	879991	151724	70687	46.6	66589	137276	+ 14448
1888	890503	154169	74665	48.4	66586	141251	+ 12918

a Mainly interest charges and dividends on preference stocks and shares.

b May–December only

c Maintenance of way, works, and stations 53.7% more than in 1872. The heavy repair and reconstruction of the timber viaducts was now under way.

Source: R1110/85–7

NOTES

1 In *VCH Essex, Leicestershire, Staffordshire* and *Wilstshire*.

2 Birmingham, Liverpool, Manchester, and Glasgow are well studied (side by side with London), by J.R. Kellett in *The Impact of Railways on Victorian Cities* (1969); York, Hull, Coventry and Birmingham in the *VCH*.

3 In T.C. Barker and M. Robbins, *History of London Transport* (1963–74).

4 A general survey of the country as a whole is offered in RTC.

5 The best general account of the railways of Cornwall is by D. St J. Thomas in chap 7 of vol i of *Reg. Hist.* (5th ed., 1981). This gives some attention to the economic and social consequences of their work. C.R. Clinker, *The Railways of Cornwall, 1809–1963*, provides a useful and accurate chronicle of events. The traffic figures for Great Western stations for the years 1903 and 1913 are in R266/45. There appear to be no such figures at all for the London & South Western company.

6 The Cornwall Railway was amalgamated with the Great Western in 1889, and the West Cornwall passed into the hands of the Associated Companies (see p60) in 1866.

7 Devon Great Consols was the only mining company in the West of England that owned the railway serving it: *Trans. Devonshire Association*, 96 (1964) 265.

8 This represented a modernisation and an extension at both ends of a mining line, the Hayle Railway, opened in 1837–8.

9 *The Route Book of Cornwall* (pub. Besley, 1853), 155.

10 The history of the Cornwall Railway is well recounted in MacDermot, vol. ii, chap 7. On its promotion and early work see the miscellaneous papers in R134/1, 134/18, and C.R. Clinker's article in *Modern Transport*, 2 May 1959.

11 The material was deliberately chosen as being low in first cost, in the knowledge that the eventual chage for maintenance and replacement would be high. If iron or masonry had been insisted on, the line could not have been built then at all.

12 Economy again: the Saltash bridge was, by comparison with its great iron predecessors, astonishingly cheap: VRY, 27.

13 For an example see the discussion between Thomas Coode and William Rashleigh in 1852–3: Cornwall RO, DDR(S) 1/848, 852.

14 A valuable collection of Brunel's own letters and reports to the directors of the Cornwall Railway relating to the construction of the line (1853–9) is in R134/17.

15 Lord Vivian to W. Longbourne, 22 November 1852: Cornwall RO, AD 267/9 (16). This was an unusual impression. Brunel's relations with the country gentlemen he dealt with were as a rule good. See for example his friendly correspondence with Sir John Kennaway: Devon RO (Exeter), 961 MS/4.

16 Cornwall RO, AD 267/9 (28): 3 January 1852 [ie 1853].

17 Vivian to Longbourne, 7 January 1853: *ibid.* (36).

18 At Truro, involving a separate part of Lord Vivian's property.

19 Vivian to Longbourne, 22 January 1853: *ibid.* (41).

20 The *Royal Cornwall Gazette* began a three-column leader on 1 February 1850 with these words: 'We announce today a great calamity. Mr Treffry is dead!' In Murray's *Handbook for Devon and Cornwall* (1850), 219–20, he is described as 'one of the most extraordinary men of his time'. See Treffry's journal, 1842–50 (Cornwall RO, DDTF/996) and the diaries and notebooks of his steward William Pease (DDX, 715/1–12); also J. Keast's biography *The King of Mid-Cornwall* (1982), esp. 147–50.

21 By a decision unusual in its liberality then he was rewarded with a pension of £200 a year: shareholders' report, August 1865 (R1110/85).

22 There is a racy account of one in 1839, salted with comments on some of the magnates, in *Barclay Fox's Journal*, ed. R.L. Brett (1979), 167–8.

23 Compare the active membership of the Railway Committee, out of which the Cornwall Railway emerged, at its meeting of 21 August 1840 (R134/1) with the board of directors when the company was constituted (R134/2, p.1).

24 The tribute paid to it by the government inspector, William Yolland, when he examined it three weeks before went well beyond the staid language that he and his colleagues generally used in their reports. He told the Board of Trade that it was a 'gigantic, magnificent, and highly scientific work'. PRO, MT6, 19/28.

25 These celebrations are agreeably recorded in the diary of Mrs Julia Yewens (Institute of Cornish Studies, MS. Lowenac F34). Prof. Charles Thomas kindly provided me with an extract from it.

26 There was at least one line from it taken up to a private house, Lanwithan outside Lostwithiel: [J. Polsue,] *Lake's Parochial History of...Cornwall* (1867–73), iv. 330.

27 P.A.S. Pool, *History of...Penzance* (1974), 153; D. Howse, *Greenwich Time* (1980), 112–13.

28 In 1887, though most of the capital was in the hands of the Associated Companies, one-fifth was still held by people living in Cornwall and Devon: calculation from R134/41. Each £20 Ordinary share raised £8 in cash when the Great Western took the Cornwall company over in 1889.

29 D.B. Barton, *Copper Mining in Cornwall* (1961), 79, 83.

30 J. Dunstan, *Origins of the Sheffield & Chesterfield Railway* (1970), 18; T. Coleman, *The Railway Navvies* (1965), 194; R. M. Barton (ed.), *Life in Cornwall in the late Nineteenth Century* (1972), 208. For an important word of caution here see D. Brooke, *The Railway Navvy* (1983), 63–4.

31 See A. L. Rowse, *The Cornish in America* (1969), esp. chap. 8.

32 Only Huntingdonshire showed a greater fall in 1861–1911: by 12.3 percent, against 11.1 percent in Cornwall.

33 Most of the large pumping-engines for the Severn Tunnel (the longest under-water tunnel then in the world) were made by Harvey's in 1880–6: T.A. Walker, *The Severn Tunnel* (1886), 26, 43, 138, 140, 159, 180.

34 R.M. Barton, *History of the Cornish China-Clay Industry* (1966), 93, 109.

35 PP 1856, liv. 660–71.

36 *Ibid.*, 1860, lxi. 154–7.

37 *Ibid.* (House of Lords), 1874, xiii. 570–5.

38 Some categories of their staff (notably drivers, firemen, and shunters) are omitted in these returns, since these men were provided, under a complicated arrangement, by the Associated Companies.

39 The 1911 figure represents 1.9 percent of the occupied male population. But the total numbers, in all branches of railway work, were certainly a good deal higher than the census returns state, as the Census Commissioners candidly admitted in 1911. For this, see RTC, 18.

40 In 1845 two mail-coaches served for the entire road traffic between Plymouth and Exeter: PP 1845, xxxix. 197. The journey from London to Falmouth had occupied about 42 hours in 1836: A. Bates, *Directory of Stage Coach Services* (1969).

41 Shareholders' report, August 1862: R1110/85.

42 R1014/3, No. 23. See W.M. Acworth's interesting discussion of the economics of the business in his *Railways of England* (1889 ed.), 271–2.

43 In the early summer of 1878 two special potato trains were running up from Cornwall daily, all other goods traffic up the main line east of Plymouth being shunted into sidings to let them pass: acc. Great Western Railway, Kingsbridge Road, 8 June 1878 (PP 1878–9, lxii. 106).

44 The trade in new potatoes from Jersey, which had a great hold on the London market, was increasing from the 1860s onwards: J.H. Lucking, *The Great Western at Weymouth* (1971), 55, 58–9.

45 Acworth, 272. See also RM 4 (1899) 311–18: *VCH Cornwall*, i. 579–81.

46 Very much the largest part of this supply came from St Erth: RM 22 (1908) 242.

47 R134/16, no. 20.

48 *Ibid.*

49 R411/7, min. 1509.

50 *Cornwall: its Mines and Miners* (1855), 1.

51 See 1861 ed., ix–x.

52 *Cook's Excursionist*, 15 May, 13 June, 1 July 1860.

53 See for example *Black's Picturesque Tourist and Road-book of England and Wales* (1846), 101: *Murray's Handbook* (1850), 155.

54 Rising rents were being paid for the quay: *Lake's Parochial History*, iii. 235.

55 Pool, *History of...Penzance*, 147, 193.

56 G.C. Boase, *Collectanea Cornubiensia* (1890), 931.

57 *Lake's Parochial History*, i. 411.

58 C. Noall, *History of Cornish Mail and Stage Coaches* (1963), 85–7.

59 *Murray's Handbook* (1879 ed.), 124; J.H. Matthews, *History of St Ives* (1892), 368; McDermot, ii. 269. There are useful miscellaneous papers relating to the hotel in R253/24–6; 266/45, 109.

60 *Lake's Parochial History*, i. 241–2; Barton, *China-Clay Industry*, 79.

61 *Watering Places of the South of England* (pub. Eyre, 1877), 760.

62 *Lake's Parochial History*, i. 241.

63 In 1910 Baedeker commended the hotels of Newquay more warmly than those in any other Cornish town: *Great Britain* (1910 ed.), 163.

64 The branch was not linked to the main line until 1901. See M.L. Messenger, *Caradon and Looe* (1978), 50–1, 60–5: an admirable study.

65 An inconvenient little journey from Par via St Blazey until the mineral line from Lostwithiel, derelict since 1879, was refurbished and opened again in 1895.

66 Barton, *China-clay Industry*, 132–3.

67 An attempt was made to build a light railway on from Helston to the Lizard (see papers in Cornwall RO, 12 M/EC/19/10), but in the end the Great Western Railway served that county by its motor-buses in 1903.

68 See *Reg. Hist.*, i. 137.

69 Matthews, *History of St Ives*, 368. For a spirited defence of the Great Western in this matter see Acworth, 270–1.

70 The mileage was in fact 80. R134/68, 65.

71 R134/72.

72 MacDermot, ii. 146: *Kilvert's Diary*, i (1938), 183: R.M. Barton (ed.), *Life in Cornwall at the End of the Nineteenth Century* (1974), 56, 59–60. No accidents of any importance ever occurred on the line that could be attributed to the timber construction of the viaducts.

73 MacDermot, ii. 153–4. Interesting papers from this arbitration are in R134/79.

74 See REW, 84–5.

75 R.A. Williams, *London & South Western Railway*, i (1968), 99–100. This tiny company deserves to have its history recounted really well. Its historian would enjoy one advantage, in the miscellaneous papers of Hayes Kyd, its manager from 1869 (R57/2): an extraordinary little archive, showing in minute detail how a country railway could come to be treated by everyone in its neighbourhood as a personal convenience of its own. Or hers: 'Miss Barnett would much prefer having a special train on Friday as it would be very inconvenient to go by the public one and hopes Mr Kyd will be able to arrange to have one at Polbrock at 12 o'clock, with steam engine for the Costislost party'. Q's delicious 'Cuckoo Valley Railway' was not a caricature.

76 Williams, ii. 271.

77 The struggle even came to play a part in the politics of the town. See A.F. Robbins, *Launceston Past and Present* (1888), 349–56; M. Robbins, *Points and Signals* (1967), 74–9.

78 For this see Messenger, *Caradon and Looe*, 49, 51, 53, 55–8.

79 See eg. its attitude towards the proposed Bude branch: Williams, ii. 268.

80 The South Western did not provide for even one conditional fish train up from Padstow (as it did from Plymouth): R948/452 (Western District), 50, 62–4.

81 *VCH Cornwall*, i. 521–2.

82 The course of the line is discussed in RM17 (1905) 141–2.

83 For an *amende honorable* see J. Hammond, *A Cornish Parish: being an Account of St Austell* (1897), 35.

84 R253/356.

85 See R.B. Wilson, *Go Great Western: a History of GWR Publicity* (1987 ed.), 25, 84; for the naming of the train, RM15 (1904), 92, 258, and MacDermot, ii. 257.

86 It was responsible similarly in Wiltshire for determining that Trowbridge became the county town, not Devizes. See *VCH Wilts*., vii. 147, x. 251.

87 M. Billing's *Directory...of Devon* (1857), 726, 769.

88 Census (1911), ix. 1, 12.

89 R.J. Woodfin, *Centenary of the Cornwall Railway* (1960), 139.

90 The journey by one of them down to Camborne in the 1870s is well described in M.V. Hughes, *A London Family* (1946), 85–91.

91 The first such services run by any railway company in Great Britain were put on there by the Great Western in 1903. See J. Cummings, *Railway Motor Buses*, ii. (1980), 24–6, 35, 38–40.

5
RUGBY JUNCTION

1

The railway towns of Britain formed a special group of their own. Most students of urban history would accept that statement, but if one goes on to ask 'what was a railway town?' or even 'which were the railway towns?' disagreement appears immediately.[1] Using the term in its strictest sense, it might perhaps be confined to those towns that became towns, where before they had been villages, solely because of the establishment in them of railway works. The classic instance is Crewe; others, which were on a much smaller scale, are Shildon (the oldest), Eastleigh and Horwich.[2] But there have also been railway towns of another kind; those that represented a grafting of new railway business on to old-established urban communities. Swindon is an especially interesting example of this type: for the railway town, New Swindon, grew up in the plain below the hill-top town of Old Swindon (as at Laon, on a smaller scale, in France), adjacent yet quite separate from the beginning.[3] There were several others – Ashford, Brighton, Darlington, Doncaster; Caerphilly in Wales, in Scotland Inverurie. Even one county town, Derby, in spite of its aristocratic associations, grew for a time at least into something like an appanage of the Midland Railway, though its industrial development came in the end to be more widely diversified.

All these places were 'railway towns' because they were the seat of railway works, for the building and repair of locomotives and rolling stock, and in some cases of a railway administration on a large scale too. But there was one other small and interesting group to which one might apply the term 'railway town' in a different sense: towns that, beyond question, were transformed by the railway, through their exceptional importance as railway junctions. There were in Britain four pre-eminent examples of towns of this kind. Three were cathedral cities, Peterborough, York, and Carlisle. The other one was Rugby.

2

Let us begin by considering what Rugby was like before the railway arrived. Here are two descriptions, very different. First the dry, precise account of it given by Samuel Lewis in 1833. Rugby, he says, is 'a market-town and parish...containing 2,501 inhabitants... The town is pleasantly situated upon rising ground, on the south side of the Avon: it consists of one street leading to the market-place, parallel with which, on the one side, is a narrower street, in which the shambles are placed,

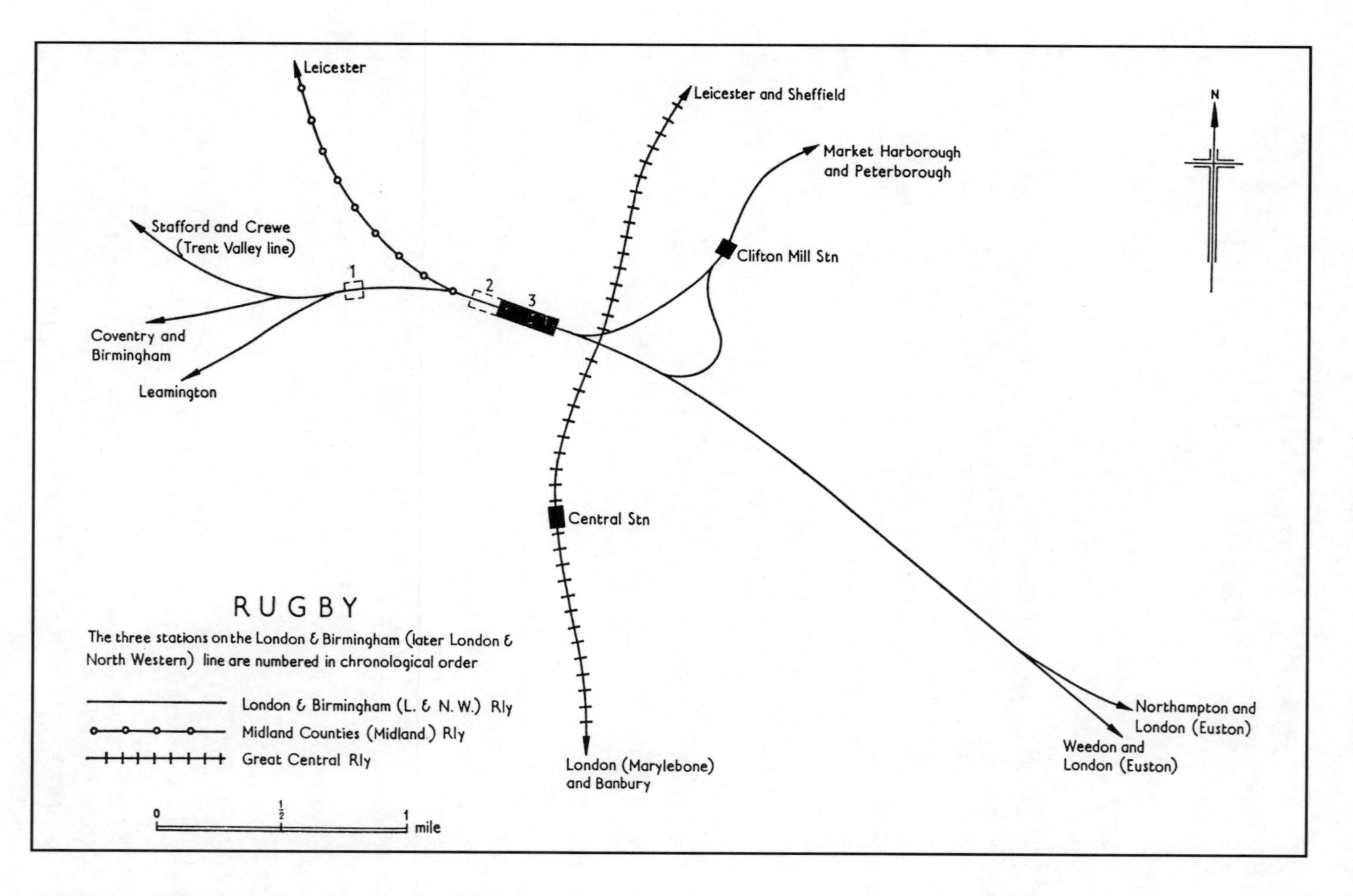
Leicester
Leicester and Sheffield
N
Market Harborough and Peterborough
Stafford and Crewe (Trent Valley line)
Clifton Mill Stn
1
2
3
Coventry and Birmingham
Leamington
Central Stn
RUGBY
The three stations on the London & Birmingham (later London & North Western) line are numbered in chronological order
London & Birmingham (L. & N. W.) Rly
Midland Counties (Midland) Rly
Great Central Rly
London (Marylebone) and Banbury
Northampton and London (Euston)
Weedon and London (Euston)
0
½
1 mile

and on the other a handsome and spacious street leading to the church. The houses are in general well built of brick, and of modern appearance, though occasionally intermixed with some of ancient character, with plaistered walls and thatched roofs. The Oxford Canal passes in the vicinity. The market, which is well attended, and abundantly supplied with corn, and provisions of every kind, is on Saturday: thirteen fairs are held annually, but the greater number are only cattle markets... The grammar school, which is the distinguishing feature in Rugby, is a noble and magnificent establishment, and has for many years maintained a high degree of reputation'.[4]

The second account is livelier, and more famous; relating to the same moment of time, but written over twenty years later. It comes from Tom Brown when, on his first journey to school, he asks the guard of the Tally-ho coach what sort of a place Rugby may be:

'Guard looks at him with a comical expression. Werry out-o'-the-way place, sir; no paving to streets, nor no lighting. Mazin' big horse and cattle fair in autumn – lasts a week – just over now. Takes town a week to get clean after it. Fairish hunting country. But slow place, sir, slow place – off the main road, you see – only three coaches a day, and one of 'em a two-'oss wan, more like a hearse nor a coach – Regulator – comes from Oxford. Young genl'm'n at school calls her Pig and Whistle and goes up to college by her (six miles an hour) when they goes to enter'.[5]

These two accounts are agreed on the main point: that Rugby was a market town, whose economy was wholly agricultural. Only one thing set it apart from scores of similar towns up and down the country, its grammar school. In this respect its situation was unique at that time: for in the 1830s it was the only nationally famous school that was placed in what was no more than a minor market town.

The first notion of building a railway to pass through the district was brought forward in 1825. In 1830 two rival plans for a trunk line linking London with Birmingham were prepared, one of them running by way of Rugby. These plans were unsuccessful; and it was not until 1833 that the London & Birmingham Railway was incorporated by Act of Parliament. This was to pass just north of Rugby, where, from the outset, it was intended to build a station. Its terminus at Birmingham was to adjoin that of the Grand Junction company, which was incorporated at the same time to build a railway northwards as far as Warrington, whence through communication would be afforded with Liverpool and Manchester. Rugby was thus to be placed on the line of the greatest railway in the United Kingdom, with the prospect of free interchange, of passengers and goods, with London, with Birmingham and the Black Country, with industrial Lancashire and the port of Liverpool.

It was an exciting prospect, to anyone in Rugby who could read it aright. But it was slow to materialise. The London & Birmingham and the Grand Junction were the first long-distance railways to be constructed in Europe, and they had to face all the difficulties that confronted pioneers. More than five years elapsed after the passing of their Acts of incorporation before they were brought into use throughout. The Grand Junction was opened first, on 4 July 1837. The London & Birmingham arrived at Rugby in two instalments. The northern section, from Birmingham to a temporary terminus at Rugby, was opened to passenger traffic on 9 April 1838. On the same day the southern part, from London , advanced as far as Denbigh Hall, a little north of Bletchley. The intervening gap of 34½ miles from that point to Rugby was closed five months later when the line was opened throughout its length from London to Birmingham, on 17 September.

The station at Rugby was sited some distance outside the town, at the point where the railway intersected the Newbold Road: a natural choice, for that was the only road leading north that the railway crossed. There seems to be no evidence to support the assertion that the trustees of the School refused to sell the land originally asked for by the London & Birmingham company, so obliging it to pass at a greater distance than it had intended. Such action is by no means improbable – it would be in line with the similar decisions of Eton College and the unhelpful attitude towards railways displayed by the Universities of Oxford and Cambridge, which are well authenticated.[6] The site of the station was not an inconvenient one by the standards of the time, however, for most railways passed well beyond the built-up areas of the towns they touched. The station itself was hardly more than a modest wooden shed; but the bridge was castellated, in the Gothic style, spanning the road with a four-centred arch. This excited A.W.N. Pugin's derision. When he wrote his *Apology for the Revival of Christian Architecture* in 1843 he attributed the decoration of the bridge wrongly to the station. It makes no difference, however, to the point of his comment: 'At Rugby, because Rugby School, as rebuilt lately, has had battlements and turrets, the old station had four half turrets with the best side turned out, and a few sham loop holes.' He went on to suggest an alternative Gothic design of his own.[7]

Pugin speaks of the 'old' station; that wooden shed lasted as a station less than three years. Its abandonment was a necessary consequence of the arrival of a second railway in Rugby.

This was the Midland Counties Railway, which was first projected in a shadowy form in the autumn of 1832, while the fate of the London & Birmingham project was still unsettled.[8] Its main purpose was to provide an outlet for the coal from Derbyshire and Nottinghamshire to the south, by a railway running up the Soar Valley and through Leicester. The route to be followed south of Leicester was at first doubtful. William Jessop and Joseph Glynn, the engineers who were advising the promoters, made it clear that there were two ways in which the Midland Counties line could link up with the London & Birmingham, when that was built: by a shorter line to Rugby or a longer one to Northampton, with a junction to the west of that town. The plan underwent important modifications before it was realised, the railway changing its character from a conveyor of coal into a passenger-carrying line, with the ambition of becoming part of the great trunk railway between London and north-eastern England.

In this second scheme the junction with the London & Birmingham line was finally fixed at Rugby, and it is easy to see why. The Rugby route required the building of only eighteen miles of new railway, whereas the Northampton route required thirty-three miles. Between Leicester and Rugby there was no major physical obstacle to be overcome, nothing more serious than the bridging of the Avon at Rugby itself. But to carry a railway from Leicester to Northampton meant crossing the Welland, climbing the steep hills on the southern side of its valley, to drop down again to the Nene. The one substantial argument in favour of the Northampton route was that it was five miles shorter between Leicester and London. On the other hand it was also argued that the Rugby route would have the advantage of providing a link between Leicester, Coventry, and Birmingham, whereas that journey would be a very much more roundabout one by way of Northampton.

There was much grumbling in Northampton when the news of this decision became known. But the promoters of the Midland Counties Railway could not be persuaded to change it, and they secured parliamentary powers to build the Rugby line in 1836. In the following year Northampton interests sponsored a South Midland Counties Railway, but it failed with ignominy.[9]

The Midland Counties line was opened to general public use from Nottingham and Derby to Leicester on 5 May 1840 and from Leicester to Rugby on the following 1 July.[10] Since the purpose of running the line to Rugby had been to provide a junction with the London & Birmingham, and since the easiest route for the Midland Counties line, descending from the high ground north of the Avon, required that the junction should be at a point nearly half a mile east of the existing station, there was nothing for it but to move the station to a new site. The first proposal, in 1839, had been that the two companies should own the new premises jointly; but this was rejected by the London & Birmingham.[11] In February 1840 that company agreed that the new station should be built at the expense of the Midland Counties and let at £100 a year for a term of 99 years to the London & Birmingham, which should exercise the 'sole control' of its management and receive an annual payment for transacting the business of the Midland Counties company.[12]

The Midland Counties line was opened on the same day as a series of others further north, linked with it, which made it possible for the first time to travel by railway from London, through Rugby and Derby, to Leeds, York, and Hull.

It thus came about that the Midland Counties and the London & Birmingham companies were established at Rugby, hardly as partners but rather side by side, as independent agents drawn together by common interests. Two things soon contributed to change their relationship.

In the first place, both companies were merged into larger units. The Midland Counties Railway joined up with its bitter rival the Birmingham & Derby Junction and with the North Midland to form the Midland company in 1844, presided over by an outsider, George Hudson. Two years later the London & Birmingham became part of the London & North Western, along with the Grand Junction, the

Manchester & Birmingham, and the Liverpool & Manchester companies. The chairman of the London & Birmingham, George Carr Glyn, was elected chairman of the new combine. As they progressed towards becoming national systems, the interests of these larger organisations moved apart; they came to treat each other as foreign powers, often fighting for position in contests far remote from the Midlands.

Secondly, the simple pattern established hitherto soon came to be changed, with the opening of three new lines, all converging on Rugby, in 1847–51: from Stafford by way of the Trent Valley, from Peterborough and Market Harborough, and from Leamington.[13] Much the most important of these lines was the first, for the Trent Valley at once became the main route from Euston to the North, a huge bypass for the old line that joined the Grand Junction at Birmingham;[14] and Rugby acquired new consequence as the diverging point between the old line and the new. From the moment when the Trent Valley line was opened, Rugby gained a train service to and from the north – that is Holyhead (for Ireland), Lancashire, and Scotland – far superior to Birmingham's. In the 1880s Foxwell observed that Birmingham was the 'the unfortunate town on the North Western system. Once it enjoyed the full blaze of railway speed; now it is left out in the cold, on a neglected "siding". The North Western arterial trains forget all about it as they sweep along the direct route of the Trent Valley'.[15]

Rugby became a frontier post, where the northern and southern divisions of the London & North Western company met.[16] This meant something more than a mere administrative demarcation. All trains to and from the north changed engines at Rugby, and the officials of the southern division were not slow to point out that the accommodation provided for their machines was inadequate:

> 'so insufficient that Mr McConnell (locomotive superintendent of the southern division) is applying for an immediate increase. The Trent Valley engines come up the line to wait close to the place where the Wolverton engines are coked, and...it would be advisable, in the present position of the lines, to provide coke sheds for all the engines at that point. The best position for the coke sheds for the northern division is evidently at the Trent Valley engine shed lower down the line – where there is plenty of room, and from whence the engines could come up to wait, ready coked'.[17]

Of the other new lines, the one to Leamington was never of much importance. The Market Harborough and Peterborough line was strategically more valuable, offering the London & North Western a reasonably direct and convenient route from Birmingham to the eastern counties. Even when a second route was developed from Birmingham via Leicester and the Midland Railway in the 1860s, the Rugby line remained the shorter (by eleven miles) and the better, with the substantial added advantage of providing easy interchange at Rugby for traffic to and from the north.

The opening of these three lines turned Rugby into a first-class railway centre. It is worth noting that none of them was a dead-end branch. Each connected with other lines, affording a service to places of importance. Rugby could now claim to be Rugby Junction indeed.

3

The second station, of 1840, soon proved inadequate for this greatly-increased traffic. Its enlargement began to be discussed as early as 1847.[18] We have an exact specification of the premises, as part of a general survey of stations throughout the London & North Western system, dating from 1 January 1848.[19] It is so detailed and precise that it is best reproduced in full:

TABLE 4

London & North Western Railway's Rugby Station, 1848

	Up (to London) side	Down (from London) side
Passenger sidings	792ft	663ft
Goods sidings	2,872ft	6,290ft
Turntables	10 x 12ft	1 x 36ft
Platform: length	392 x 10ft	111 x 10ft
Goods shed		3,586 sq ft
Spare carriage shed		1,824 sq ft
Engine shed		20,568 sq ft
Station shed		1,400 sq ft
Booking offices	570 sq ft	450 sq ft
Waiting-rooms: Ladies	228 sq ft	228 sq ft
Gentlemen	570 sq ft	510 sq ft
Refreshment room		570 sq ft

This statement excludes the separate, though closely adjacent, station of the Midland company, which provided the only refreshment room on the up side of the line. It was then in process of enlargement.[20] In the following month the London & North Western company was negotiating for the acquisition of additional land, at a price of some £9,000 – though, with an eye to economies that might well be necessary at that time of great financial stringency, it was noted that the purchase 'need not be paid for for a considerable time'.

The work of enlarging the station had already begun, on a small scale. In January 1848 a new waiting-room was being built, and the goods shed extended.[22] Larger works followed, on which nearly £10,000 were spent between March 1849 and

January 1852.[23] This was hardly more than a beginning, however, and the company's manager, Mark Huish, was well aware of that. Before these works were completed, in November 1851, he was urging the traffic committee to contemplate a radical change in the arrangement of the station, based not on piecemeal alterations but on a considered long-term plan.[24] To be completed satisfactorily this required the full co-operation of the Midland company; and when it appeared that that was not sure to be forthcoming, or at least that it would be delayed, he pressed his company to go ahead on its own.[25] A plan costing £26,000 for the gradual improvement of the down side of the station had already been produced by then;[26] and three months later the tender of Messrs Branston & Gwyther was accepted for an instalment of the work, in the sum of £9,240 12s 10d.[27]

Huish's bold vision of a completely replanned station at Rugby was not fulfilled until 1886. For the present, the hand-to-mouth reconstruction he deplored had to suffice. These were difficult years for the railways, with much clearing-up still to be undertaken arising out of the boom and crash of the 1840s, followed by high prices and a shortage of labour in the 1850s. The enlargement of the station at Rugby, such as it was, had been forced on the London & North Western management by the arrival of the three new lines, in 1847–51, followed by the continuing expansion of the Midland company's business. No further lines were opened into Rugby for many years; and in 1853 the Midland company took the important step of promoting a second line from the north to London, through Bedford and Hitchin. It was opened in 1857. The pressure on Rugby, which had increased at a formidable rate in the 1840s, was eased in the two decades that followed. Though the station was still inconvenient for the business it had to transact, it remained just adequate until the 1870s.

One of the most constantly troublesome problems in the management of the London & North Western station arose from the refreshment rooms. Such difficulties were not confined to Rugby. In 1850 a special committee was set up by the board to investigate the rooms there and at Euston and Wolverton.[28] They were leased to a company, which also managed the hotel at Euston, for an annual rent fixed at £1,250 in that year.[29] The worst trouble at Rugby arose, it is plain, form the inadequacy of the premises. There was, for example, only one room there for all comers, and in 1853 Huish pointed out to the traffic committee that, 'in consequence of there being no second-class refreshment room at Rugby, labouring men, bricklayers, hodmen, and similar persons used the new refreshment room to the great inconvenience of passengers and injury to the general character of the rooms. It appearing from the report of the Superintendent that a tap is kept in the room, which is unusual and objectional (*sic*), the Committee decided that Mr Edwards be requested to remove the tap altogether from the first-class refreshment room and that the Company's servants under the rank of Inspectors be instructed not to use the refreshment room'.[30]

This provision remained unsatisfactory, and in the following decade the refreshment room brought Rugby into the full glare of the limelight, in one of the sketches that Dickens wrote in the autumn of 1866, to be published in the Christmas number of *All the Year Round* under the title *Mugby Junction*. Though the association of the title is inescapable, it must be said at once that there is very little in the sketches that is really local to Rugby. The brilliant prose-poetry of the description of the railway at night could have been inspired by any great junction:

'A place replete with shadowy shapes, this Mugby Junction in the black hours of the four-and-twenty. Mysterious goods trains, covered with palls and gliding on like vast weird funerals, conveying themselves guiltily away from the presence of the few lighted lamps, as if their freight had come to a secret and unlawful end. Half miles of coal pursuing in a Detective manner, following when they lead, stopping when they stop, backing when they back... Unknown languages in the air, conspiring in red, green, and white characters. An earthquake accompanied with thunder and lightning, going up express to London. Now, all quiet, all rusty, wind and rain in possession, lamps extinguished, Mugby Junction dead and indistinct, with its robe drawn over its head, like Caesar'.[31]

The third sketch, however, is based on a real experience at Rugby that had befallen Dickens himself.

On 25 April 1866 he was travelling down from Euston to Liverpool, accompanied by W.H. Wills and Chappell's manager, George Dolby, in the course of one of his reading tours. At Rugby the carriage in which the party was travelling was found to be on fire. It therefore had to be detached, and the passengers transferred to another vehicle. While this was in progress, Dickens walked into the refreshment room with Wills to get a cup of coffee. Dolby was engaged in looking after the removal of the luggage from one carriage to the other, when Dickens came along the platform to him, greatly excited, and asked him to join them in the refreshment room.

'Then [says Dolby], standing in the doorway, and pointing with his finger, he described the picture he particularly wished to impress on my mind. "You see, Dolby – stove to right hand – torn cocoanut matting on floor – counter across room – coffee-urn – tea-urn – plates of rusks – piles of sawdust sandwiches and shrunken-up oranges – bottles – tumblers – and glasses on counter – and, *behind* counter, *note particularly* OUR MISSIS"...

'When the train was fairly off again, Mr Dickens proceeded to explain. Entering the refreshment room, he and Mr Wills had each asked for a cup of coffee, which was supplied to them. While Wills was feeling in his pocket for some small change wherewith to pay, Mr Dickens reached across the counter for the sugar and milk, when both articles were suddenly snatched away from him and placed beneath the counter, while his ears were greeted with the remark, made in shrill and shrewish tones, "You shan't have any milk and sugar till you two fellows have paid for your coffee".

This speech was delivered by the woman he had pointed out to me as 'our Missis', and it gave infinite amusement to a page in buttons, who, with that demoniacal spirit which seems to seize some boys at the idea of somebody else 'catching it', was so overjoyed that he burst out into an uncontrollable fit of laughter. The discomfited travellers left their coffee on the counter, after an apology for making so free with the sugar basin'.[32]

So, in 'The Boy At Mugby', we have for our eternal entertainment that refreshment room and its assistant manageress, Mrs Sniff: 'She's the one as you'll notice to be always looking another way from you, when you look at her. She's the one with the small waist buckled in tight in front, and with the lace cuffs at her wrists, which she puts on the edge of the counter before her, and stands a-smoothing while the public foams'.[33]

Dickens had old scores to settle with railway refreshment rooms. Mrs Sniff is a composite figure, made up of many originals. One of them he had encountered ten years earlier, in the small hours of the morning, on the Great Northern station at Peterborough. And as for the food that these railway rooms purveyed, he had written in 1860: 'I cannot dine on shining brown patties, composed of unknown animals within… I cannot dine on a sandwich that has long been pining under an exhausted receiver. I cannot dine on barley-sugar. I cannot dine on Toffee'.[34]

His comments on the Rugby refreshment room made his readers laugh; but they angered some people too. David Stevenson, for example, a senior railway official living there, with no particular axe of his own to grind, wrote to a friend when he had read that Christmas number:

'Rugby is not to be sneezed at – although our refreshment rooms don't come up to the wants and wishes of cold, tried, ill-tempered, over-pampered travelling authors, who, in a Christmas book, which should be all charity and forgiveness, choose to wound and pain hard-working women, who have to stand all day in the draught, about which Mr Dickens is so funny, and to put up with the insolence and impudence of the British Public, who, be it said with all deference, is too often rude to young persons behind a counter'.[35]

As it happened, the London & North Western company had been considering an extensive change in the amenities of the station not long before Dickens saw it. In 1864 the board had resolved to erect an hotel and stabling there, but it evidently took alarm at the cost, and only a few weeks later it deferred expenditure on the refreshment room.[36] The hotel project disappeared.

Once made, Dickens's comment stuck; and in the next generation successive writers thought it necessary to point out most explicitly that the Rugby refreshment rooms had been improved out of all recognition since he described them.[37]

4

Meanwhile the population of Rugby was growing steadily, rising from the 2,500 of the census of 1831 to nearly 7,000 within 20 years and 10,000 in 1881. It was generally recognised that this growth was due in part to the rising fame of the school, but even more to the railway. In the words of a local *Almanack* for 1854, 'the town derives a great benefit from the Big School, but its chief support and present position may be fairly attributed to the various railroads that junction here'.[38] Indeed, as a distinguished Old Rugbeian put it, the advent of the railways directly brought about 'a perceptible increase of boys to the school'.[39]

The town was beginning to become conscious of its needs as a community. New streets were being laid out, a number of them feeling northwards in the direction of the railway. The London & Birmingham company had itself made Railway Terrace, in a straight line from the old town centre to the second station; and in 1851 Albert Street was added, with James Street behind, which became a colony of railway workers.[40] The London & North Western company provided some housing of its own. It was not always of a high standard, and there was trouble with the inspector of the Rugby Board of Health over some of the railway's cottages in 1854.[41] In later years the provision of houses was facilitated by the Rugby Freehold Land Society (founded in 1866) and two local building societies.[42] Gas works were established on Railway Terrace, by the Rugby Gas & Coke Company, in 1838;[43] the town's first newspaper, the *Rugby Advertiser*, began to appear in 1846.[44] The place remained under parish government, however, until 1849, when a Local Board of Health was established, under the terms of the Public Health Act of the preceding year. Rugby and Croydon were the first places to take this step.[45] As in most other Early Victorian towns, the sewage and water supply were notoriously deficient. The town took some advantage of the Sanitary Act of 1851 to improve its drainage; but quarrels over the water supply were noisy and incessant from 1849 to 1864.[46]

Although these were years of striking growth in Rugby, they did not produce any important change in the town's economy, except that deriving from the railway. It had, as we have seen, no industries on a large scale; of those it did have, some were damaged or wholly destroyed by the arrival of the railway, with the open competition it introduced. The town had formerly been noted for its manufacture of Windsor chairs, but that now disappeared; and there had been a sizeable factory for the making of hats in Union Street, which quietly decayed. On the other hand, from the 1860s onwards Rugby builders began to get a name for themselves, securing important contracts like those for Keble and Mansfield Colleges at Oxford. Portland cement works were established at New Bilton, on the western outskirts of the town, in 1865. Though they were not at first very successful, in the 1870s they began to forge ahead; towards the end of the century they were employing some 300 men, and a second, smaller quarry was being exploited on the Newbold Road. No other factory of any significance appeared, however, until 1882, when Messrs Symington of Market Harborough set up a branch of their large corset-making business in Rugby, which came to employ 250 hands, with four subsidiary branches in the villages round about.[47]

One manufacture connected with railways began to emerge shortly afterwards. Thomas Hunter, junior, makes his first appearance in the directories as a railway wagon repairer in 1887. Three years later he has become a 'railway wagon builder'. He set up his works on the north side of the railway line, on Glebe Farm, until he sold the site, of 25 acres, in 1900 for £10,000. The purchasers were the British Thomson-Houston Company.[48]

5

When the Midland Railway opened its entirely independent line to London, through Luton to St Pancras, in 1868, its old line from Leicester to Rugby lost its former importance, becoming little more than a country branch. Although this eased the pressure on Rugby station, the relief was only short-lived, since the traffic on the main line of the London & North Western continued to grow steadily during the 1870s, and towards the close of that decade a new line began to be planned, the arrival of which could be expected to impose an additional strain on the existing arrangements. This was the loop running from Roade through Northampton and Long Buckby, which was important in two ways: it offered Northampton, for the first time, main-line communication, where hitherto it had been uncomfortably dependent upon branches; and at the same time its additional pair of tracks in effect completed the quadrupling of the line from Euston to Rugby. The work was completed in 1882. It had two consequences at Rugby itself. The approaches from the south had to be reorganised, and this was done boldly, carrying the down Northampton line and that from Market Harborough aloft over bridges, so as to avoid, as far as possible, the interference of the movement of one train with another. Even more important, the London & North Western board recognised that the time had now come when Rugby station must be entirely rebuilt; and in February 1882 they voted £70,000 for this improvement.[49] The need for it was growing imperative. In 1884 the *Builder* thought it necessary to urge the railway to make a good job of it, for the existing station was 'poor and shabby'.[50]

The third Rugby station was again on a new site, and it was built to a quite different plan from its predecessors. It stood immediately to the east of the second station, which was therefore able to continue in use while the new one was taking shape. It followed a pattern then becoming fashionable – still to be seen today also, for example, at Darlington (opened in 1887): that of a huge island platform, with bays set into it at either end, one of them used by the Midland company's trains. At Rugby the platform was long enough to accommodate, if necessary, two main-line trains on one face at the same time, which could approach and leave independently of each other by means of scissors crossings in the centre. Outside ran two further tracks in each direction, which came to be used for goods trains, and for passenger trains not stopping at Rugby. Before 1888 very few trains ran through.[51] Thereafter, the practice became increasingly common.

The new station was brought into use by stages. The first came in July 1885, when the down side was completed. No formal ceremony took place, but a dance was held on the platform on the third of the month. An admission fee of sixpence was charged, the proceeds going to the Hospital of St Cross, and 2,000 people paid. The Steam Shed Band, we are told, was in attendance, mounted in two wagons standing in front of the refreshment room. Public traffic began into this part of the station two days later. The up side was opened on 10 April 1886, and the whole work was completed that June.[52]

The number of London & North Western men employed in and around Rugby was now rising towards its peak. The last important addition to the company's establishment there was the erecting shops, which were brought into use in 1892. The directors were cautiously extending the provision they made for their men's welfare. In 1887 they established a Railway Institute on the company's own premises. It was a modest venture, designed to provide an elementary technical education, and it was not confined wholly to railway employees. Other people could avail themselves of its services, on payment of 1s a quarter for the use of the reading room, or 2s for attendance at one or more of the classes provided.[53] In 1891 the work was taken up on a broader basis, and a Technical Instruction Committee was formed in Rugby, containing townspeople and railway servants. Under its auspices, classes in art were arranged at premises it rented in the town, while those in science continued to be provided at the Railway Institute. This plan provided a good start; but its very success in attracting a growing number of students meant that the accommodation became less and less adequate, and in 1903 a new proposal was put forward for the building of a much larger Institute in the town, and the union there of the whole of the work, in art and science alike. The case for this had been greatly strengthened by the establishment in Rugby of two large engineering firms, Willans & Robinson and the British Thomson-Houston company. The demand for instruction meant that the premises available were grossly overcrowded, and the Board of Education did not consider that the Railway Institute was any longer suitable for the purpose.

Accordingly, an appeal was launched for funds. The Warwickshire County Council promised £1,000 if at least an equal sum was raised from local sources; the governors of Rugby School indicated that they would give £500, and probably provide a site. Both the big engineering firms undertook to contribute, and the London & North Western company agreed – on the recommendation of F.W. Webb, its chief mechanical engineer – to subscribe £200, and £25 a year thereafter.[54] The scheme was not carried out, however, in this form. Four years later another, bigger plan was proposed. The cost had now risen to £5,400, for it included physics and chemistry laboratories. Again the promoters approached the London & North Western company, arguing that the project would benefit principally students from its works and those of the other large engineering firms. This time the company's attitude was different. It pointed out that the promoters now said nothing specific about the participation of British Thomson-Houston or of Willans & Robinson; nor did they mention the attitude taken up by the other large railway companies, the Midland and the recently-arrived Great Central. George Whale, who had succeeded Webb in 1903, was much less sympathetic to the idea than his predecessor. To him 'the extension of manufacturing firms in the town employing far more skilled artisans than the company renders those firms far more interested in the question than the London & North Western'. The scheme would clearly have to be aided through the rates, and the company was a large ratepayer. (This was, of course, true. In 1903, when the matter had been previously discussed, it had been stated that its property was assessed at twelve percent of the total rateable value of the town.) In short, Whale advised that the company should decline, on this occasion, to subscribe to the cost of the scheme. His recommendation was accepted and the original promise was withdrawn, on the grounds that the nature of the plan had changed so materially in the meantime.[55] It would be wrong, however, to conclude that the company did little for education in the town. Even though it played only a small direct part in the development of the Technical College, it had done much to lay the foundations on which that institution came to be based. As T.H. Simms put it, in his study of the growth of modern Rugby, out of the Railway Institute 'developed a wide provision of adult education in the town'.[56]

6

Up to this time Rugby had been virtually in the hands of a railway monopoly. Apart from the line to Leicester – and that, as we have seen, had lost most of its importance in 1868 – all communication was in the hands of the London & North Western company. On the whole this must have worked to Rugby's advantage, for it meant that the North Western, with so much plant and so many employees concentrated there, had a substantial stake in the town's property and amenities. Rugby was better provided with express trains at this time than any other town in Britain. In 1871 it had 27 daily to and from London; in 1883, 50.[57] By 1887, when the whole work of rebuilding the station was completed, the quickest trains ran up in 105 minutes at 48.4mph.

But among commercial men there were always some ready to argue that the services they needed would be improved by competition; and several of those in Rugby therefore supported a project, first brought forward in the 1880s, for the construction of a new trunk line from Sheffield to London, laid out to serve the town *en route*. The driving force behind this plan was Sir Edward Watkin. He was chairman of the Manchester Sheffield & Lincolnshire and the Metropolitan companies, and the essence of the idea consisted in building a line to link up those two railways, from Annesley in north Nottinghamshire to Quainton, a little north of Aylesbury, where it would join the Metropolitan. This would provide a new trunk route from Sheffield, Nottingham, and Leicester to London, running roughly parallel to the existing line of the Midland company. To the charge that it presented merely a wasteful duplication of existing facilities, which would in the end prove uneconomic, the answer given was that traffic was constantly increasing, as was proved by the expensive additional works then in progress or contemplated by the three great railways running between London and the north; the Midland, for example, having been engaged in quadrupling its tracks, piecemeal, for a continuous stretch of 75 miles from London. The Midland was the company most immediately aggrieved by this new scheme, though at one stage in the acidulated correspondence that followed between its chairman, Sir Matthew Thompson, and Watkin, Thompson indicated that the Midland might be prepared to come to terms if the Sheffield company would make use of the old Midland Counties line from Leicester to Rugby rather than building one of its own.[58] There was some good sense in this proposal, even though it would have involved costly works at Rugby, in order to pass the line through the North Western station, or clear of it in a great arc to the north, high above the Avon and the Oxford Canal. But economy interested Watkin and his colleagues very little. What they wanted was an independent route. They may well have decided that, if the new line were built in any form, it would be chiefly at the expense of the Midland, which would do all it could to hamper its free operation when it was at work; and in that perhaps they were right.

The first attempt at securing parliamentary powers to construct the line failed, in 1891; but the second, in the following year, was successful, though the Act authorising it did not come into force until 1893. As sanctioned then – and again, in a slightly different form, in 1894 – the projected line was to include a junction with the Market Harborough line of the London & North Western at Rugby;[59] but that was never in fact built. It is interesting to find Rugby as the point at which, for engineering purposes, the northern and southern divisions of the new line met when it was opened in 1899. Here again we can see the town standing on a railway frontier between the north and south of England. In building the railway, the Manchester Sheffield & Lincolnshire company (its name was changed to Great Central in 1897) was obliged to enter into numerous arrangements to protect established interests. At Rugby they included the reconstruction, at considerable expense to itself, of the very large signal gantry controlling the junctions east of the London & North Western station, so as to render the semaphores clearly visible high above the Great Central's steel girder bridge. The result was said to be the second largest signal gantry in Britain; the Great Central's signal superintendent, A.F. Bound, nicknamed it 'the Rugby bedstead'.[60]

The new station was a modest edifice on the Hillmorton Road, at the westernmost limits of the built-up area of Rugby. It stood as far from the town's centre as the existing station; and it was therefore preposterous that the self-advertising practice of the company required that the name adopted for it should be 'Rugby Central'. The reference was, of course, to the company's name, but many hapless visitors to the town – and to others, like Leicester and Brackley, where the same policy was followed – thought the description a vile misnomer. For, as Betjeman said,

> ...quite where Rugby Central is
> Does only Rugby know.[61]

The opening of the Great Central line brought Rugby a material improvement in its communications. Since the building of the Midland extension from Leicester to St Pancras in 1868, the Leicester–Rugby line had become a backwater, giving a slow service to and from north-eastern England, always demanding a change of trains at Leicester. The Great Central provided Rugby with half-a-dozen through expresses a day to and from Sheffield, with services also to Bradford, York, and later Hull and Newcastle. In addition it offered an alternative route to and from London – not very important perhaps, since the Euston service was so good. But it put right the greatest defect in the facilities supplied by the North Western company: the lack of any through service to the south and south-west of England. Hitherto, a journey from Rugby to Bristol had required a change at Birmingham. Now there were through trains running to Bristol, as well as useful direct services to Oxford and Southampton.

All this added further to the ease with which passengers could move in and out of Rugby. But the Great Central company was predominantly a carrier of freight traffic, and the route it took, along the eastern edge of the town, kept it right away from the industrial area. None of the engineering firms had any siding connection with it, and that must have denied the new line a large amount of profitable business that it could otherwise have handled. A goods yard, of a size appropriate to a small country town, was provided on the south side of the station, together with a little cattle dock and siding on the north. No enlargement was ever called for; an indication that they had been found adequate to the demands made upon them.

The Great Central was the last railway to be built that served Rugby. One further proposal was made, in 1897, for a new line in connection with it to Coventry and Birmingham, but nothing came of that scheme.[62] The railway system of Rugby reached its fullest extent when the Great Central line was opened in 1899.[63]

7

The advent of the new railway coincided, quite by accident, with a change of critical importance in the town's economy. Apart from Hunter's wagon works, the corset factory, and the cement works at New Bilton, the industries of Rugby (excluding those dependent on the London & North Western Railway) had been on a small scale. In 1895–6, however, the firm of Willans & Robinson, makers of motor-launches, decided to move their works from Thames Ditton, where they had previously been established, to Rugby. They set up in North Street, with siding access to the London & North Western Railway. Their business grew fast, and they were soon manufacturing turbines and other engineering equipment on a large scale. In 1900 they were joined by the British Thomson-Houston Company, which acquired Hunter's wagon works, immediately outside the North Western station, within the arc of the Midland line on its approach from Leicester. Hitherto the company had carried on its business in London, manufacturing there on a small scale but concerning itself chiefly with the distribution of electrical plant imported from the United States. The Rugby works began to manufacture in March 1902. They were designed for the employment of 800 hands.[64]

These two engineering establishments together provided more work than the railways. The official guide to the Rugby Urban District could still open in 1907 with the words 'Rugby is one of the Railway Towns of England'.[65] Already that was ceasing to be true, even in the limited sense in which it had been true in earlier years.

Rugby was certainly now an engineering town; it remained, as it had long been, a scholastic town; and it was now being selected as a leading centre of fox-hunting, on account of the good railway services it enjoyed. 'There is perhaps no place in England', wrote a well-recognised authority on the sport in 1903, 'where horse boxes are so much used in the hunting season as at Rugby'[66] But, at the same time, the London & North Western Railway still employed some 1,400 men there altogether, 220 in and around the station and 850 in the locomotive department.[65] The large engineering works continued in business, while the railways first ceased to grow and then, very notably, contracted. It would not be fair to say that they no longer introduced anything new to Rugby. The London Midland & Scottish and London & North Eastern companies set up a locomotive testing plant there jointly, brought into use in 1948: an excellent collaborative enterprise, and a proof that the railways were earnest in their fostering of research.[68] When the former London & North Western main lines were electrified in 1967 they afforded a service between London and Manchester that was as fast as that between Paris and Brussels, and faster than any other comparable service in Europe. Rugby remained the critically-important point of divergence between the Birmingham and the Trent Valley lines, with a service of its own much quicker than those it had ever enjoyed before. By 1969 the fastest trains were timed to run up to London in 63 minutes, at 80.7mph.

On the other hand, the old minor lines to Leicester, Peterborough, and Leamington had all been closed in 1959–66, so that the North Western station had to deal only with main-line traffic. It soon became, once more, *the* station, as it had been at the beginning: for the Great Central line, having been run down to carry an exceedingly thin service, was closed south of Rugby in 1966 and completely three years later.

Rugby has been transformed since 1830 from a 'werry out-o'-the-way place' of 2,500 people into a busy, substantial town of 80,000. Though the writer of a guide-book to Rugby now could not possibly characterise it as a 'railway town', it owes that transformation, and its present consequence, primarily to railways.

NOTES

1. For a general treatment of these towns see RTC, chap. 6.

2. On Crewe see W.H. Chaloner's admirable study, *The Social and Economic Development of Crewe* (1950). There are no satisfactory accounts of Shildon or Eastleigh. On Horwich see B.J. Turton, 'Horwich: the Historical Geography of a Lancashire Town', *Transactions of the Lancashire and Cheshire Antiquarian Society*, 72 (1962) 141–50.

3. On Swindon see H.B. Wells in *Studies in the History of Swindon* (1950), 94–157; *VCH Wiltshire*, iv. 183–219.

4. S. Lewis, *Topographical Dictionary of England* (1833), under Rugby.

5. T. Hughes, *Tom Brown's Schooldays*, chap. 4. The Regulator coach seems to have run not daily but only three times a week: W. West, *Topography and Directory of Warwickshire* (1830), 737.

6. See MacDermot, i. 13–14, 30–2, 97 (Eton), i. 86–7 (Oxford); R. B. Fellows, *London to Cambridge by Train* (1976 ed.), 11–12.

7. Pugin, 11. The trustees of Rugby School gave £1,000 towards the cost of erecting this bridge; perhaps, if they had put difficulties in the way of the construction of the line, this was a gesture of compensation? 'In its style of architecture', we are told, the bridge 'harmonises with the school house at Rugby': A. Freeling, *London & Birmingham Railway Companion* (1838), 156.

8. For the history of this company see *The Midland Counties Railway*, ed. P.S. Stevenson (1989).

9. The whole of this story, with its curious details, is told by V.A. Hatley in 'Northampton Hoodwinked?', JTH 7 (1965–6) 160–72.

10. Stevenson, 57.

11. R384/3, mins. 682, 932; 490/3, min. 93.

12. *Ibid.*, min. 205. During the later stages of the construction of the line Dr Arnold wrote to the chairman of the company 'expressing a desire on the part of himself and the other masters of the Rugby School to be made useful to the labourers employed on the railways which pass close to Rugby, by giving them an opportunity of attending the church service at such time and place as would be most convenient'. The company thanked Dr Arnold and his colleagues for the offer and assured them that they could rely upon 'the best efforts of this directory being used to second their exertions': R490/16, min. 776 (6 March 1840).

13. The dates of opening were: Trent Valley line, 15 September 1847; Market Harborough line, 1 May 1850; Leamington line, 1 March 1851.

14. P.H. Elliott, *Rugby's Railway Heritage* (1985), 22.

15. E. Foxwell and T.C. Farrer, *Express Trains English and Foreign* (1889), 16.

16. When the central district was created in 1860 Rugby formed its southern termination and Samuel Grew, who had been stationmaster at Rugby, was appointed its superintendent: Neele, 62.

17. R410/137, p.3 (10 January 1848).

18. The earliest reference I have found to the matter is in the minutes of the Rugby & Stamford construction committee on 4 March 1847: R410/506, p.22.

19. R410/137.

20. *Ibid.*, 4 February 1848.

21. *Ibid.*, 16 February 1848.

22. *Ibid.*, 14 January 1848.

23. The exact total was £9,967 3s 2d, authorised piecemeal, at seven different times: R410/506,

pp. 164, 181, 182, 190, 208, 211, 217. A valuable plan of the station and the adjoining premises appears on sheet 3 of the Ordnance Survey map made for the Rugby Board of Health in 1850–1 to the scale of 10ft to the mile (copy in Rugby PL). There is another good one, dating from 1840 but revised from time to time, in R384/192.

24. R410/140, min. 120.

25. *Ibid.*, min. 173.

26. *Ibid.*, min. 170.

27. *Ibid.*, min. 201.

28. R410/282, p.15 (12 April 1850).

29. *Ibid.*, pp 19–20 (10 May 1850).

30. R410/140, min. 410 (10 June 1853).

31. *Mugby Junction* (1866), 1–2.

32. G. Dolby, *Charles Dickens as I knew Him* (1885), 29–31.

33. *Mugby Junction*, 18.

34. Dickens, *Letters*, ed. W. Dexter (1938), ii. 736; *The Uncommercial Traveller* (Oxford Illustrated ed.), 57.

35. *Fifty years on the London & North Western Railway, and other Memoranda in the Life of David Stevenson*, ed. L. Turner (1891), 126. At least two sequels to *Mugby Junction* were written: 'Lyulph', *A Girl at a Railway Junction's Reply* (1867), and J. Astle, *The Gal at Mugby* (privately printed, Cheltenham, 1867). Prof. P.A.W. Collins, who kindly mentioned these titles to me, had not seen copies of either pamphlet. Nor have I.

36. R410/25, mins. 4329, 4334. Plans for the enlargement of the refreshment rooms were, however, submitted to the Rugby Board of Health on 14 August 1869 (Minutes, Rugby Town Hall).

37. See for example *Murray's Handbook of Warwickshire* (1899), 2; RM24 (1909) 3.

38. A.T. Read, *Companion to the Almanacks for 1854* (Rugby, 1854), [ii].

39. M.H. Bloxam, quoted by W.O. Wait, *Rugby: Past and Present* (1893), 163.

40. T.H. Simms, *The Rise of a Midland Town* (1949), 5.

41. R410/141, min. 3789; 410/282, mins. 600, 632.

42. Simms, 23, 26.

43. F. White, *History, Gazetteer, and Directory of Warwickshire* (3rd ed., 1874), 896.

44. For the early history of the Rugby press, see Wait, 170–3.

45. Simms, 9. Rugby became an Urban District in 1894 and a Borough in 1932.

46. Simms, 12–16.

47. Wait, 165–6. For Symingtons' business see *VCH Leicestershire*, v (1964), 142.

48. Hunter's first appearance is in J. Hopewell's *Rugby Almanack* for 1887; his last is in the direc-

tory for 1918. For the purchase of Glebe Farm see H.A. Price-Hughes, B.T.H. *Reminiscences: Sixty Years of Progress* (1946), 14.

49. There had already been a protracted argument with the Local Board of Health and the rector of Rugby about the enlargement of the bridges passing beneath the railway to the north. These objectors carried their opposition so far as to instruct parliamentary agents to draft petitions against the company's Bill; but agreement was reached when the company had made some concessions. (Rugby Town Hall, Board of Health Minutes, 15 January, 26 February, 21 May 1881; also Committee Report Book, 1880–8, pp. 11–13, 15, 17, 26.)

50. *Builder*, 47 (1884), 252.

51. Two Birmingham expresses had been booked to run through the station, however, as early as 1847: Neele, 3.

52. H. Lodge, 'A Short History of the London & North Western Railway at Rugby', *Rugby Advertiser*, 26 December 1908.

53. *Midland Times Almanack* (Rugby, 1891), 45.

54. R410/38, min. 18, 886 (5 February 1903).

55. This story is clearly summarised in a memorandum in the company's archives, dated 7 August 1907: R410/712.

56. Simms, 27.

57. H.B. Willock in *Journal of the Royal Statistical Society*, 47 (1884) 295.

58. Dow GC, ii. 240. This book gives a very full narrative of the building and operation of the new line.

59. See plan in *ibid.*, ii. 280.

60. *Ibid.*, ii. 321.

61. *High and Low* (1966), 23.

62. Dow GC, ii. 302, 305.

63. For passengers on 15 March, and fish and goods trains on 10–11 April: *ibid.*, ii. 340–1.

64. Price-Hughes, 24.

65. *Mate's Illustrated Rugby* (2nd ed., 1907).

66. T.F. Dale, *Foxhunting in the Shires* (1903), 96–105.

67. RM 24 (1909) 2, 3, 8.

68. Elliott, 45, 47–8.

6
SUBURBAN TRAFFIC *at* KING'S CROSS, 1852–1914

The London terminus of the Great Northern Railway at King's Cross, opened in 1852, was cursed by inherent weaknesses in its site. It was squeezed into a space only 600 yards deep from north to south, between three highways, both already established and immovable: the Regent's Canal and the Euston and Pentonville Roads. The railway had to pass under the canal by dipping through the Gas Works (or Maiden Lane) Tunnel, into which trains plunged almost immediately they left the station, first down a short incline and then up at 1 in 107. All the manoeuvring required in moving engines or vehicles from the up to the down tracks and vice versa had to be conducted within the space of about 250 yards between the end of the train shed and the tunnel mouth. Nor was this the worst. When the Great Northern became linked with the Metropolitan Railway in 1863 the ascent from the underground line on the west side of the station was by another tunnel, sharply curved, up one of the steepest gradients on which passenger trains worked anywhere in London; part of it at 1 in 35. The whole station was, almost from the beginning, very awkward to operate.[1]

The passenger traffic running in and out of it was relatively small at first. But the King's Cross complex included also large goods and coal depots. Although they were separate from the passenger station, lying north of the canal, they had to be reached through the Copenhagen Tunnel, much longer than the Gas Works one and equally steep, into which all traffic – main-line and suburban passenger, goods and coal trains – jostled for admission from the north. This tunnel was the critical point, the most constricting bottleneck.

Table 5 shows the number of trains entering and leaving King's Cross at an irregular series of dates between 1857 and 1909. Its figures have been drawn from the company's working timetables.

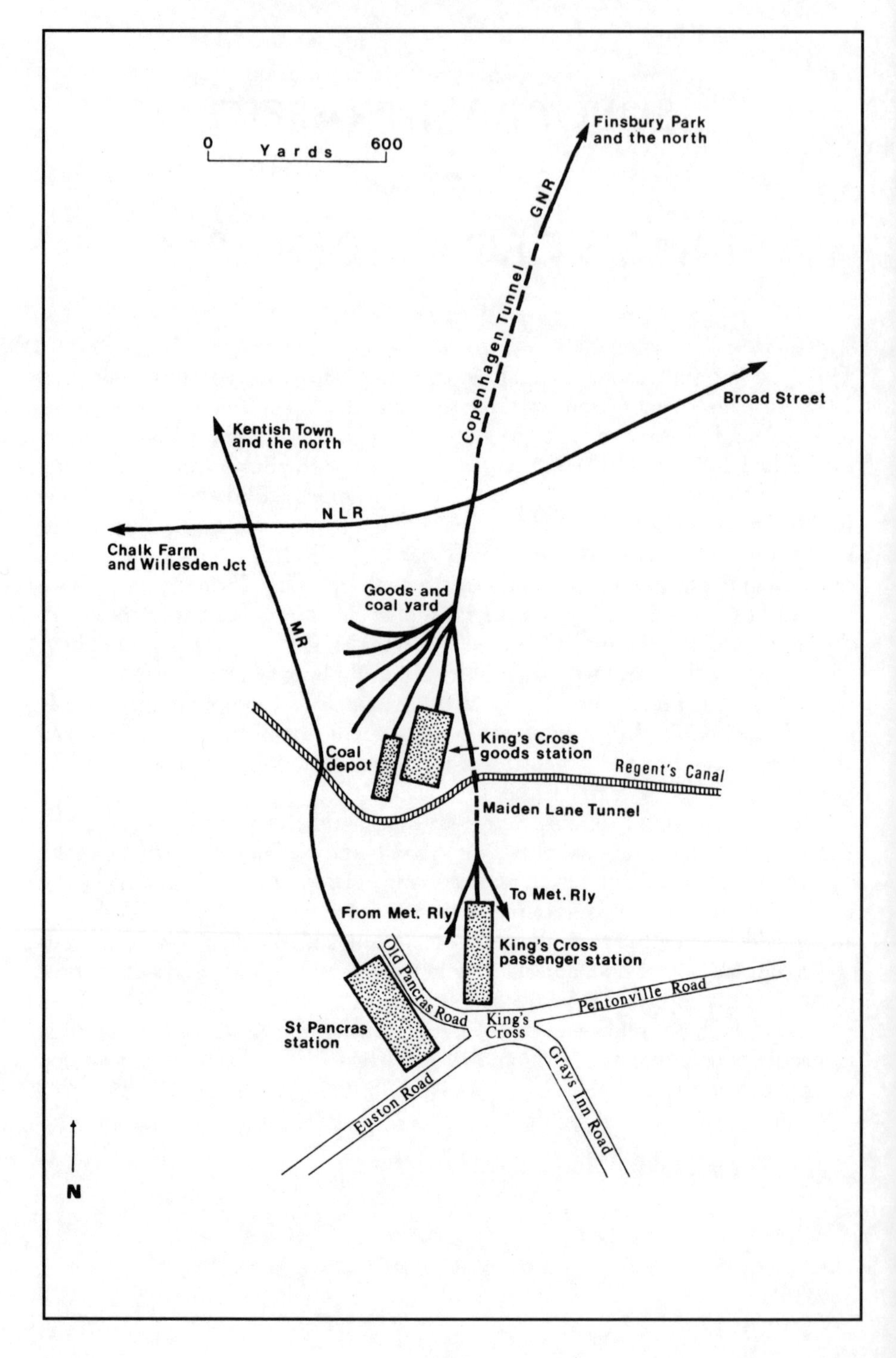
0 Yards 600
Finsbury Park and the north
GNR
Copenhagen Tunnel
Broad Street
Kentish Town and the north
NLR
Chalk Farm and Willesden Jct
Goods and coal yard
MR
King's Cross goods station
Coal depot
Regent's Canal
Maiden Lane Tunnel
To Met. Rly
From Met. Rly
King's Cross passenger station
Old Pancras Road
Pentonville Road
King's Cross
St Pancras station
Euston Road
Grays Inn Road
N

TABLE 5

Traffic At King's Cross, 1857–1909

Trains arriving and departing 7am–midnight

	Main line		Suburban a		Goods		Coal		Empty stock b		Total
	No.	%	No.	%	No.	%	No.	%	No.	%	
September 1857	13	36.1	7	19.4	5	13.9	11	30.6	?		36
November 1882	19	11.0	101	58.7	36	20.9	15	8.7	1	0.6	172
July 1884	33	15.2	125	57.6	32	14.7	6	2.8	21	9.7	217
October 1903	43	15.6	150	54.5	29	10.5	6	2.2	47	17.1	275
July 1909	44	14.2	158	51.1	34	11.0	8	2.6	65	21.0	309

Notes

a Trains starting at Hitchin and stations south.
b Including light engine workings.
Source: Working timetables, R935/59, 62, 65, 70, 71

The Great Northern began to encourage suburban traffic early. By 1861 it had seven intermediate stations on the 17¾ miles of its main line out to Hatfield, and it then began to consider branches. The following year it agreed to work the projected Edgware Highgate & London Railway, as well as an extension to Watford (never built) and other branches to Muswell Hill and High Barnet in 1864–6.[2]

When shareholders first questioned this policy in 1867 the doubts they expressed concerned the economic merits of branch lines as such, not the complications they might entail in working the main line. In June 1868 the chairman was delighted by the profitability of the whole business, proclaiming that the traffic from (New) Barnet to London alone was worth £29,060 a year.[3] Eighteen months later the shareholders were warned that nearly £30,000 would have to be spent in quadrupling the tracks up to Wood Green. In August 1871 Seneca Hughes, a crusted character much in evidence at their meetings, asserted that the Edgware branch (which had been opened in 1867) had proved a 'disastrous speculation' and attributed the error of constructing it to 'persons who have an immense deal of influence upon our directors – engineers, parliamentary agents, solicitors, landed proprietors'. In response to a direct question whether the line paid or not, the chairman replied, 'Above two percent *per se*, and what it pays to the main line is very considerable indeed'. Of course he repudiated the charge that the directors were improperly influenced.

After this exchange the board did not find it necessary to refer to these matters again in any detail for another ten years. The High Barnet and Alexandra Palace branches were opened in 1872–3. A link from Finsbury Park to the North London

Railway at Canonbury (1875) eased the flow of traffic to the City, by allowing Great Northern trains to be taken to the North London terminus at Broad Street. Nonetheless in February 1882 the chairman announced that the main line must be quadrupled from Wood Green to Potter's Bar, which would require the provision of five additional tunnels. To support his case, he stated that the company's suburban traffic had increased in 1867–81 from £39,000 to £195,000 a year in value, and the number of passengers from 1.7 million to 12.9 million.[4] The bill for these operations was to be £745,000, with a further £124,000 (approved in February 1883) for enlarging the capacity of the Copenhagen Tunnel.[5] No one complained. It was evidently accepted as a charge that had to be met if a profitable traffic was to be carried satisfactorily. The chairman gave no hint, from the managerial side, that a point of saturation might lie ahead. And yet it could surely be discerned. Even with six tracks through the tunnels outside King's Cross, and with all the relief that came from the arrangement with the North London company and the development of a large goods yard at Ferme Park, the Great Northern was still in a tight straitjacket.

Adequate provision for the relentlessly-increasing traffic could be made in three ways, all of them expensive: by a total reconstruction of King's Cross station and its approaches; by the building of some new avoiding line; or by the adoption of electricity as a motive power. The first of these solutions seems never to have been entertained. All that was done in that direction was to add short additional platforms on the west side of the station, for suburban traffic, in 1875 and 1895.[6] An opportunity offered, however, to adopt the second and third in combination, and it was in the end rejected.

In 1891 the engineer Sir Douglas Fox discussed with the Great Northern's general manager, Sir Henry Oakley, the idea of building a tube railway (the City & South London had been opened the previous year) from Euston and King's Cross to Charing Cross. Oakley persuaded him to change the plan to comprehend a line from Finsbury Park to the City, with tunnels large enough to accommodate not merely the small rolling stock used on the City & South London Railway but full-sized Great Northern trains, passing from steam to electric traction at Drayton Park.[7] The scheme was authorised by Parliament in 1892. In February 1894 the chairman told the shareholders that if the railway were built 'it would be an immense relief to the Great Northern company'. Nevertheless that company refused to give the project any financial assistance, beyond undertaking to run a minimum of 50 trains a day over the line, for which it would pay at least £20,000 a year; and the capital was not raised for some years to come. It is true that the Great Northern was then being forced to find much money to meet the demands arising from the activities of the Manchester Sheffield & Lincolnshire Railway in promoting its London extension. But that project was no new one, against which the Great Northern had now suddenly to defend itself. It had been under discussion for two years before the meeting between Fox and Oakley took place. Oakley behaved most discreditably in repudiating the full support he had pledged to the

Great Northern & City tube railway, and he made matters much worse by remarking with gratuitous spite that his company was 'tired of being connected with a thing which has been marked by failure almost from its birth'. The real truth was that he had now become interested in the idea of another tube railway, of a different pattern: one designed to run from Wood Green beneath the main line to King's Cross and thence due south, not into the City at all. It was to be a separate railway, with small-bore tunnels, which ruled out any question of accommodating through trains from the Great Northern system. In the end the Great Northern laid it down that the line should not extend northwards beyond Finsbury Park. One of the company's motives was perfectly clear, in relation both to this tube and to the Great Northern & City. It was determined to prevent the penetration by another railway, of whatever kind, into a suburban territory that it valued and regarded as its own. Both tubes were now built according to these plans, to arrive from the City and the West End of London below Finsbury Park station and to stop there in terminals owned by the Great Northern, in 1904–6.

For some time past it had been said that the Great Northern laboured under a 'suburban incubus', a phrase that has become one of the best-known clichés in English railway history, most tediously repeated down the years.[8] Like all clichés this one has become a substitute for thought, but it is worse than most because it is, in a very positive sense, misleading. It plainly implies a burden thrust upon the Great Northern, whereas in fact it was one that the company had deliberately chosen to assume. Unlike the Great Eastern it had never been subjected to any special obligations by Parliament, requiring it to develop a suburban traffic. It had done so because it found that traffic profitable. The Great Northern now had a clear chance to free itself of a substantial part of the 'incubus', in a way that would have improved the quality of the whole of its main-line and suburban service. The unpunctuality of the service into and out of King's Cross was much complained of; it was hardly avoidable as long as the trains, of all descriptions, had to be pushed through those tunnels at minimal intervals every morning and evening.[9] The journeys the suburban passengers made were among the most unpleasant in London.[10] The track layout and the buildings of King's Cross station itself were a hopeless muddle. All this could have been rationalised, and the restricted space used to much better purpose, if the quantity of suburban traffic (amounting in 1894, as the table reveals, to 58% of it all) had been reduced. But the company chose to retain it in the old way, even when it had the chance to let part of it go, on terms it was in a position to dictate. The records seem to disclose no serious argument on the loss and gain involved in a thorough reorganisation of the suburban traffic, in full partnership with the tubes. The shareholders were given no assurance that such an appraisal had been undertaken (to be fair, none of them asked for any); and there is nothing to indicate that the company was more precisely informed in this matter than in many others concerning its operations.[11] Its determination to hold on to existing traffic could be justified only by a conviction that that traffic was highly remunerative – not an incubus at all (except to the company's passengers and servants) but a gold mine. When in the succeeding years the company complained bitterly, as others did, about the competition of the electric trams – they began to invade the Great Northern's district in 1904 – it must be supposed to have been bewailing the loss of business that it had found profitable. Relief was indeed given to the manifestly inadequate King's Cross through the abstraction of traffic by this triumphant competitor. The Great Northern gained from that relief, and its lamentations were therefore to some extent humbug. Still, a railway could scarcely be pleased by a fall in receipts from any part of its business.

For all the loss to the trams, the traffic went on growing. In 1906 – the date is significant: just when the effects of the new tram services were beginning to become clear – the company launched a campaign to advertise the attractions of living on the 'Northern Heights' of London and the cheapness of its season ticket rates.[12] In the same year it took up powers it had long held to construct a new line northwards from Enfield, partly in order to open up an empty tract of country to suburban development. When the first five miles of that line were opened, as far as Cuffley, in 1910, the company started to publish *The Great Northern 'Where to Live': an Illustrated Descriptive Quarterly*, well produced, with many Photochrom pictures in colour, a mine of information about the prices and availability of houses.[13] It boasts confidently that 'the high-class suburban traffic of this company exceeds that of any other of the leading lines', and of King's Cross it says (with a side glance at the tube railways opened in 1906–7) that it is 'the most accessible station in London… *All* lines now lead to King's Cross'.

We have no means of knowing how much additional business these efforts brought; but the traffic into King's Cross certainly continued to mount. It mounted faster, indeed, than the table reveals, for in 1907–8 a group of trains that had long been run from the Great Northern system through King's Cross and over the Thames by the Metropolitan line to Victoria and Woolwich, south of the river, were taken off, on the grounds that their traffic had passed to the trams. Since there had been 21 of these trains in 1903, the number of the Great Northern's own suburban trains had evidently increased by a further 22% (from 129 to 158) in 1903–9. All this in the face of the trams' competition and of the diversion of the passengers (their numbers are not known to us) who changed to the tubes at Finsbury Park.

It is a story of makeshift expedients and a good deal of deception – perhaps of self-deception too. There is nothing to show that the company's managers had a well-considered policy for meeting the demands of this business in advance, or a clear perception of the proper relationship between it and the other kinds of traffic for which they were responsible.[14] The chief public statements on the matter come in the repeated complaints of the chairmen at shareholders' meetings, wringing their hands over the expense incurred by the growth of suburban traffic. But was that traffic truly profitable, or was it not? We shall never know. Did the company itself know accurately?

The social interest, the interest of the suburban communities that had grown up on the Northern Heights in association with the Great Northern Railway, called out for a thorough reform of its arrangements. The opportunity for that, springing from a new technology, arrived in 1891. The company rejected it, and there was no more to be said: its decision in the matter was final. 'Final' in a very absolute sense, for in 1902 the Great Northern secured a right to prevent any extension of electric railways into what was accepted as its own territory north of Finsbury Park.[15]

The analysis offered here stops with the first World War. In the 1920s the whole situation began to change. The London & North Eastern company, into which the Great Northern passed in 1923, waived the 'veto' secured by the Great Northern in 1902. Though it still opposed the admission of underground railways into its district, it was obliged to see them arrive there and extend (partly over its own tracks) in 1924–41. Then, a whole generation later, came the redemption of the Great Northern & City from 'failure', when in 1976 the nationalised railways converted it into a branch of the main system, precisely in accordance with the intentions of its original promoters; and when, at the same time, they carried through the electrification of the surviving parts of the old Great Northern suburban system.[16] The improvement of the comfort and efficiency of life in this tract of suburban London has in consequence been beyond calculation. The country would surely have done better to impose a firmer hand on the railway companies, at the end of the Victorian age, instead of leaving them completely under the control of the Oakleys. And the shareholders, who deserve some of our sympathy too; would they have suffered from a thoroughly planned and economical reorganisation of their company's business? The opportunity for that arose in 1891. It took 85 years to seize it.

King's Cross station has been further altered, and in some important respects improved from the passenger's point of view. The traffic, of all kinds, has been much thinned out – partly by the diversion of suburban trains, to run through, by the old Great Northern & City line, to Moorgate. The dreadful tunnels to and from the Metropolitan line at King's Cross are no longer used. The suppression of steam has eased working in the tunnels north of the station; so have improvements in signalling. No workings of light engines are called for any more. But the fundamental defects of the site remain. This great station may still have to be closed to all traffic when a sudden violent storm floods the dip in the Gas Works Tunnel. To many passengers, travelling over long distances as well as short, and no doubt to some operating men in their hearts, King's Cross continues to be, as it has been for well over a century, a 'sad jumble'.[17]

NOTES

1. See A.A. Jackson, *London's Termini* (1972 ed.), 72–3. This book gives an excellent account of the difficulties of working the station. See also J.N. Young, *Great Northern Suburban* (1977).

2. See A.A. Jackson, *London's Local Railways* (1978), 15–16, 112–14.

3. The proceedings at the company's meetings are fully and carefully recorded in its *Reporter*, of which there is a set in R1110/172–4.

4. In February 1884 it was said to have grown by 46.5% in the previous seven years.

5. None of this work was in fact executed there at this time beyond New Barnet.

6. Jackson, *London's Termini*, 73, 77.

7. For what follows see T.C. Barker and M. Robbins, *History of London Transport* (1963–74), ii. 48–50.

8. C.H. Grinling uses the expression in the first edition of his *History of the Great Northern Railway* (1898), 406. He prints it in quotation marks. Who coined it, and when?

9. There may have been some exaggeration here. For alternate months of the year 1890 we have some precise figures to go on, given in a parliamentary return concerned with the punctuality of trains arriving at all the main London terminal stations (PP 1890, xvi. 802–25). They show that, on average, 80.5% of the Great Northern's suburban trains were less than three minutes late in reaching King's Cross. That was the best rate of punctuality achieved by any company at its London terminus except the Great Eastern at Liverpool Street, where the average for all trains (main-line and suburban) was 82.2%. The physical difficulties at Liverpool Street were only a little less than at King's Cross. The level of punctuality achieved by long-distance trains running into King's Cross was very low, however. Even allowing for adverse weather conditions and for waiting for connections from the trains of other railways, it was under 50%. That must have been due in part to delays caused by suburban trains.

10. See Jackson's graphic account of the ascent from the Metropolitan line: *London's Termini*, 72–3. Among the complaints addressed to the company may be noted a memorial of 1898 (R236/724/3); one sheet contains the signatures of 70 members of the Stock Exchange.

11. See J. R. Kellett, *Railways and Victorian Cities* (1979 ed.), 60–1.

12. Jackson, *London's Termini*, 80.

13. There is a set of the first four volumes in the British Library, running down to January 1914.

14. Even Grinling, the company's loyal and intelligent apologist, observes (303) the aimlessness of its suburban policy in the 1870s.

15. Barker and Robbins, ii. 251–2.

16. This process, staggeringly slow, is recorded in Young, chaps. 7–9.

17. Jackson, *London's Termini*, 84.

7

ENGINEER, CONTRACTOR, *and* WRITER

In spite of the efforts of biographers, we know little that is truly personal about the engineers who built and equipped the British railways. Most such men led a hard life – above all those who were at work during the principal age of construction, in 1830–80. Not many of them lived to be old. They were men of action, and when action was past their work was over. They did not feel the need to defend themselves by setting down recollections or embarking on any self-justification. It is true that George Stephenson devoted much time in the closing years of his life to relating his own early history, at public celebrations and wherever he saw a chance to proclaim the moral lessons he drew from it. He also talked privately about the past, to Thomas Summerside and others. Robert Stephenson conversed with his father's biographer Samuel Smiles and drew up his own account of the Conway and Britannia Bridges.[1] But neither of the two Stephensons wrote reminiscences. Only one of the leading men of the earlier days did that: Daniel Gooch, who recorded the story of his own life as far as 1867. He also kept a diary, which he continued to 1885.[2] So did three other well-known railway engineers, his brother Thomas Longridge Gooch,[3] G.P. Bidder,[4] and C.B. Vignoles;[5] but not, so far as I know, any more of them.[6]

F. R. Conder's *Personal Recollections of English Engineers* represented an effort of a different kind. They were the work of a man who left no mark on railway engineering but moved after a time into the business of contracting. When he returned to engineering in later life he concerned himself with other things than railways. Although he published the book anonymously in 1868 as the work of 'A Civil Engineer', he made public acknowledgement of it as his own in 1874.[7]

I

Francis Roubiliac Conder was the son and grandson of London booksellers. His father Josiah had just moved into St Paul's Churchyard when he was born on 26 November 1815.[8] His mother was a granddaughter of the great sculptor Roubiliac; hence his second Christian name. He was educated at Mill Hill School. In 1819 Josiah Conder sold his bookselling business and moved out of London to devote himself to literature as a profession. From 1824 to 1839 he lived at Watford, and the *Personal Recollections* open with an amusing sketch of that town as it then was, before the railway got to work and changed it.

At the age of eighteen the boy was taken on as an articled pupil of Charles Fox (less than six years older than he was himself), to work on the London & Birmingham Railway under Robert Stephenson. We can piece together a rough outline of his successive railway employments from the narrative he puts before us in his book. From the London & Birmingham he moved to the Eastern Counties Railway in 1835, and then he went to the Birmingham & Gloucester, to which he devotes four interesting chapters. Another young assistant who served there with him as a junior engineer was Herbert Spencer, who wrote his own brief account of the undertaking many years later, with which Conder's may be compared.[9] After that railway was opened in 1840 he worked again for Charles Fox, who had moved into partnership with John Henderson in the manufacture of ironwork and in general contracting at Smethwick, outside Birmingham. Conder's duties with the firm included the supervision of one of the most curious pieces of construction in these years: the running of a railway through the long tunnel of the Thames & Medway Canal in 1844–5. In 1848–55 he was engaged intermittently as a contractor for works on the South Wales Railway, under Brunel, in Pembrokeshire. He also went over to Ireland, to represent Fox Henderson in the construction of the Cork & Bandon Railway, which afforded him wryly entertaining recollections. Next he set up his own firm, Conder Goode & Co., and went to look for railway contracts abroad, securing one in south-western France and negotiating for another in Portugal that he did not get. It would have been well for him if he had failed in a third bid he made, for the construction of part of the long line between Naples and Brindisi. That took him out to Italy in 1856, and there he was engaged for almost nine years in an increasingly hopeless struggle, which cost him all the capital he had accumulated from his work at home and brought him to brain fever, very nearly to death.[10]

The elements of risk in this enterprise must have been obvious from the start. Its success depended entirely on the good will and good faith of the government of Naples, a rigid autocracy endangered by the hatred of a large number of its people and notoriously treacherous in its dealings. Although it promised Conder its support and encouraged his survey in Apulia, in fact it obstructed him and presently seized the sum of £50,000 that he had been required to lodge with it as a deposit at the beginning. The government itself was overturned in 1860 by Garibaldi; but in spite of diplomatic support from England Conder never recovered anything of what he had lost from the new Kingdom of Italy. Late in 1864 he returned home, ruined.

He had now 30 years of engineering and contracting behind him, and he must certainly have hoped to pick up the threads of it all again quickly, for the third and last wave of feverish railway promotion was then rising in Britain. But he had been out of the way for a long time. Before he could get far in his quest for work the crash of May 1866 arrived, and all railway promotion was delayed, cut back, or stopped. For the moment he turned his energies to writing, to produce in quick succession two substantial books: *The Trinity of Italy* and his *Personal Recollections*.

Englishmen were taking a great interest in Italian politics at that time, and it was sensible for Conder to turn his experiences there to some account. *The Trinity of Italy* is a vivacious piece of work, and it was well received on its publication in 1867. By that time railways were much in the general news in Britain, and Conder decided to record something of what he had observed of them in his earlier life. He wrote quickly, and the *Personal Recollections* came out in 1868.

These two books must have helped to make a place for him in high-class literary journalism, on the revenue from which he seems to have lived in his later years. Nearly all that he published here was anonymous. In 1872–88 he wrote much for the *Edinburgh Review*, as well as for *Fraser's Magazine* and the *Art Journal*; he commented on politics for the *St James's Gazette* and for some time had a weekly article in the *Builder*. The books he produced – slighter than the two of 1867–8 – reflected an old interest in philosophy and a new one in the history and archaeology of Palestine, stimulated by the work of his son Claude Reignier Conder, who was at the beginning of a distinguished career in that field.

In the last decade of his life he spoke out, and now for the first time openly in his own name, on the part that he thought canals could, and should, play in the commercial life of the country. He supported the case for the Manchester Ship Canal zestfully with two publications in 1882: a *Report on the Comparative Cost of Transport by Railway and Canal* and *The Actual and the Possible Cost of Conveyance between Manchester and Liverpool*. In the second of those writings he contended that the cost was then higher than it had been in 1829, before the opening of the Liverpool & Manchester Railway.[12] In the following year he gave evidence to a Commons committee on canals, designed to show what might be done with them in England from Continental examples.[13] We can detect in his questioners a certain impatience with this elderly witness, who was obliged to admit that he had never had anything to do with the making or management of a canal in his life. His work was not confined to writing and talking, however. He had by now found an active and successful role as a sanitary engineer, making himself a recognised authority on the deodorisation of sewage. (A system devised by him was installed at Windsor Castle.) He died at Guildford from angina, reading quietly in his chair, on 18 December 1889.[14] He had never recovered the fortune he lost in Italy. He left a personal estate of no more than £534.

2

Conder's life was curiously fragmented. His interests were wide, diverse, and at some points hardly consistent with one another. The religious strain in him was strong, and stoutly Protestant. Southey had written of his father that he held 'most of the opinions which were in fashion under Cromwell – a thorough Independent'.[15] Francis Conder was vehemently opposed to the Roman Catholic church, to ultramontanism and to the claims of the Popes to universal dominion.

He looked back with relish over 'the 29 schisms which have rent their communion'.[16] His mistrust of Catholics, and of the Tractarians who seemed to him Catholics in disguise, was never concealed. That dislike had doubtless been sharpened by his experiences in Italy, in the realm of the most bigoted Catholic monarch in Europe, Ferdinand II of Naples. And yet his account of that ruler is not uniformly unfavourable. It is rather different from the portrait of the cruel and sinister King Bomba that was accepted by conventional Protestants and Liberals in Britain.

We can see quite plainly, from his own recollections and from all the other evidence, that Conder did not succeed as a railway engineer. With his varied experience and obviously quick, intelligent mind he would have been a well-qualified candidate for at least a senior assistant's post, as deputy or resident engineer, in the 1840s, during the great boom in projection, when such men were most in demand. But he got nothing of the kind, and turned to contracting instead. It is worth comparing him with William Baker, his junior by a year or two, who joined the London & Birmingham Railway service with him.[17] In 1852 Baker became engineer of the southern division of the largest railway in the country, the London & North Western. Seven years later he succeeded Robert Stephenson as engineer of that company's whole system. By the side of this former colleague and of other contemporaries, Conder is an evident failure. When he returned to England in 1864, poor and in need of work, even his old chief Sir Charles Fox never found anything for him to do. He published his recollections not only in order to make money by them but also in some degree – it is clear – for the purpose of justifying himself, of explaining failure away.

Yet the recollections are not embittered. He too, like his father, was a thorough independent, in the broad, not merely sectarian sense of the phrase; a man who delighted in forming opinions for himself, shaded according to his own principles. Scarcely anybody who is described in his reminiscences, whether by name or indirectly, is accorded Conder's unqualified admiration. But equally, his most unfavourable accounts of the men he disapproved of or disliked nearly all include some effort to recall what he thought were their good qualities.

He kept his own name most strictly out of the book. His rule, as he explains at the beginning of it, was to put names to the men he praised but to withhold them from those he attacked. He names the most distinguished: Robert Stephenson and Brunel, the Irish contractor William Dargan, the government inspector Sir Charles Pasley. Nearly all the rest of the figures in the book are anonymous, and many of them – it must be admitted – elude any search for their identity now. That sort of mystification used to be a not uncommon practice in memoirs, but it was seldom pursued so thoroughly by anyone as by Conder. It is clear that he enjoyed mystery for itself, the mystery of his own authorship most of all. That does not impair the value of his book. In one sense the method he pursued may even have increased it; for it allowed him to record exactly what he wished to say, however unfavourable, without the need to pay much attention to the laws of libel. By the time he wrote, most of the leading men he spoke of were dead,[18] and were therefore beyond the scope of those laws; but it would have been impossible for him to trace many of the smaller fry, to discover which of them were still alive, and so he covered them all with a blanket of anonymity. These men survive in his pages as types, sometimes resembling others we meet elsewhere in his book. The types are not fictional, however; Conder persuades us to accept them as portraits sketched from the life.

At the head of those he attacks stands W.S. Moorsom, the engineer of the Birmingham & Gloucester Railway: 'a man too full of contradictions to be dismissed in a line', he remarks; 'perhaps difficult to be judged with fairness'.[19] He allows him some personal virtues, but he sees those as quite cancelled out by three defects. In the first place, Moorsom had come to the full responsibilities of a chief engineer without any adequate experience. He had been in the army, mainly in Nova Scotia, until 1832 and had been brought in to work on the London & Birmingham Railway at the instance of his brother, who was a director of the company. There he attracted Robert Stephenson's notice by a meritorious piece of surveying, and he was set on a new path. He sensibly tried to repair his deficiencies by an extended tour of the most important English railways in 1835–6, but when the Birmingham & Gloucester company appointed him he knew very little of the duties that the post of a chief engineer demanded. Although that was a serious shortcoming, it could have been remedied if he had chosen for his assistants men who had the knowledge and experience that he himself lacked and if he had been willing to trust them. The second charge Conder makes against him is that he did nothing of the kind: 'his professional knowledge was limited, to use the most favourable term; but his chief hostility was evinced towards those who, in perfect good faith, would have enabled him to supply the defect'. Here were two grave faults. In Conder's eyes Moorsom had a third, however, much graver still. He was devious, shifty, and unreliable: 'he managed to teach all his staff that they would meet fairer dealing from anyone than from himself… He was more likely to say nothing *to* the defaulter but much *of* the default where it might most turn to his disadvantage'.[20]

How far are we to believe these charges? Conder was opinionated. Did he quarrel with Moorsom, and were these statements made in revenge? We have no evidence directly on that point, but we can test Conder's assertions on another, linked with it. He observes that Moorsom had been 'borne well forward on the flow of the first railway mania' (ie in 1835, when he secured his appointment with the Birmingham & Gloucester company) and was therefore 'on the very crest of the wave' in the second, ten years later. 'He took in one year into Parliament more railway Bills than almost any other engineer. He lost them all but one, and that one was secured by the exertions of the experienced contractor who intended to make the line'.[21] Those statements are, broadly, true.[22] The one important English railway that he carried through after the Birmingham & Gloucester was completed was the Southampton & Dorchester, and the contractor there was one of the biggest men in the business, Peto, who did indeed give him very effectual support.[23] To that must be added the Waterford & Kilkenny Railway in Ireland. However, the survey there, on which the authorising Act was based, seems to have been deeply discreditable to him, and the work of construction was quickly taken out of his hands.[24] He then almost disappeared from the roll of railway engineers practising in the British Isles.[25] He never constructed any other line except the Ringwood Christchurch & Bournemouth, eight miles long, in 1860–2. That was at the end of his life. He died in 1863.

Reviewing Moorsom's career as a whole, it must certainly be judged a failure. He was not incompetent. The erection of the Birmingham & Gloucester's cast-iron bridge over the Avon at Defford won him a Telford medal from the Institution of Civil Engineers. In 1850 he gained first prize, against 60 competitors, for his plan for a road and railway bridge over the Rhine at Cologne. That it was not built to that plan, but to other men's designs later, was not his fault. But his work was seldom satisfactory. The Lickey incline (at 1 in 38), which the Birmingham & Gloucester Railway adopted on his advice in preference to more circuitous routes recommended by George Stephenson and Brunel, was a serious mistake. It is to be noted that both the Cornwall and the West Cornwall Railways' lines were taken away from him and given to Brunel to revise and execute.[26] Conder's judgement on Moorsom's public performance as an engineer may be taken as well-founded and reliable. It is harder to assess the truth of what he says about Moorsom's character. But the extremely discreet Herbert Spencer went some way towards confirming the unfavourable opinion of it that Conder expressed.[27]

The *Recollections* afford us briefer glimpses of other well-known engineers. He sets down Braithwaite, Vignoles, and Rastrick, all alike, as 'hard swearers'. Towards Rastrick he is unjust in saying that he 'came to the front of his profession rather in virtue of Parliamentary tactics than by any other form of introduction'. No doubt he was referring there to Rastrick's skill as a witness before committees, but the remark ignores his work as engineer for the construction of the main system of the London Brighton & South Coast Railway[29] as well as his important part in the development of the steam locomotive.[30] The Gravesend & Rochester line, discussed in Conder's book, was one of Rastrick's last undertakings, carried through when he was 64. He may well have grown testy by that time. Indeed if we were to judge solely by what Conder tells us, it would seem surprising that any railway engineer managed to avoid an early death from apoplexy. But his account of this railway finishes with a smiling portrait of Rastrick, 'his face and eyes glowing under his snowy hair', pouring forth reminiscences at a fish dinner given to celebrate the successful inspection of the line. The inspecting officer was Sir Charles Pasley (see pp218–19), and Conder's accounts of him are vivid and memorable. His physical courage and his sense of humour stand out in them, as well as – in a railway engineer's eyes – the limitations of his knowledge, and his bureaucrat's timidity.[31]

The sketch Conder gives of William Dargan, the Irish contractor, accords him very warm praise.[32] He appears as a just man, both in his dealings and as an employer of labour; decently modest, and a notable benefactor of his country. That verdict, broadly speaking, stands. All that Conder found to regret in him was that he shortened his life with 'Irish sherry'.

He is at his best on Robert Stephenson and Brunel, expressing his admiration for them and recording quite fairly what he sees as their defects. He brings out Stephenson's energy, his endurance, his extraordinary strength, and his integrity, together with his autocratic temper and his fieriness when he was crossed. His modern biographers have recognised the merit of this account of him. Here are 'the words of an admirer but not a worshipper', says one of them; 'and they ring true'.[33]

The treatment of Brunel in the *Personal Recollections* is more complex and quite as interesting. It may even be better because it is based on more mature and intimate observation. The first thing that struck Conder was Brunel's insistence on keeping control himself of the whole of the enterprises that were going on under him, compared with Stephenson's devolution of authority to his subordinates;[34] the second, Brunel's 'extreme and unprecedented insistence on excellence of work'.[35] He must have been right in saying that that added substantially to the expense of building Brunel's railways; not only because the engineer required a high and therefore costly standard of materials and workmanship but also because contractors came to tender for his undertakings only at top prices.[36]

Brunel was a perfectionist, for whom the best was sometimes the enemy of the good. Many people have said that, in admiration or criticism, from his day to ours. But Conder's professional experience enabled him to take the measure of Brunel, not of his art and intellect alone but also of the science and observation on which they were founded. He spells it out plainly for the lay reader. A difficulty arises, for example, from a slip in the wall of the harbour he is building for the railway at Neyland in South Wales. Conder indicates for us in words, with almost the accuracy attained by the best television, the process of looking and thinking by which Brunel solves his problem.[37] In the end, with no disloyalty to Robert Stephenson, Brunel stands out for him as 'our greatest engineer'.[38]

3

This book of Conder's bore exactly the right title. His recollections are indeed *personal*; personal to the men he talks about, personal to himself. They therefore present us with highly individual judgements, sometimes prejudiced. By the time he wrote them down he was out of the railway world, and he could say what he chose with full freedom because he wrote anonymously. They are *recollections*, of things he had observed from 12 to 35 years before he published them. Their interest for us is not confined to what he has to say about railway work. His eighth chapter is one of the best accounts we have of the pleasures of travelling by coach, free of commonplace romanticism and carrying with it entire conviction. The weaknesses of the book are obvious: the temptations to malice, to a little paying-off of old scores, the insidious tricks of memory. But there is great strength here too. Conder was able to write with detachment. He could look back coolly on his earlier experiences, reflect on them and place them in perspective. At the same time these recollections were not, like so many others, set down in old age. The writer was in his earlier fifties when he recorded them, with a fully alert mind ready to seize new opportunities as they came his way. The succeeding 20 years of his life prove that.

As we are able to look at it now, more than a century later, the book represents Conder's greatest stroke of good luck: the chance to set down a first-hand account of railway construction in the British Isles at the time of its fullest intensity. Our knowledge of that story is already considerable, from official records of many kinds, and what they have to tell us is by no means exhausted yet. Those records are dry and formal, however. If some of the biographies of the leading men involved, written shortly after they died, are useful, the writers of them were inhibited from entirely plain speaking. Conder was not himself a leading man, but he worked with those who were, and he watched them closely. Although his book is full of anecdotes, they are not – like so many others, handed down from one writer to another – stale. Some of them are misleading, some difficult to interpret. Conder made no claim to be a judicious historian. He was setting down personal recollections, no more. They come out here fresh and alive, recorded with spirit by a man who knew very well what he was writing about, and who also knew how to write.

NOTES

1. Printed in J.C. Jeaffreson, *Life of Robert Stephenson* (1864), ii. 285–304.

2. Sir D. Gooch, *Memoirs and Diary*, ed. R.B. Wilson (1972).

3. See M. Robbins in *Transactions of the Newcomen Society*, 56 (1984–5).

4. Extensively used by E.F. Clark in his *George Parker Bidder* (1983).

5. The original is in the British Library, Add. MSS. 34528–36, 35071. His diary is a work of remarkable detail, to have been written up almost daily by an engineer in extensive practice. It has been used in the recent biography of him by K.H. Vignoles (1982).

6. There are diaries of some lesser railway engineers, such at that of R.B. Dockray (between 1850 and 1860, discontinuous; ed. M. Robbins, *JTH* 7 1965–6), and the young Henry Swinburne's of 1842–3 (Northumberland Record Office, ZSW539/2, 3). *John Brunton's Book* comprises an interesting set of reminiscences, written down for the author's grandchildren and published 40 years after his death, in 1939.

7. On the title-page of his *Child's History of Jerusalem*.

8. The main source of information about Conder's life is his obituary in *Proc. ICE* 100 (1890) 379–83. It does not entirely agree with what he himself says in his *Recollections*. See also E.R. Conder, *Josiah Conder: a Memoir* (1857), 112, 118, 236.

9. *Autobiography* (1904). He mentions Conder twice (i. 131, 138), recording a remark made to him by Charles Fox that 'he [Conder] has not got his wits about him nearly as much as you have'.

10. The dates of his Italian employment are given in his book *The Trinity of Italy*, xi–xii.

11. In 1850 he had produced *Elements of Catholic Philosophy, or Theory of the Natural History of the Human Mind.* He followed this up with a short work in German, published at Leipzig in 1879: *Drei Ideale menschlicher Volkommenheit.*

12. Copies of these pamphlets are to be found in the library of the Institution of Civil Engineers: Tracts, vol. 350.

13. PP 1883, xii. 127–44.

14. Very brief obituary in *The Times*, 19 December 1889.

15. *Selections from the Letters of Robert Southey*, ed. J.W. Warter (1856), iii. 275.

16. *The Trinity of Italy*, xviii.

17. p. 11. All references given in this form are to pages in the text of my edition of Conder's *Recollections*, published under the title *The Man Who Built Railways* in 1983.

18. The chief exceptions are John Braithwaite and Sir Charles Fox, who did not die until 1870 and 1874 respectively.

19. p. 78. It is worth noting that in Moorsom's case Conder comes near to departing from his rule of anonymity, by calling him 'Captain Transom'. (p. 85).

20. pp. 78–9.

21. p. 87.

22. Reading between the lines, we can see that they are borne out even in the very circumspect obituary of Moorsom in *Proc. ICE*, 23 (1863–4) 498–504 (esp. 501).

23. See J.C. Cox, *Castleman's Corkscrew* (1975).

24. The government inspector's report on the first section of it to be finished (10 September 1847: PP 1847–8, xxvi. 438) says: 'The parliamentary section…according to the statement of the present engineer [Charles Tarrant]…is completely wrong, the surface of the ground as it exists being entirely of a different form from that delineated on the parliamentary section'. Compare that with the sentence in which Conder describes (p. 185) the care taken by Brunel to secure a correct and economical survey of the South Wales Railway's line.

25. He was engineer to the Cromford & High Peak Railway for a time and began its modernisation, but the company found itself too poor to retain his services, and he was dismissed in 1856: J.D. Marshall, *The Cromford & High Peak Railway* (1982), 12–13.

26. The cracks were papered over. On the Cornwall Railway the change was ascribed primarily to Moorsom's excessively large commitments to other railway companies; but see J. Keast, *The King of Mid-Cornwall* (1982), 147–9. On the West Cornwall he proved personally acceptable. He served as chairman of the company in 1847–50.

27. *Autobiography*, i. 183–5.

28. pp. 36, 154.

29. He executed the main Brighton line to Sir John Rennie's plan. He was sole engineer for the lines from Brighton to Chichester and Hastings.

30. His notebooks in the Goldsmiths' Library of the University of London show what a serious

student he had been of both the civil and the mechanical engineering of railways.

31. pp. 142–4, 154–5. Conder's account can be checked by Pasley's own. His reports on three inspections of this line and its tunnel in 1844–5 are in PP 1846, xxxix.

32. pp. 165–6.

33. M. Robbins, *George and Robert Stephenson* (1981 ed.), 44.

34. This is borne out in ways of which Conder himself cannot have been aware. Brunel even conducted some of the negotiations for the purchase of land for his railway companies himself. See for instance his dealings with Lady Georgiana Fane's solicitor concerning Brympton d'Evercy (summarised in RTC, 306–7), with Sir John Kennaway (Devon Record Office, 961 M/54), and with Lord Vivian's solicitor concerning Glynn in Cornwall, recounted on pp. 59–60 of this book.

35. p. 119.

36. p. 122. Brunel did not disregard the need for economy. The cost of his Royal Albert Bridge at Saltash was extraordinarily low. See P.S.A. Berridge, *The Girder Bridge* (1969), 61, and *The Works of Isambard Kingdom Brunel*, ed. Sir A. Pugsley (1980), 178; also VRY, 27.

37. pp. 129–30.

38. p. 187.

8

THE DIARY *of a* LONDON & NORTH WESTERN ENGINEMAN 1855–62

We seldom learn anything directly from those who managed or worked the Victorian railways. A few of the men at or near the top kept diaries, wrote letters that have survived, or produced memoirs.[1] But they are a few only, and their attention is given, very properly, to their own tasks, to planning and direction. Their writings do not often have much to show us of the lives of the men who worked under them. A retired locomotive inspector of the London Brighton & South Coast Railway, Michael Reynolds, published a popular book, *Engine-Driving Life*, in 1881, but it has not very much to tell us that is really useful. It is sentimental and rather slipshod, in marked contrast with his admirably lucid manual *Locomotive Engine-Driving* of 1877. H.A. Simmons's two little volumes, published under the title *Ernest Struggles* in 1879–80, have a good deal to say about the working of stations, much of it from the under-dog's point of view.[2] But this is overlaid everywhere with satire and complaint, and though that makes what he says more amusing it also makes him, at many points, less informative about normal practices and procedures, about ordinary life. Though there has been some investigation by modern writers into the work of railwaymen in the twentieth century, very little has been written as yet about that in the nineteenth, with the exception of one pioneering study, P.L. Kingsford's *Victorian Railwaymen*.

Where then are the voices from the ranks to be heard? To some extent in the early trade-union journals, though there, like Simmons's, they are usually voices of complaint. They sound out from time to time in the reports on accidents investigated by the inspecting officers of the Board of Trade. Under their patient probing a good deal emerges about the conditions of railway service, particularly about the hours the men worked. But since these were inquiries into irregularity, when something had gone wrong, they do not always help us to understand the day-by-day routine of the men's employment. Unfortunately, the staff records surviving from the British railway companies are patchy and defective.[3]

Here and there some alert journalist troubled himself to set down the recollections of an ancient railwayman; but then it was as a rule because he *was* ancient, rather than because he had anything very remarkable to say,[4] and being recollections, they were subject to mis-statement, and to all the colourings that arise from distant memory.

So even a small and simple detailed record of a railwayman's work, made at the time, may be of considerable value when it ever turns up. The diary kept by Thomas Baron as a fireman and engine-driver in the service of the London & North Western Railway is for the most part a bare catalogue of daily work done, with very little comment. But it is worth attention, as a clear and evidently truthful account of a routine. It is contained in a bound notebook, and though many of the later pages have been removed the diary itself seems to be as Baron left it, running from 5 December 1855 to 30 November 1862, when he apparently decided to bring it to an end. The history of the document seems to be unknown. It went with the British Transport Historical Records to the Public Record Office at Kew, where it is now.[5]

Although there are large gaps in the diary at the beginning, from 12 January 1857 onwards it is the record of the work of almost every day when the writer was employed. The entries usually comprise no more than the date, the name or number of the engine, the name of the driver that Baron was working with until he became one himself on 28 April 1862 (at the age of 27),[6] and the work done: the trip – that is to say the time of the train's departure, to a named place – and the distance travelled in miles. As a fireman, Baron seems to have had one day off in the week. When he became a driver he worked all seven days, with Sunday usually spent on shed, looking after his engine. His absences from work were infrequent, and they were from causes he sometimes notes, rarely extending to more than a single day at a time. Other information appears here very seldom. He notes down nothing, for example, about his pay, whether for his normal work or (if he got any) for overtime. He glances aside from the footplate only when something happened that struck him as worth special record.

The regularity of the entries is remarkable. The diary has, at first sight, the appearance of a fair copy made from rough notes – possibly based on the diarist's pay sheets.[7] The handwriting is even and consistent throughout, and I believe it to be Baron's own, not a copyist's. The inscription on the inside of the front cover (it will be quoted later) is plainly the writer's own statement, and the hand in which it is written is the same as that in the rest of the book. This seems to me to indicate that the whole record as it stands was written up, if not daily then at least at frequent intervals, by Baron himself, not by anybody else on his behalf, using his notes. The argument here is fortified by one change in spelling. Down to 18 October 1860 the diary often refers to 'Cendal' when it records a journey to or from that Westmorland town. Then the writer seems to have discovered that the accepted spelling was 'Kendal', for the name appears in that form consistently thereafter. If the present record is a fair copy, why should the original wrong spelling have been preserved and then, at this point, changed? It is surely probable that the writer would have made it 'Kendal' throughout.

We know very little of Baron's life. From notes appended to the diary we learn that he was born at Adlington in Lancashire on 5 April 1835, the eldest son of Robert Baron and his wife Betty (Markinson), that he became a cleaner with the London & North Western Railway in its engine sheds at Preston in June 1855, and then quickly a fireman. He was moved to Crewe in October 1861, and in September 1862 to Abergavenny. He continued to drive there for fifteen years until, at 42, he was promoted to become night foreman at Abergavenny shed. The surviving staff records of the company do not seem to allow us to follow his career any further, or to tell us when he died.

Now and then he would take a day's holiday, which probably meant loss of pay. 'At Morecame & Lancaster Pleasur', he records on 26 September 1860; 'to Crumblen Vieadock [Crumlin Viaduct] off Work', on 21 July 1862.[8] On 4 March 1859 he notes: 'My Mate Killed at Stafford. I worked the train Back'; five days later he went to the funeral at Bolton. The entry for 12 December 1860 – it was a Wednesday – reads: 'Shead [ie on shed] and Buring [burying] Child'. On 4 January 1862 he 'saw Maddox hung at Stafford'.[9]

The few pages that have been preserved after the conclusion of the diary have nothing to do with his employment on the railway at all. They include some addresses, among them those of a decorator and two house agents at Wigan. (Did Baron come to own the house he occupied, or perhaps more than one?) Some fragments of family history are set down here, concerning his parents and the births of himself, his brothers and sisters; a number of the christenings and burials took place at the parish church of Standish, north of Wigan. Baron also preserves a few simple prescriptions in case of illness. The first is perhaps too laconic to be useful: 'Reciet for Stomak and Hepatite 5 New Egs'. But the last is more specific: 'A Reciet for the yellows [ie jaundice]. Boiled Ormric[10] and Goos Greace. Aply it on a plaster on the Crown of the Head'.

In general the account is of work done to a very steady routine, seldom varied. When the line from Abergavenny to Brynmawr was completed he was detailed to drive the government inspector over it, on 19 September 1862. With its opening on 1 October he was set to work conveying passengers three times daily up and down the line, which was 9½ miles long. His record shows that during the seven months April–November 1862 he drove a little over 12,000 miles, an average of 78 for each of the days on which he worked.[11]

The tasks he had to perform were varied. When he was a fireman he had several spells of 'coaling'. I suppose that to mean taking coal trains (perhaps from the collieries themselves?) along the main line. Sometimes his engine was set to bank trains up the steep incline northwards from Wigan. Occasionally he went with passenger excursions, from Preston or Crewe to Rugby, to Liverpool and Manchester and Chester, and to Knowsley Hall. His engine might be one of a pair used on express trains, quite often the Irish Mail to and from Holyhead. From Preston and Crewe he worked entirely within the northern division of the railway, running occasionally to its southernmost limit at Rugby, but never going any nearer than that to London.

He fired for long periods with the same driver. The London & North Western Railway followed the practice of allocating an engine to a single driver for a substantial length of time, though not for many years on end as the Midland and the Brighton companies came to do. From 1 to 22 September 1862, working between Hereford and Newport, his engine happened to be *Columbine*: still to be seen today, not much altered, in the National Railway Museum at York.[12] A student of the working of the London & North Western Railway at this time, or of the service performed by its individual locomotives (Baron worked on 100 of them, each specified by name or number) will find it worth while to turn up the record set down in this book.

But the diary is not interesting solely as an account of one man's work. It throws a little light on a general question, which has not been much discussed: how far were railwaymen, and engine-drivers in particular, literate in the Victorian age?[13] That trains might still be driven at this time by men who were totally illiterate appears from a report on an accident on the Newport Abergavenny & Hereford Railway on 12 November 1856. The occasional driver employed on an express train derailed at Nantyderry said he could not read or write, and as the official commentator pointed out he 'could not therefore make himself acquainted with the book of regulations, with a copy of which he was supplied'.[14]

Baron's first words, appearing inside the front cover of his book, are these: 'Dairey from the year 1855. Acount of Work don. name of Engine I whent with and the Drivers I Fired for. and places runt to from Preston. Comenced Cleaning at Preston June 1855'. The spelling is phonetic, and irregular here and there: 'whent' appears several times, 'of' and 'off' are used interchangeably. When he moves house to Abergavenny he takes his 'Wife & Furnuter'. Naturally, a number of the names of his engines are mis-spelt: 'Sirius' becomes 'Serrious', 'Fury' is rendered 'Fewrry'.

The penmanship (if it is, as I think, Baron's own) is admirable, quite as good as that of many men of some education; and surely it was not much easier to learn to write than to spell. This man may have had no formal education at all. But he had certainly picked up a good deal before he became a railwayman at the age of 20, and as the small matter of 'Cendal' seems to demonstrate, he continued to be capable of learning.

He was evidently a man of good natural intelligence. His rise in the railway company's service – steady, if slow – is confirmation of that. The diary proves that he was determined in a rather exceptional degree. How many of us now would manage to keep a careful record like this, when working long hours for six or seven days in the week? Baron gives no indication why he undertook this labour; nor why, having kept it up for quite a long spell of time, he abandoned it. Perhaps we may guess that his additional work and responsibilities as a driver left him too tired to manage the careful recording day by day, at the end of his task.[15]

The value of what he has to tell us is greater than he could ever have imagined it might be. The official records that were once maintained – of rosters of work and of allocations of staff to sheds, for instance – have now almost all disappeared. There can never have been many enginemen in the Early-Victorian age who kept records of their own like this one. A few other diaries of the same kind may still await discovery. If they are found, they will be very welcome. Meanwhile, we should be grateful to Baron for showing us a routine of employment that is hard to find set out so clearly and regularly anywhere else, except by chance now and then in some accident report, and for doing it with the occasional asides he affords us, in a way that makes his simple account worth our attention still.

NOTES

1. See p.107 above and VRY, 106–9, 116–18.

2. The first volume was reprinted under the title *Memoirs of a Station Master* in 1974; the author's initials being wrongly given on the title-page of this edition, as 'E.J.'.

3. The most voluminous, by a long way, are those of the Great Western; the least satisfactory perhaps those of the Great Northern, the Lancashire & Yorkshire, and the Southern. (There must surely have been a deliberate destruction of these records from the Southern very soon after nationalisation.) All this information comes from Tom Richards's invaluable publication *Was your Grandfather a Railwayman? A Directory of Railway Archive Sources for Family Historians* (Federation of Family History Societies, 2nd ed., 1989). Its meticulous listing of staff records (company by company), held in the national collections and in local libraries and record offices, makes it a tool that every serious student of the history of British railways should have at his hand.

4. Among the more useful recordings of this kind may be noted the recollections of the engine-driver Joshua Slowen, extending from 1838 to 1903, published in the *Sheffield Independent*, 9 October 1903. See D.L. Franks in the *Railway World*, 44 (1983) 350–1.

5. R1015/4.

6. He had previously driven a shunting engine sometimes within the yards at Crewe.

7. I owe this suggestion to Mr P.D.J. Roos, who kindly discussed the diary with me at Kew. The paper used in the book carries no watermark, which would perhaps have helped us in determining its dates.

8. This great iron bridge had been completed in 1857 and at once became a justly famous sight.

9. Maddocks (that is the more probable spelling of his name) was one of three young men convicted of the murder of John Baggott at Bilston. Only one of them (David Brandrick) was hanged; the other two were reprieved. So it must have been Brandrick's death, not Maddocks's, that Baron witnessed at Stafford. I am grateful to John Bourne and Tony Hutchinson for disentangling this story.

10. The most probable identification of this plant (spelt here phonetically) seems to be with *armoracia*, or horseradish. I owe that suggestion to a pharmacist, Mr John Hind.

11. This figure agrees almost exactly with the one given by Dionysius Lardner in his *Railway Economy* (1850), 78: he works out the average 'daily distance worked per head' by drivers and

firemen on the London & North Western in 1848–9 as 75 miles.

12. It used to be supposed that *Columbine* was the first locomotive built at Crewe, but that is a mistake. The first was No 32, *Tamerlane*, completed on 20 October 1843. See D.H. Stuart and B. Reed, *Locomotives in Profile*, ed. B. Reed (1971–4) 54–6, 70.

13. Men employed in railway work – mostly navvies – figure in R.K. Webb's important article on working-class literacy in the Victorian age: *English Historical Review*, 55 (1960) 333–51. See also VRY, 188.

14. PP 1857, session 2, xxxvii. 145, 170.

15. We cannot be quite certain that he gave up the record at this point, for a large number of pages here have been torn out of the book. But the concluding paragraph, written below the entry for 30 November 1862, seems to indicate very clearly a termination.

9

THE REMOVAL *of a* NORTH EASTERN GENERAL MANAGER, 1871

The servants of Victorian railway companies enjoyed no contractual security of tenure in their employment. The men who worked the lines were always liable to dismissal, without any compensation, at times of financial stringency for instance, or when small companies were absorbed into larger units. Historians of labour have revealed a number of sudden dismissals of railwaymen, arising from various causes, and commented on them.[1] As trade unions developed and grew stronger, from the 1870s onwards, they were sometimes able to contest the decisions that the companies had taken in such cases, or at least to bring them to public attention.

It has not been widely noticed however that the same practice applied everywhere in railway employment: to the officers at the top as well as to the rank and file. The dismissal of one of those senior men could be made less abrupt, and sweetened if the directors of the company thought fit by some monetary recompense; or, supposing the officer concerned had committed some gross fault, he might be asked to send in his resignation in order to save his face. (The railways here inherited a practice well known in the army and navy.) But these were no more than subterfuges. The officer was dismissed all the same.[2]

The case to be looked at here is a curious one, and it seems to have passed without any public notice, either at the time when it occurred or since. It concerns Capt. William O'Brien, the general manager of the North Eastern Railway. He had held his post since 1854 and was of quite good standing in his profession; his probity was never called into question; he was apparently well liked by the company's men; he is not known to have been in ill health. Yet he retired suddenly, to be replaced by a much younger man; and this change, affecting the conduct of every part of the great company's business, was carried through in a profound and unbroken silence.

2

His earlier career had been successful, in a very straightforward fashion. He was born in or about 1805, the fifth son of an Irish gentleman, Lucius O'Brien of

Cratloe House, Co. Clare. He went into the army but soon turned to civilian life, enjoying as it appears some influential connections. He is stated to have been a cousin of Augustus Stafford O'Brien, Conservative MP for Northamptonshire from 1841 to 1857, and also of another more distinguished politician, Sir James Graham, to whom he may perhaps have been for a short time private secretary.* In 1841 he became secretary to the Great North of England Railway, and he went on to serve three other companies in succession, in the same capacity, the South Eastern, the Wilts Somerset & Weymouth, and the York Newcastle & Berwick. The last of these was one of the units that made up the North Eastern Railway, created by amalgamation in 1854. O'Brien was appointed secretary to that greatly-enlarged new company,[3] and three months after its formation he became its general manager, continuing to serve as secretary also for two more years until the offices were separated and John Cleghorn became secretary in his place.[4]

There had been nothing suspicious or unusual in his frequent changes of employment in the 1840s, a time of great upheaval in everything to do with railways, above all in their management. Each of the moves he made in those years had been occasioned, wholly or chiefly, by changes in the control of the companies he worked for, which took place over his head. He now settled down at York, in his mid-forties, to grapple with a task very much bigger than any he had undertaken before, and he appears to have discharged his duties without arousing any opposition or complaint. An engraving made from a photograph of him in 1861 depicts a sensible man, seated firmly and comfortably in his chair.

He had necessarily to involve himself in many troublesome matters – the North Eastern enginemen's strike of 1867 among them, as a result of which the company ruthlessly dismissed 900 of its servants, many of them of great value to it.[5] He seems to have been a quiet man, by nature and by preference; perhaps he was even a trifle colourless. We hear little of him in the railway world at large. (But then the North Eastern company always kept itself to itself as far as it could, and went its own way.) He seems to have had talents as a diplomat. In 1855 he played a considerable part in the making of the second Octuple Agreement, apportioning the receipts from the traffic between England and Scotland among the companies that were handling it; acting virtually as an arbitrator, to persuade the Great Northern and the Midland Railways to temper their rival claims.[6] He bore much of the weight of the protracted and difficult negotiations that led to the fusion of the Newcastle &

*Unfortunately two Capt. O'Briens figure in the early history of railways, and they have frequently been confused with each other. Possibly some confusion remains even now. Capt. Donatus O'Brien, William's brother (Boase suggests that he was no relation, but that belief is dispelled by William's will), was the first secretary of the Railway Department of the Board of Trade in 1844–6. After being displaced there he turned his back on railways for good and went to the Home Office, serving as an inspector of prisons and director of convict prisons in 1849–64: GR, 64–5, 82; Boase, vi. 314. It seems probable that it was Donatus, rather than William, who was secretary to Graham, in spite of the statement made in the *Post Office Railway Directory for 1847*, 321.

Carlisle and Stockton & Darlington companies with the North Eastern in 1862–3. He had also to be at times a fighter: with one enemy within the company's gates, the West Hartlepool Railway, and with a number outside that were striving to enter its territory, the London & North Western and the North British in particular. The threats from these quarters were all defeated, or contained within acceptable limits, and much of the credit for his company's success here must certainly have belonged to him.

The North Eastern and the companies amalgamated with it were, on the whole, prosperous throughout the 1860s. Like all others, they were adversely affected by the collapse of the stock market in London in 1866, but that brought none of them anywhere near to bankruptcy and by 1869 they were all paying higher Ordinary dividends than they had paid four years earlier. The stocks of the once-separate companies were combined together in 1870 to form North Eastern Consols, and the first dividend on that new stock was at the rate – high by the standards of British railway companies – of 7⁷/₈%. That was not a flashy demonstration, but a sign of an assured and long-lasting prosperity; the dividend was maintained at just that figure, on average, down to 1883.

Through all these years O'Brien worked under one chairman only, Harry Stephen Thompson,[7] and there was no public evidence of any disharmony between them. In one important matter indeed, as will become plain later, they are known to have been broadly in agreement. All in all, the man seemed to sit just as comfortably in his managerial chair in 1870 as he had in 1861. But the chair had perhaps grown easier to him than was quite desirable. Two groups of very serious problems confronted him as general manager in the 1860s, and he appears to have made no strong or sustained effort to solve either of them.

3

The first may well have been the more difficult of the two. The creation of the company in 1854 had involved what was, in all aspects other than the financial, a complete amalgamation of the four units that were then joined together. When the West Hartlepool Railway was added in 1865 it was the same – this amalgamation being more absolute, however, because the smaller company was a good deal at the mercy of the larger one. But with the Newcastle & Carlisle and the Stockton & Darlington companies, when they came into the hands of the North Eastern, it had been another matter. They were both prosperous corporations, established long before the North Eastern was created, each with secure command of the district it served, which lay almost entirely outside the scope of the North Eastern when they came to join it. Neither of them entered into union with the bigger company in a spirit of whole-hearted enthusiasm; within each there was strong opposition to that policy. Long wrangles went on between them and the North Eastern before acceptable terms could be agreed. The North Eastern succeeded in getting its Bill for the absorption of the Newcastle & Carlisle company passed in 1862 only after two previous attempts to secure the consent of Parliament had failed. Some of the older men who were powerful in the affairs of the Stockton & Darlington were very uneasy about the fusion. While the business was under discussion in 1861 the Stockton company's solicitor Francis Mewburn wrote to its secretary, John MacNay, in these terms: 'we [the Stockton & Darlington company] pay dearly for our connection with the North Eastern company, the most unpopular and unaccommodating line in the Kingdom. See and keep you out of the way of temptation'.[8] When the measure was going through Parliament two years later he noted that Joseph Pease was not at all surprised by the objections that were taken to it and was far from eager for it himself; he had agreed to support it only 'after great deliberation'.[9] The amalgamations were sanctioned nevertheless. O'Brien's diplomacy must have done a good deal – perhaps very much – towards securing this achievement; and the achievement was of great value to the North Eastern in extending its territorial monopoly and so helping to protect it against encroachment from outside.

But while the legislative act of union brought the bargaining to an end, it opened up new difficulties concerning the organisation and working of the greatly-enlarged North Eastern Railway; a company that now belied its name, with long tentacles stretching out westwards into Cumberland and Westmorland. There were three seats of power within the company. Its administrative headquarters were at York; but much of its day-to-day business was dealt with at Darlington, or on the Tyne at Gateshead and Newcastle. Each of the companies brought into it in 1862–3 had its own arrangements, differing from those established on the North Eastern. Some of them could be changed without much trouble: the Newcastle & Carlisle trains, for instance, could be made to travel on the left-hand rails, not on the right, and that order was enforced in 1864.[10] The Stockton & Darlington lines were placed, under the terms of the Act of amalgamation, in the hands of a Darlington Committee, the majority of whose members were directors of the old company. That arrangement lasted for thirteen years, and the disturbance of practices long established there was, in consequence, slow. By 1870, whilst the North Eastern had successfully resisted threatened invasions of the territory it considered its own and had achieved a new and impressive financial strength, the differences that necessarily arose from the variety of operating practices of the constituent companies remained, steadily increasing as the years passed. For those practices the general manager was ultimately responsible, and there seem to be no signs that he recognised the drawbacks arising from this diversity or sought to bring them to an end.

It was in day-to-day operation, in matters concerning machinery and techniques, that O'Brien came to confront the second group of his problems. Late in 1870, four serious accidents occurred on the North Eastern system, the last three of them within the space of eight days. William Yolland (see p.216) was the inspecting officer who reported on them all to the Board of Trade.

The first was at Scotswood Bridge, outside Newcastle, on 10 November; a collision that would not have occurred, so the inspector considered, had the lines at this point been worked on the block system. He was evidently growing indignant at the company's delay in extending that system, and he now discharged a heavy broadside at it. Nearly 18 months earlier, in May 1868, the Board of Trade had sent out a circular to all the railways, asking on what parts of their lines the block system was not in use. 'The North Eastern company', Yolland now observed caustically, 'could have replied in two words "the whole"' – saving some sections of line in tunnels and one short stretch of the old Stockton & Darlington system. Instead, it chose to leave the inquiry without any reply.[11] That was surely a serious mistake; the Board's records were well kept, and its memory long.

Next came another accident, at Cargo Fleet, east of Middlesbrough, on 30 November, and Yolland attributed it in part to the variety of rules framed by the constituent companies of the North Eastern, still in force seven or eight years after amalgamation; obliging drivers on this section of the line to carry two rule-books with them and to adjust their practices as they travelled along, out of one division of the company's system into another. 'There seems to be no unity of purpose', he wrote, 'in the management of the traffic on the different sections of this railway'.[12]

A week later, on 6 December, there was a disastrous collision between trains, meeting head-on, at Brockley Whins, causing five deaths. The company was treated with remarkable leniency by the coroner's jury at the inquest that followed. Its members understood none of the technical matters that the inspector came to discuss when he examined what had happened and analysed it in his report. They chased after a red herring instead: the presence of a man conversing with the signalman in his box as if he was a casual waster of time, when in fact it was his duty to be there. Yolland slapped that misapprehension down very firmly in his report, using it as a prime example of the misconceived thinking common to most coroners' juries when they inquired into what happened on railways.

More than one kind of mismanagement stood out plainly in the inspector's report.[13] The first and worst was the exceedingly bad layout of the station and of the adjacent junctions, clearly shown on a plan included in it; standing at an important point in the system, where lines from Newcastle, South Shields, and Sunderland converged. It had always been a troublesome place, which was understandable when those three lines were owned by three separate companies, but they had passed into the hands of one as early as 1846.[14] Twenty-four years later, when Yolland conducted his inquiry, he was told that a radical improvement of these arrangements was on the way – but it had still not even begun. Long overdue though that alteration now was, the dangers of the junction could have been much reduced (and, as he pointed out, this particular accident entirely avoided) if the points and signals had been interlocked, to prevent their movements from conflicting with one another.

So here the company's servants were set to work a notoriously dangerous junction with none but the most primitive pieces of equipment. The inspector had no doubt that these men were undisciplined and ill-directed, and that led him to his resounding conclusion: 'Nothing can more plainly exhibit the entire absence of responsibility that exists on the part of railway directors, their officers and servants, for the occurrence of preventable disastrous accidents than this very serious collision'. And then, with a final trenchant brevity: 'it appears to me that the company's management is wholly to blame'.

The last of these accidents followed on 8 December, at Seaton, north of Thirsk, and Yolland demonstrated that it would not have occurred if the block system of signalling had been in force on that section of the company's main line. In his report he took the opportunity to refer to some comments lately made by O'Brien, who in the previous June had publicly remarked that the whole block system was 'premature' and no more than 'experimental'.[15] O'Brien used these words as a witness before the House of Commons Select Committee on Railway Companies. It considered the application of the block system with care and may perhaps have chosen O'Brien as one of the railway managers to be examined because he was known to think ill of it, in order to ensure that that point of view was put before the members, even though it had already grown old-fashioned. The purpose of all that he said on the subject was to discredit the increased use of mechanical appliances to secure safety on railways. His method had a kind of cleverness about it. It was to throw a mist of uncertainty over everything of the kind. But the committee was not taken in, for its report came to a firm conclusion that the adoption of the block system had 'materially conduced to the safety of the public'.[16]

Yolland's words in these four reports were carefully selected, incisive and unanswerable. He had here exactly the chance he wanted to demonstrate the need for the re-equipment of the whole of the main lines of the North Eastern system, and he seized it. More than that: he may be said almost to have forced the board's hand. In the Brockley Whins report he included a warning that if railway companies persisted in refusing to adopt adequate machinery for ensuring safety on their lines they might find themselves compelled to do so by the government. His words were: 'I can only hope that the legislature will either compulsorily impose the introduction of the absolute block system on all railway companies or empower some public department to order it to be done when necessary'. That was a threat especially dreaded by the North Eastern Railway, which had come out strongly against the nationalisation of the telegraphs in 1868, moved by a desire 'to keep the government officials off their lines'.[17] Yolland was now turning that weapon round in the board's hands, in an effort to persuade it to incur essential expenditure voluntarily, lest it should find that expenditure forced on it by an inquisitive and determined government.

This was not quite the last shot in his locker. At the close of his report on the Seaton accident he made what can almost be seen as an appeal to the board himself. Referring again to the words that O'Brien had addressed to the Commons committee, he wrote: 'Of course it is natural that his opinions should completely outweigh with the directors anything which I can state or the experience of other railways can prove – if proof be sought for'. It may well have been those words which decided the issue.

The reports on these four accidents were completed between 23 December and 3 January. Copies of them were sent by the Board of Trade to the company, as usual, the first on 14 January and the last – the longest of them, on the Brockley Whins accident – on 11 February. Exactly a fortnight later, on 25 February, O'Brien retired.

4

That might of course have been a straightforward act of voluntary resignation, and no more. But the records, by a most remarkable silence, altogether forbid us to accept that idea. O'Brien's departure is not mentioned in the board's minutes at all, nor even – this omission is extraordinary – the decision to appoint Henry Tennant, the company's chief accountant, to succeed him in his office. Such important changes as these, on the North Eastern as well as on any other well-regulated railway, were always put to the board for its approval. As it happened, the company's secretary, Cleghorn, and Thomas Cabry, one of its divisional engineers, both retired in the normal course just at this time. The directors minuted both these events, inviting Cleghorn to become one of them while at the same time ratifying the appointment of C.N. Wilkinson to succeed him, and awarding Cabry a handshake of £1,000.[18] They had nothing to say of O'Brien whatever. By a special irony, his name figured in the board's minutes for the last time on 30 December 1870 as a signatory, along with Tennant and the chief engineer, T.E. Harrison, of a report recommending the installation of that block system which he held in contempt, on two important sections of the company's main line: a clear acceptance of the lesson that had been taught by the Seaton accident.[19]

In the same way, at the meetings of the company's shareholders, held as usual in February and August 1871, O'Brien's name seems never to have been mentioned.[20] Some of those who attended regularly may have been puzzled to find that he was not there, that Tennant had taken his place on the platform. No doubt explanations of this change, true or mistaken, passed round among them by word of mouth, but that was all.

When Mark Huish had resigned from the office of general manager of the London & North Western Railway in 1858, it was because his conduct of the company's business was too positive – indeed, overbearing – to please a group of powerful directors with whom he had been at variance for five years past. But there was no overt breach. He was given £3,000, together with a gold pass allowing him to travel free of charge over the whole of the company's system, and he was still called in occasionally to advise on one or two minor matters.[21] Little more than six months before O'Brien's departure, Seymour Clarke had retired as general manager of the Great Northern company at the age of 56, with a present of £2,000; but it was well known that he had been ill for a long time.[22] Had O'Brien's health been impaired, even a little, it would surely not have been difficult for the North Eastern board to persuade him to retire on the same grounds, and to paper over the cracks of disagreement by paying him something, as they did Cabry. Nothing of that sort happened. The directors simply turned their backs on him. It is surely impossible to avoid the conclusion that he was in fact dismissed – though permitted, for the sake of appearances, to send in his resignation. It was not O'Brien's attitude towards the block system that had brought him down. The chairman of the company, Thompson, took occasion at the shareholders' meeting in February 1871 to express his own belief that 'the whole line might be made perfectly safe without the general introduction of the block system', and he took the same ground as O'Brien had done with the Commons committee in the previous June by reiterating the hoary warnings that its extension served to decrease the enginemen's vigilance: so at least at that time chairman and manager were substantially in agreement. Thompson's mind must surely have come to be made up, along with those of his senior colleagues, by the general display of slack management, in several different quarters at once, that was presented by the inspector's reports, as powerful public statements of dangerous weaknesses that they already recognised. In the course of the next five months Thompson changed his attitude towards the extension of the block system, merely telling the company's shareholders in August that in his opinion there was no need to install it on minor branch lines.[23]

The directors had of course to take heed of their own position. On a number of other railways – the North British and the Brighton, for example, in 1866–7 – palace revolutions had broken out, leading to changes of chairmen and the reconstruction of boards. The North Eastern directors had themselves passed through a very awkward passage in 1867 when a shareholder, H.J. Trotter, alleged that it had been found necessary for the company to pay a dividend out of borrowed money, and that the cost of renewing its permanent way had been shown in the accounts at a fictitiously small figure. Though Trotter reaffirmed his charges pertinaciously, the chairman, the engineer, and the accountant were able to rebut them with entire success.[24] As the news of these four accidents arrived in the autumn of 1870, followed by the inspector's damaging analysis of their causes, the chairman and the directors may well have been tempted to put the blame for them entirely on to the company's manager.

If they were throwing O'Brien overboard in order to protect themselves, he certainly had hard measure, and that would entitle him to some sympathy. But the tone of the evidence he chose to present to the committee of 1870 gives no indication whatever that he was really a progressive, thwarted in his desire to adopt improvements by stingily-minded directors. The board took a certain risk in accepting what must have been the chairman's recommendation, given to it verbally at its meeting (in the absence of any written record, we can do no more than guess that it was made in that way), to accept Tennant as O'Brien's successor. Although the whole operation of the company's lines clearly called for reappraisal and reform, Tennant had had no recent experience of the working of traffic, at first hand. But the chairman and the board knew him to be conscientious, untiring, and astute. They judged that he would set himself to learn what he did not know, and master it; and they judged rightly.

At the time of his retirement, O'Brien had been general manager of the company for more than sixteen years, apparently adequate and blameless, though never as far as can be seen responsible for any large improvements in the conduct of its traffic. In this respect he was unlike his colleague Harrison the engineer, who was the same age but kept constantly abreast of them. Technical changes affecting the whole management of the railway (for which he was responsible) had evidently passed O'Brien by, as they passed by a number of other senior railway officers too: Bruyères on the London & North Western for example,[25] Tyrrell on the Great Western;[26] perhaps we should add, on the North Eastern itself, its much-loved locomotive superintendent Edward Fletcher.[27]

O'Brien's memory seems to have remained popular. A total of £5,500 was subscribed by 5494 of the company's servants to make a presentation to him on 14 September 1871.[28] He had then left his house on the Mount at York and gone to live in London, in Gloucester Gardens, Hyde Park. There he died on 6 September 1872, leaving a personal fortune of £45,000 (over £1 million in our money today):[29] a quite unusually large sum at that time for a man who, as far as we can tell, inherited nothing but made the whole of it by what he had earned as the salaried servant of railway companies.

NOTES

1. See for example P.L. Kingsford, *Victorian Railwaymen* (1970), 19–22, 44.

2. I have referred briefly to the dismissal of some railway engineers and locomotive superintendents in 1847–75 in VRY, 109–10.

3. Tomlinson, 549.

4. *Ibid.*, 648, 772.

5. P.S. Bagwell, *The Railwaymen* (1963), 40–2; Kingsford, 66–7.

6. Tomlinson, 555.

7. James Pulleine served as a stop-gap chairman on the formation of the new company in 1854–5.

8. *Memoir of John MacNay by his Son* (1867), 68.

9. Francis Mewburn, Diary (Darlington Public Library), 186.

10. J.S. Maclean, *Newcastle & Carlisle Railway* (1948), 109.

11. *Ibid.*, 306.

12. *Ibid.*, 307.

13. PP 1871, lx. 308–14.

14. See Tomlinson, 415–16.

15. PP 1870, x. 248.

16. *Ibid.*, 212.

17. See VRY, 228.

18. R537/13, minutes 5557–8, 5689.

19. *Ibid.*, minutes 5554, 5560. It may be added that the chairman's business books (R527/138–9) have nothing to say about O'Brien's removal either. Thompson's personal papers have either been destroyed or are inaccessible. Thompson pointed out to the shareholders that the company was fortunate in the possession of numerous alternative routes, by the use of which the pressure of traffic could be relieved when it was at its heaviest, without delays, which might lose the company business. He was presumably implying that its lines were less crowded than, for example, most of those running into London; and that was true.

20. *Railway Times*, 34 (1871) 207–8.

21. T.R. Gourvish, *Mark Huish and the London & North Western Railway* (1972), 54–6.

22. Wrottesley GNR, ii. 12.

23. *Railway Times*, 34 (1871) 836.

24. See Tomlinson, 630–2. For Trotter, see Boase, 1023.

25. Neele, ix.

26. 'Probably the most unprogressive traffic chief of that or any other time' (MacDermot, ii. 193). He retired in 1888 at the age of 72.

27. See R.J. Irving, *The North Eastern Railway Company 1870–1914* (1976), 90.

28. Tomlinson, 848n.

29. Will: Somerset House, London.

10

A POWERFUL CRITIC OF RAILWAYS: *John Tenniel in* PUNCH

Punch was first published in 1841 as a weekly comic paper modelled on the *Charivari* of Paris, which had taken its title from an old French word meaning a loud noise, accompanied with cries. That is just what *Punch* was at the beginning and long remained, though it soon developed other characteristics too, becoming a chronicler of politics, of fashion, of popular ideas and moral judgement. Some of those qualities could still be observed in it 100 years later.

The paper had one other feature at the outset, which it constantly retained. It was pre-eminently an organ of London, commenting chiefly on London matters and looking at everything it touched from the point of view of the capital, having little to say about the provinces. As for Welshmen, Scotsmen, and Irishmen, they seldom figured in it except as people who were thought to speak versions of the English language that Londoners enjoyed because they found them grotesque.

Certain assumptions governed the conduct of *Punch* throughout the Victorian age; some of them remained in force far into the twentieth century. It was always primarily a spokesman of the middle classes (in the plural; it thought of them very broadly), and everyone concerned with the journal – proprietors, editors, contributors, and newsagents alike – acted in accordance with the attitudes, the known wishes and prejudices of that division of society. *Punch* depicted people who were socially above most of its readers with jealous envy, longing greatly to live as they did but often concealing that desire behind a mask of obsequiousness. Their social inferiors were a constant source of merriment to its readers, and *Punch* fastened on that too; their dress, their accents, their misdemeanours, even their proprieties – the paper poked fun at them all weekly. Anybody who takes up one of the early volumes now is apt to be incredulous at first – can such crudities really have formed the stuff of the thinking of ordinary, decent people 150 years ago? But if these early Victorians' prejudices and snobberies and humbug are translated into those of our own time, they will perhaps appear less surprising.

The prejudices were just what might be expected. All foreigners tended to be presented in *Punch* as wicked or absurd, sometimes both. In religion its governing principle was a detestation of the Church of Rome and a contemptuous ridicule of the Puseyites, together with all other kinds of Anglo-Catholics. In politics it was not an organ of either of the two main parties. It commended Peel as Prime Minister almost exactly in accordance with the movement of his mind towards the adoption of free-trading policies. It treated his opponent Disraeli rather tenderly, however, as a striking human oddity; he was a wonderful gift at all times to caricaturists.

Punch was never of any account as an originating force, a protagonist of new ideas. Its success (and that did not come its way easily at first) arose largely from its skill in depicting the prevalent opinions and attitudes of its time. It was, and it remained, a reflector.

Mark Lemon, who edited the journal for the first twenty years of its life, drew in a talented team of writers and artists – in early days, for instance, Thackeray, Douglas Jerrold, and John Leech. Foolish items of news or comment were soon being culled from daily papers and sent to it in a constant stream, spotted by correspondents and the office staff. It greatly relished absurdity in public life and fastened on certain exponents of that with a sure grip, for years on end. Alderman Humphrey was one, Sir Peter Laurie another. Among those who come into the history of railways were Colonel Sibthorp ('when Parliament is without its Sibthorp', said *Punch* in 1844, 'may Pantomine lose its Clown!') and the odious and crazy G.H. Whalley, MP for Peterborough in the 1860s.[1] The contractor Peto too, as his rascally doings with the London Chatham & Dover company came to be exposed in the courts: 'who could know better what mismanagement means than Sir Morton?', the paper inquired contemptuously.[2] *Punch* treated a bigger man, Brougham, with an interesting kind of discrimination, noting the wild eccentricity of his self-centred political conduct and never pretending to think that anybody could trust him, yet quite often paying tribute to him for his energetic promotion of ideas that appeared valuable. The moral faults it hated most were fraud, false pretences, and what it thought unjust oppression. As an organ of the middle classes, it could not be a leveller. But it disliked landlords and landlordism and particularly enjoyed exposing tyrannies alleged to be exercised by the aristocracy on their estates – always fair game to those who lived in London and knew nothing of such matters at first hand.

These are generalisations about *Punch*'s notions and attitudes. But they were not totally rigid; it was never a doctrinaire. Much as it detested Catholicism, it was happy to take the devout Irish Catholic Richard Doyle on to its staff in 1842; when he suddenly left it in 1850 it was solely because he felt the paper was insulting the Pope.[3] It was quite prepared on occasion to give credit to the politically-minded aristocrats in the House of Lords when it thought that a policy they advocated was more praiseworthy than one favoured by the Commons. An example of that will be given here later, concerned with railways.

2

Being a London paper, founded in 1841, *Punch* was bound to pay some special attention to railways: for the trunk system was emerging just then, in its rather haphazard fashion, as one based primarily on London – not, as a carefully-planned

THE MOMENTOUS QUESTION.

"Tell me, oh tell me, dearest Albert, have *you* any Railway Shares?"

Leech: *Punch*, vol. 9 (1845) p.47

national system for the whole of Great Britain might have done, on Birmingham or perhaps on Sheffield. Two of the main trunk routes, from London to Bristol and Brighton, were completed close to the time of the paper's birth. It refers to railways twice in its opening number, published on 17 July 1841. Almost at the beginning, a contributor notices a young man in the train between London and Birmingham reading a three-volume novel on the way, and that prompts him to go home and write one himself, designed specifically to be read on a railway journey. Later in the same number, *Punch* offers its first railway picture: a little cartoon in silhouette entitled 'Grand Junction Trains', showing four of them converging on a level crossing of lines.[4] It does not seem to be intended to carry any message. No text accompanies it, so it looks like a neat piece of pattern-making, hardly more. It is unsigned, but can certainly be ascribed to H.G. Hine, who excelled in this delicate technique and continued producing such 'blackies' for the paper until 1844.

Constantly on the look-out for abuses and follies to expose and attack, *Punch* soon turned its attention to railway accidents, resulting from carelessness or

Doyle: *Punch*, vol. 17 (1849) p.52

mismanagement . Late in 1842 it offered 'Recommendations for the Prevention of Railway Accidents', having been 'particularly struck by the infernal smashes that have recently taken place on several railroad lines'. The alarming collision between a train and a stage-coach at Bridgwater on 11 September (though no serious injuries resulted from it) must pretty certainly have been in that writer's mind;[5] his comment was made only five weeks after the accident had occurred. Intermittent references to accidents continue from this point onwards, all treated as examples of the misconduct of railways.

In the first twenty years of the paper's life, John Leech, its principal cartoonist, contributed to it a fair number of full-page drawings concerned with railways. Several of them, dealing with speculation and speculators in 1845–9, have remained famous: 'The Railway Juggernaut' of 1845 for example, and 'Off the Rail' depicting George Hudson's fall in 1849.[6] Among those that are also good, but less well known, are 'Lord Brougham's Nightmare' and 'The Momentous Question', showing Queen Victoria timidly inquiring of Prince Albert whether or not he holds any railway shares.[7] Another of Leech's pictures, of 1850, shows us a nervous old lady who has at length made up her mind to travel by train, confronted with a placard concerning insurance against accidents, with the premiums to be paid for compensation on account of different sorts of injuries, from broken legs to broken necks. This notice is 'the first thing she beholds on arriving at the station'.[8] Here is perfectly fair comment on the wooden-headed concept of public relations that characterised railway managements throughout the Victorian age, and frequently characterises them still.[9]

Richard Doyle, Leech's second-in-command on the staff of *Punch*, had his own delectable and entirely individual way of commenting on railways.[10] But when he left the paper at very short notice, although there were plenty of clever draughtsmen who might be considered eligible to replace him, the proprietors and editorial staff must have felt they needed to inquire carefully into the outlook and opinions of any artist they thought of engaging to succeed him, and they had no very high payment to offer. They appointed John Tenniel to fill the vacant post quickly, however, in December 1850.

3

Tenniel was a Londoner through and through, born in Kensington in 1820 and dying there in 1914. His father, John Baptist Tenniel (his name suggests a French descent), made his living as an instructor-at-arms and drawing-master. The boy was educated privately and then studied at the Royal Academy School from 1837 onwards. His first work to attract wide notice was his set of engraved illustrations to Thomas James's edition of *Æsop's Fables*, published in 1848. Mark Lemon noticed and admired these drawings, and that must have helped Tenniel to secure the position that had to be filled on Doyle's departure.

Tenniel's signed work did not begin to appear in the paper until the issue of 15

February 1851. That included a full-page picture by him, 'Smithfield as it is to be. A Pastoral', designed to comment on the plan for a new meat market for London, the artist showing his delight here at once in animals, as he had already done in illustrating Æsop. The drawing is signed 'J.T.', the letters made up into a neat monogram. Tenniel continued to use it, with no more than slight changes in the decoration of the letters, for the rest of his life.[11] The monogram did not appear frequently to begin with. But when the 20th volume, in which Tenniel's work first figured, drew near to completion in June 1851 and it had to be provided with a title-page, together with a decorative heading to its preface, both were entrusted to him. His work had evidently pleased his paymasters and fellow-artists.

Tenniel was a shy, quiet man, who grew to be much liked and respected by his colleagues and close friends, though he cut scarcely any figure in public life. In the portrait he drew of himself in 1889 he remains inscrutable to us now; rather formidable too, behind the barrier of his elaborate, well-tended moustache.

The most important decisions on the attitude to be taken up by *Punch* towards current events were arrived at by its proprietors and senior staff in a discussion that took place at a dinner held every week on Wednesday evening. In each issue its most striking announcement of that attitude was conveyed in a full-page cartoon. (Occasionally it broadened out to fill two facing pages, or there were two separate large cartoons in one issue.) The artist was never at liberty to decide on the subject of the cartoon by himself. Though, like the rest of the diners, he was fully entitled to propose one, he had in the end to draw a picture of some event, real or imaginary, that had been fixed on by the assembled company as a whole. In his 50-years' service on the paper Tenniel came to produce a much larger number of these drawings than any other artist. Of all the full-page cartoons that *Punch* published in 1841–94, 96 percent were the work of three men: Leech, Doyle (who might well have succeeded Leech, had he not resigned), and Tenniel. Tenniel's share of them came to be 2,750, two-thirds of the entire number.[12]

4

After the excitement of the wild speculation in the 1840s had subsided, and the losses incurred by many of the less lucky or skilful investors had been reckoned up, a journal like *Punch* naturally tended to turn its eyes away from railways, and for the first eighteen months of Tenniel's service there it had little to say about them. Many of its readers must have lost money in the business and would not have wished to be reminded of railways at all, except perhaps in one way. They might now applaud with special gusto the criticism of the directors and managers of railway companies that arose from all kinds of malpractices when they came to light. Suddenly, in August 1852, *Punch* began to open fire on them, and it went on peppering them for several weeks to come. Most of the onslaught was in words alone: damning little phrases – 'Parsimony leads to Smash', 'Railway Signals – Signal Extortion, Signal Neglect, and Signal Impudence'. Here and there came something more extended, like 'The Railway Nursery Rhymer', set to the tune of 'Hush-a-bye, Baby':

> Rock away, passenger, in the third class,
> When your train shunts, a faster will pass.
> When your train's late your chances are small,
> Crushed will be carriages, engines and all.

But drawings play there part here as well. In two successive issues (11, 18 September) there are full page cartoons concerned with the dangers of railway travelling. One, by Leech, shows a station bookstall offering medical literature on the treatment of broken limbs as well as the latest number of a fictitious periodical, *The Railway Operator*. In the other, which is unsigned but may, I think, be attributed to Tenniel on stylistic grounds, an undertaker offers one of his professional cards to a passenger before he sets out on a journey by train, to be useful to his relatives in case of his being killed in the course of it.

These assaults on railways, coming so close together, formed a group that stood on its own. Perhaps a few readers intimated that they had grown tired of the subject, or disgusted by it; or somebody connected with the railway interest may have remonstrated with the proprietors of the journal. At any rate the barrage dies down, not to be resumed in full force for more than ten years. But during that interval it still rumbles occasionally, as when in 1857 a small cartoon suggests that a seat should be provided on the front of every locomotive to be occupied by a director, who will then be the first to be killed in a collision. This device is called 'The Patent Safety Railway Buffer'.[15]

The business of satirists is to search out and expose follies and crimes, only rarely to praise merit, and then by making demerit look worse by contrast. *Punch* had no favourite among railway companies, whose practice it steadily approved.[16] Indeed, it seldom praised anything that was done by a railway. But it selected several for repeated and long-continued denunciation. In early days it enjoyed itself very much with the absurdities of the West London Railway, which thoroughly deserved its half-affectionate banter. The paper conducted its most energetic war against the Eastern Counties company, in a series of campaigns from 1846 to 1862 when its name disappeared on its merger into the new Great Eastern combination. Someone then seems to have persuaded the editor of *Punch* that serious efforts were being made to reform the old company's misdeeds; it never attacked the new Great Eastern in the same way. By 1868 it was able to tell its readers that this was not the worst British railway company. That distinction had now passed, it thought, to the London & South Western. Already, four years earlier, it had associated with that railway a statement that 'the company will hold themselves responsible for nothing'. Now it referred to the South Western as 'the common enemy of mankind' and said roundly that it was 'the worst managed railway out of London'.[17]

THE PATENT SAFETY RAILWAY BUFFER.

Anon: *Punch*, vol. 33 (1857) p.25

?Tenniel: *Punch*, vol. 23 (1852) p.129

5

Tenniel had no special interest in railways in themselves. It seems likely that he always agreed with the fiercely critical view of their management that was expressed by *Punch*. As far as I have observed, his first full-page cartoon to be devoted to them (apart from the one of 1852 that has been mentioned) appeared on 9 September 1865. Its subject was the proposal of the Great Western Railway to set up works for building carriages and wagons at Oxford, close to Worcester College and the western edge of the city. *Punch* opposed this plan loudly and contemptuously – one of its articles was headed 'The Great Western Vandals at Oxford' – and it was in the end defeated. The cartoon did not assault the proposal directly, merely indicating one of the ludicrous results that might be expected to spring from it if it was carried out.[18]

Tenniel had now risen to the full height of his powers. The Oxford cartoon appeared immediately after the publication of a set of his woodcuts, entirely different in kind, which has brought him permanent fame: those for *Alice in Wonderland*. Lewis Carroll chose Tenniel as an illustrator of his text himself. 'Of all artists I should prefer Mr Tenniel', he wrote when he began his search for the right man in December 1863. The book was delayed in the press a long time, largely on account of the burden of Tenniel's other work, and when it was completed in 1865 the whole first edition had to be withdrawn from sale owing to the artist's dissatisfaction with the printing of it. He was always, in his own fashion, a perfectionist. When Carroll planned to write a sequel he turned again to Tenniel, who at first refused him and then accepted the commission. It was completed in 1871 and, as *Through the Looking Glass*, was published in the following year.[19] These pictures should never be out of one's mind as one looks at Tenniel's subsequent work for *Punch*.

Punch was still occasionally prepared to treat railway matters in the spirit of comedy. Just while its attack on the Oxford proposal was at its height, it published a 'Guide to Bradshaw' in six instalments, containing good fun poked at the timetables' obscurities (see pp.178–9) and most merrily illustrated by Charles H. Bennett.[20] But the paper's indignation against railway companies was now growing steadily once again, to become an assault upon their relentless expansionism, which was displaying itself in every direction. It saw London being invaded by them, as they pressed in from all sides, closer and closer to its centre; not without reason either, for Bills were presented to Parliament in 1860–6 seeking to permit the construction of some 850 miles of line in Greater London.[21] It suggested that St Paul's Cathedral might be converted into a station[22] and savagely opposed the line that the London Chatham & Dover company hideously thrust across Ludgate Hill (a miserable blot on the City of London that was not removed until 1991).[23] In 1864 it published a series of bogus advertisements 'rendered necessary by the Railway Invasion', all of them relating to that company and its voracious purchases of property.[24]

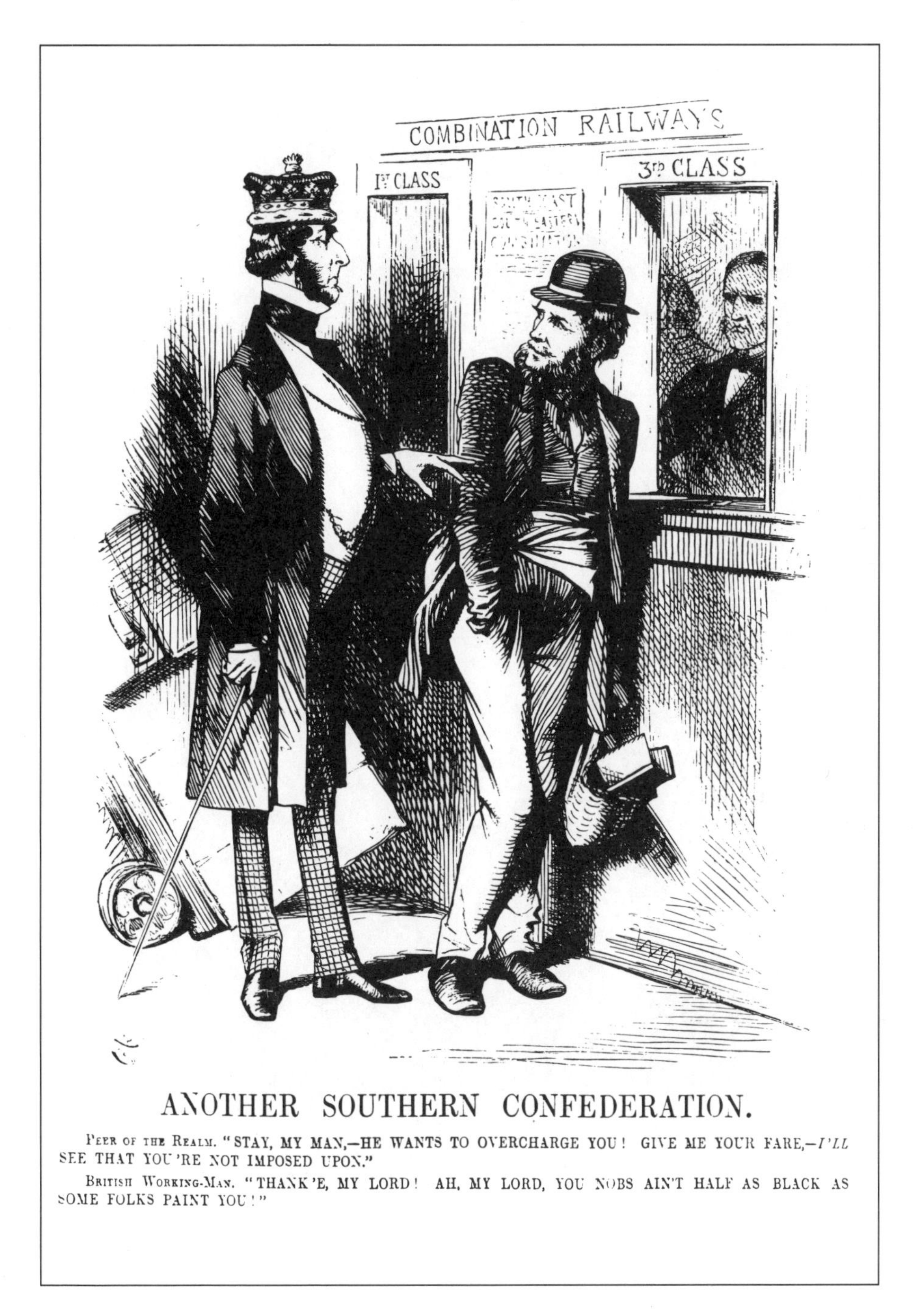

ANOTHER SOUTHERN CONFEDERATION.

PEER OF THE REALM. "STAY, MY MAN,—HE WANTS TO OVERCHARGE YOU! GIVE ME YOUR FARE,—*I'LL* SEE THAT YOU'RE NOT IMPOSED UPON."

BRITISH WORKING-MAN. "THANK 'E, MY LORD! AH, MY LORD, YOU NOBS AIN'T HALF AS BLACK AS SOME FOLKS PAINT YOU!"

Tenniel: *Punch*, vol. 54 (1868) p.279

Tenniel: *Punch*, vol. 55 (1868) p.70

This wild extravagance met its death in the financial crisis following the failure of Overend Gurney & Co in 1866, for which the promotion of unsound railway companies had been largely to blame. *Punch* had by now taken its own measure of the whole railway interest –MPs, directors, shareholders, managers, and projectors alike – and from this point onwards it had almost no kind words to say about railways throughout the rest of the Victorian age.

It attacked them now on a very broad front, concentrating its attention particularly on two evils: the sinister power that it saw them wielding through the activities of their directors in Parliament, expressed for instance in a biting poem entitled 'The Railway Despots', trampling everybody under their feet, published in March 1866;[25] and assailing the plans for amalgamating companies together to make them form stronger, monopolistic corporations.[26] The most prominent effort of this kind in the later 1860s was that made by the Brighton and South Eastern companies to unite. A Bill to allow this fusion was passed by the House of Commons in 1868, but the Lords insisted on including a provision to forbid the new combine to raise passenger fares, whereupon the companies abandoned the plan. Little as it liked aristocrats, *Punch* was prepared to salute their action here, and Tenniel produced an effective cartoon, showing one of the peers preventing a workman from being overcharged for his fare by a clerk in a booking office that bears the inscription 'Combination Railways', with a board specifically naming the two companies placed beside it.[27] Seven weeks later Tenniel attacked Disraeli's government and the directors of railway companies, both together, by means of one of his very best pictures: a double-page spread, referring to the Regulation of Railways Act, only a fortnight after it had gone into force. 'The Modern Dick Turpin' it was called, showing the highwayman riding up beside a train, with a director astride its engine, who exclaims to him 'Ha! Ha! You were hanged. *We* rob by Act of Paliament'.[28]

Next year he provided a strong comment on the Overend Gurney affair. The unravelling of that company's murky and labyrinthine business went ahead very slowly. It was not until January 1869 that the directors of the firm were sent for trial – two and a half years after the crash. Tenniel shows us a 'ruined shareholder' in the company standing outside the court, embracing his daughter and saying 'Yes, they are committed for trial; but we, my child, to *Hard Labour for Life*'.[29]

The fearful increase in the number of railway accidents that was appearing at this time (see pp.221–7) produced a return to an already-old theme. Tenniel's comments on them showed how little precise knowledge he had of railways. When he came to treat the Kirtlebridge accident on the Caledonian Railway (20 October 1872), his drawing (see frontispiece) bore only a vague relationship to what had happened in it.[30] However, it must be remembered that he was depicting an event that had taken place only a fortnight before he set to work on it, when nearly all the information he had to go on was supplied by newspaper reports and the proceedings at the inquest. The inspector's report, giving a much more full and careful account of the conditions in which the accident occurred, was not published until the following March – far too late to give a commentator like

THE GOLDEN WEDDING.

(MR. PUNCH'S *present to Vulcan and Vapour on the 50th Anniversary of their happy Union.*)

MR. P. "LET'S HOPE, MY DEAR FRIENDS, THAT BEFORE THE NEXT ANNIVERSARY YOU'LL HAVE BROUGHT BLOCK AND BRAKE BOTH TO PERFECTION."

Tenniel: *Punch*, vol. 69 (1875) p.141

RAILWAY RESPONSIBILITY.

MR. PUNCH. "NO, NO, MR. DIRECTOR, *THEY*'RE NOT SO MUCH TO BLAME. IT'S *YOUR* PRECIOUS FALSE ECONOMY, UNPUNCTUALITY, AND GENERAL WANT OF SYSTEM THAT DOES ALL THE MISCHIEF."

Tenniel: *Punch*, vol. 67 (1874) p.129

Tenniel any guidance or help.

These technical misapprehensions do not at all affect the force of the moral that he wished to be drawn from his pictures. In one sense they even help to strengthen it by showing that Tenniel was not in any respect a railway buff demonstrating exactly what had been done wrongly in technical terms, but an austere judge, concerned to point out broad causes and consequences and to suggest their implications. His depiction of the dreadful Thorpe collision on the Great Eastern Railway in 1874 is again quite generalised (it does not even show the accident as a meeting of two trains head on, which made it specially alarming), but the lesson it tries to inculcate is plain enough: the responsibility for the accident rests mainly on the directors, not on the company's servants.[31] Significantly, the whole comment made by *Punch* in September of the following year on the celebrations at Darlington to mark the 50th anniversary of the opening of the Stockton & Darlington Railway is an admonition to the companies to press on with the improvement of their signalling and braking systems – conveyed by Tenniel in a milder tone than usual.[32]

6

His cartoons were not always concerned with accidents and irresponsibility. Now and then he was set down, by the general wish of his colleagues, to illustrate a change of policy that might be both criticised and defended. When in October 1874 the Midland Railway announced that it had decided to discontinue the provision of second-class accommodation on all its lines from the following New Year's Day, going over to a two-class system (first and third), other competing companies denounced the change loudly as a financially reckless arrangement, and threatened severe retaliation. Those matters were nothing to do with *Punch* but, mindful as always of its main *clientèle*, it addressed itself to the dilemma that this policy presented to many middle-class travellers. Tenniel called his cartoon 'A Railway Revolution' and depicted a stout and indignant mamma confronting a Midland official on a station platform and protesting to him: 'I can't afford to go first, and I won't go third. What am I to do?' She and her dutiful daughter are admirably characterised in the picture; so is the railway man, regretful but smilingly inflexible.[33] A little later, Tenniel also glances at the extreme slowness of Parliamentary trains, only three years before they were virtually done away with by the Cheap Trains Act.[34]

Though *Punch* continued to dislike and mistrust railway management in all its forms, it did occasionally relax for a moment, so that it appeared to forgive an old foe – or was the editor perhaps taking a nap? In 1885 it allowed Harry Furniss to provide the London Chatham & Dover company (the paper's deadliest enemy 20 years before) with a fine gratuitous advertisement, in the shape of a half-page drawing to depict the Granville Express waiting at Victoria station on a Friday afternoon to carry a distinguished company down to the north Kent coast for the

A RAILWAY REVOLUTION.

SCENE—*Platform on Midland Railway.*

MATERFAMILIAS. "WHAT, NO SECOND CLASS! NO RETURN TICKETS! I CAN'T AFFORD TO GO 'FIRST;' AND I WON'T GO 'THIRD.' WHAT *AM* I TO DO?"

Tenniel: *Punch*, (1874) p.17

week-end; among them Archbishop Benson of Canterbury and the actor Henry Irving.[35] Moreover, since Furniss's object here was not caricature he was able to offer a lively and well-observed picture of the interior of a large railway station. That was something seldom attempted by any draughtsman or painter in the Victorian age after Frith had shown how it might be done, in another more elaborate way, at Paddington in 1862; and it lay outside the usual scope of photographers, from the difficulties they were confronted with in these smoke-filled, dark interiors. So the *Punch* cartoon here is of direct interest to students of railways (they should pay attention to the electric light fittings, for example), as well as to those who are interested in the development of the week-end holiday as a social institution.

Again, in August 1888, when *Punch* felt impelled to offer some comment on the Railway Races to Edinburgh, then arousing a good deal of excitement, it was of course directed at the dangers these high-speed trains brought with them. However, Linley Sambourne, in his cartoon, did not go for the competitors as Tenniel would probably have done. He makes the speed exciting and conveys his cautionary words only in a small caption, where a shareholder cries out 'Stop! Stop! More haste, less dividend!'[36]

But Tenniel had not turned away from the railways altogether. He could still be stirred to do battle with them again. On 1 May 1891, as an express was crossing the Portland Road bridge at Norwood Junction on the London Brighton & South Coast Railway, that bridge collapsed under it, derailing the whole train. Neither the engine nor any of the vehicles fell off the embankment or down on to the road below, and no one was seriously injured. Had that miracle not occurred, the company might well have had to pay out an unexampled sum in compensation: for this train was the 8.45am from Brighton to London (first-class only), carrying a load of richer commuters than any other, in Britain or anywhere else in Europe.

The inspecting officer, G.S. Hutchinson, had some disquieting revelations to make in his report. The cause of the accident was clearly the fracture of a girder beneath the track, which had been in place since the bridge was reconstructed in 1859–60. One of these girders had already failed fifteen years earlier, and the company had then been strongly recommended by the inspector to strengthen them; but it had done nothing of the kind. They were all made of cast-iron, which by 1891 had come to be generally recognised as an undependable material for such purposes as these. Now, at last, the Brighton directors were really frightened – if anyone had died in the accident, they might well have been prosecuted personally for manslaughter – and that drove them to order the reconstruction of all similar bridges throughout the system. Here was an epitome of the cynical misconduct of railway directors that *Punch* had been attacking for nearly half a century; misconduct towards the public, towards their shareholders and their employees, all alike. Nothing, it seemed, could rouse these men to do their duty except fear for the safety of their own skins.

Hutchinson's report and other papers concerning the accident were laid before

THE RAILWAY TAM O' SHANTER.

Shareholder. "STOP! STOP! MORE HASTE, LESS DIVIDEND!"

Furniss: *Punch*, vol. 95 (1888) p.96

Parliament on 18 June, and then put on sale to the public.[37] To *Punch*, with its long record of exposing the criminality of railway directors, they presented an obvious opportunity. Its comment on these very serious revelations did not appear for more than another six weeks. This delay looks curious at first, but it can I think be explained. Those who directed the paper could not have decided to allocate a main cartoon to this subject before 24 June (the Wednesday following the presentation of the papers to Parliament), and the cartoon could not therefore have been published, at the earliest, until Saturday 4 July – already two months after the accident had occurred. The nature of the drawing itself makes it clear that Tenniel was not asked to produce one related directly to the Brighton company or to Norwood Junction: the scene he depicts is a tract of wild and lonely moor. Many other railways also had bridges with cast-iron girders, similar to those in the one crossing Portland Road, and some companies were known to be already setting about the replacement of them, at whatever cost might be necessary. The purpose of Tenniel's cartoon was to make of the Norwood bridge accident a striking example, which could be applied to the railway system as a whole.

We can perhaps go further, to see a positive purpose in the timing of the cartoon's publication. It came out on 1 August: two days before the Bank Holiday, and the first day of what had become the busiest holiday month in the Victorian year. *Punch* had been trying for a long time to dissuade people from using railways at all. Mr Punch's Golden Rule, enunciated in 1871, had been: 'Travellers should as seldom as possible travel by railway'.[38] Was not the first day of August the most effective date in the year to take up that plea again, and would not a drawing by Tenniel, relating to a recent event that would still be in the minds of many readers of the paper (but generalised, so as to refer to all railway companies, not one alone), be the best way of conveying the message? The cartoon, and an unsigned article that went with it, were both entitled 'On the Bridge!'[39] Tenniel depicted what he had to say in stark and simple terms. The skeleton figure of Death, mounted on one of the cracked side-sheets of an iron bridge, eagerly beckons a train as it approaches. There is nobody near. Even though the skeleton is seen from behind, Tenniel contrives to make us feel that it is gloating in anticipation of the collapse of the unsound structure. As the accompanying text puts it, here is 'Insatiate Death waiting for Inevitable Accident!'

It so happens that Sir Arthur Elton acquired a preliminary sketch for this picture, and it is now in his collection, presented to the Ironbridge Gorge Museum.[40] Comparing it with the one that was finally published, we can see that Tenniel cast aside some of the detail he originally included. The printed cartoon is bare, straightforward, strong and easily understood. In both versions, however, the cracked sides of the bridge figure prominently in the foreground. Tenniel must have known that the girder that failed and caused the Norwood Junction accident was below the train, and not beside it. But there was no way in which he could depict it effectively in its true place, and he conveyed what he wanted to say clearly enough by this means instead.

ON THE BRIDGE!

Tenniel: *Punch*, vol. 101 (1891) p.55

Tenniel: Self-portrait
from H. M. Spielmann, *History of Punch*, (1895)

Here was the end of his career as a cartoonist of railways.[41] That was not, we can be quite certain, because he changed his mind about them. But over the next few years before his retirement the number of railway accidents much decreased, under the effective precautions adopted in the Regulation Act of 1889 (see p.217), and Tenniel's work for *Punch* was now steadfastly addressed to the national and international politics of the time, where he discerned some of the dangers that were multiplying, for Britain and the world, as they lay ahead. He was knighted in 1893, and that was an unprecedented tribute to a professional newspaper artist. His last *Punch* cartoon appeared on 2 January 1901. In the farewell of him taken by the paper it was stated that he had now made up his mind to abandon all such work for good. He died on 25 February 1914, just before his 94th birthday, leaving a personal estate of £10, 684.

7

Tenniel's commentary on railways, as it appears in the pages of *Punch*, bears out very well the observation on him passed after his death by one of his colleagues on the paper. 'It was his mission', wrote Sir Henry Lucy (a famous parliamentary journalist, the Toby of *Punch*), 'to shoot at folly, to strike at fraud and corruption'.[42] Moral disgust, at what he saw as the greed and cynical irresponsibility of railway directors and managers, impelled him on his task. In all the years during which he worked for *Punch*, he saluted nothing with any respect that the railways did. That perhaps did a little to weaken the impression produced by his drawings. Here he was nearly always prosecuting counsel.

The proprietors of *Punch* and some of Tenniel's colleagues may possibly have come to feel that he had said enough there about railways by the 1880s. Two signs of that can perhaps be detected. Though the paper's criticism of the railways continued in the later Victorian age, its usual form changed from indictment to a milder ridicule; the ridicule directed at an old and tiresome acquaintance who needs to be reminded frequently that he is in the wrong. And very little of this criticism was by then provided by Tenniel. He continued to be the paper's principal cartoonist, highly admired and a great asset to it; but his full-page cartoons were now generally directed strictly to political subjects. And may it not be significant that when selections from Tenniel's cartoons in *Punch* were made (especially for the volume issued on his retirement in 1901) the railway pictures figured there very little? Considering the total amount of time and thought he had given to them, we may find this omission rather strange. But then, by that time people had quite forgotten about Kirtlebridge and Norwood Junction, whereas Bismarck and the Kaiser, to whom Tenniel gave so much attention, were still very much in their minds. The choice made by the compilers of these collections seems to suggest that Tenniel's railway cartoons had now come to be disconsidered.

Nevertheless, his work here must certainly have had its influence when it was first published. How great that influence was, and who felt it, we cannot of course say with any precision.[43] No other observer of the railway's doings attacked them, in words or in pictures, with so much persistence over an equally long period of time. The audience he addressed was a big one; when he retired the weekly circulation of *Punch* was 90,000, and many single copies must have been read many times over, in hotels and clubs, in doctors' and dentists' waiting-rooms. Taking all that into account and looking at his work as a whole, one may well give Tenniel a place among the most powerful and effective critics of railways in the Victorian age.

NOTES

Unless otherwise indicated, all references here are to *Punch*, by volume, date, and page.

1. 6 (1844) 83; 50 (1866) 208, 218, 242, 257; 51 (1866) 88.
2. 51 (1866) 181, 206, 212–13.
3. *Richard Doyle's Journal, 1840*, ed. C. Wheeler (1980), xiii.
4. 1 (1841) 165.
5. For the accident see PP 1842, xli. 99–102, 365.
6. 9 (1845) 47; 16 (1849) 191.
7. 8 (1845) 207; 9 (1845) 183.
8. 18 (1850) 4.
9. See VRY, 259.
10. See his brilliantly comic pictures of a railway shareholders' meeting and of the refreshment room at Swindon: 17 (1849) 32, 52.
11. The signatures attached to many *Punch* drawings are shown in H.M. Spielmann, *History of Punch* (1895) 573–4. But the drawings were not invariably signed when they were published.
12. *Ibid.*, 172.
13. 23 (1852) 132, 209.
14. 23 (1852) 157.
15. 33 (1857) 25.
16. It did however commend the London Brighton & South Coast company in 1853 for upholstering some of its second-class carriages: 24 (1853) 197.
17. 47 (1865) 63; 55 (1868) 57, 61.
18. See MacDermot, ii. 16–17, where the cartoon is reproduced.
19. *Letters of Lewis Carroll*, ed. M.N. Cohen (1979), 62. The story of the relations between author and artist is conveniently summarised in a note there (119–20). In the end Tenniel found Carroll 'impossible' to work with. See A. Clark, *Lewis Carroll* (1979), 242.
20. 49 (1865) 33 onwards. Bennett died young in 1867: 52 (1867) 151.

21. REW, 121.

22. 44 (1863) 128.

23. 44 (1863) 175; 45 (1863) 62.

24. 46 (1864) 27.

25. 50 (1866) 96.

26. *Punch* had already expressed uneasiness about the consequences of amalgamation much earlier, in 1852.

27. 54 (1868) 279.

28. 55 (1868) 70.

29. 56 (1868) 45.

30. 63 (1872) 161. For the accident itself see L.T.C. Rolt, *Red for Danger* (4th ed., 1982), 63–4.

31. 67 (1874) 129. The cartoon was published only 16 days after the accident occurred.

32. 69 (1875) 141.

33. 67 (1874) 17.

34. 79 (1880) 126.

35. 89 (1885) 178.

36. 95 (1888) 96–7.

37. pp 1890–1 lxxiv 449–58. Another very clear account of this accident is given in P.S.A. Berridge, *The Girder Bridge* (1969), 36–9.

38. 69 (1871) 65.

39. 101 (1891) 54–7.

40. AG 185. 62.

41. He does however glance at a threatened railway strike (though not in any satirical spirit) in 1897: 103 (1897) 283.

42. Article on Tenniel in *Dictionary of National Biography, 1912–21*.

43. I have not noted anything, in letters or diaries or memoirs, or in the railway press, to prove that any of the people whose minds he must have desired to reach paid the least attention to the messages Tenniel addressed to them. But then, if one of the cartoonist's barbs had hit him in a tender place, the victim might well have preferred to say nothing, and so appear unscathed.

11
RAILWAY PROSPECTUSES

The company prospectus is an oddity among historical documents. It is a record not of fact but of declared intentions, which may have been correct and well-founded or frivolous, even fraudulent. On the face of it, the prospectus forms part of the ephemera of history. If the project it announces was successful, then one's attention is apt to move away from it immediately, to what was achieved rather than to what was only promised. If it failed, the project itself disappears from view unless it survives in the form of some later one, which succeeded. Occasionally, the scheme may be worth remembrance as a curiosity, a might-have-been; and in that case the prospectus too becomes a curiosity, but hardly more than that. What useful purpose then is served by the attempt made here to investigate the survival of railway prospectuses and to comment on some of the things they say?

The account just given of these documents does not represent the whole truth. It looks at the prospectus from the wrong end; from our point of view, with our knowledge of the success or failure of the project it related to, rather than through the eyes of the man who drafted it, or of one who received it through the post in solicitation of his support. The hesitating investor, say of 1844, had to make up his mind about buying shares in it, and his decision might to some extent depend on the presentation of the scheme in the prospectus. It is wrong to dismiss all these documents sweepingly, without noticing the valuable hints and information they may contain, even if they are sometimes embedded in a good deal of what is foolish or false.

I

When a body of promoters decided to launch a scheme for building a railway, they usually proclaimed their intention by two methods. They had a duty to discharge, laid on them by parliamentary standing orders, to advertise the project in the newspapers of the localities that the railway was intended to traverse, listing the parishes through which its line or lines would pass and the places where plans and books of reference, showing the owners of the land in detail, could be inspected; giving notice also that the promoters were seeking powers for the compulsory purchase of the land that their work would need. All this procedure had been laid down in order to protect the interests of landowners, large and small, and with a view to ensuring as far as possible that the promoters acted openly, not by stealth.

The second action the promoters took was to issue another advertisement, of a quite different kind; not at the command of Parliament but for their own advantage, to announce and explain what they intended to do and to invite public support – particularly the support of those who might invest in the scheme – for the achievement of their task. This second advertisement took the form of a prospectus.

As a rule a Victorian prospectus was printed on a large double sheet of paper, folded, and comprised seven elements:

1. The proposed title of the undertaking.
2. A list of its prominent supporters, usually described as 'The Provisional Committee'.
3. The names of its chief advisers and officers.
4. An announcement of the capital to be raised, with the number of shares into which it was to be divided.
5. A general statement designed to justify the project, setting out the route the railway was to take, giving indications of the nature and quantity of the traffic it might hope to carry, and – deduced from that – of the profits that its promoters expected it to bring in.
6. A form of application for shares.
7. Something valuable when present, but often omitted: the date of issue.

In addition, many prospectuses carry maps, showing the course of the projected line and sometimes its relationship to others, already built or proposed.

These elements do not appear in all prospectuses in the same order, nor are all of them found in every one.

1. The title may declare the main purpose of the scheme simply and plainly. A Salisbury & Swindon[1] or a Birmingham Erdington & Sutton Coldfield Railway[2] is obviously intended to run between the places named. But such bare descriptions did not satisfy the projectors of many railway schemes, particularly during the Mania of 1844–6, when the system was still in the making and it was possible to bring forward enormous projects of the vaguest description, often with the sole purpose of occupying and pre-empting large territories in advance of possible rivals. So other titles came to be chosen, far less precise or not precise at all: the Great East & West;[3] the Grand London & Dublin Approximation – even the Great European – Railways;[4] as late as 1865 the North of England Union.[5]

Titles of this kind were sometimes adopted in place of more precise ones, even at a very late stage, during the passage of the company's Bill through Parliament. A famous example is that of the London & York, which announced itself in its prospectus under that name in 1845[6] but in May 1846, a month before its Bill received the royal assent, turned itself into the Great Northern.

2. The lists of persons supporting these projects vary greatly in length and

character. Their purpose was to indicate the strength of the backing that the promoters claimed to command. If the line was a local one, it was obviously necessary to announce, as far as possible, that it was looked on with favour by landowners, especially those with whom it would have to deal in purchasing their property. A prospectus announcing a trunk line had also to show this as far as it could, but at the same time to give some general indications of sympathy and support from people representing large commercial interests that could be expected to make use of the railway when it was built. There might also be some special interest to be placated, and the name of one of those prominently associated with that, appearing among the promoters of the railway, would be likely to help it forward.

The drawing-up of lists of those persons and the composition of provisional committees was, if it was taken seriously, a laborious and responsible task. Well-informed people who lived in the locality that the railway proposed to pass through would be likely to make their own assessment of the real strength of the undertaking from the names appearing in the prospectus, observing their affiliations with approval or dislike, and often we may be sure giving their adhesion to the project or opposing it largely according to the judgement they had formed of the persons named. Some of these committees, as listed, were absurdly large. The provisional committee of the Cambridge & Lincoln Extension Railway of 1845 had 179 members. That of the Wolverhampton Chester & Birkenhead Railway contented itself with no more than 100 members, the prospectus specifying not only their addresses but also the other commercial undertakings with which they were connected.[7]

These lists, like all other parts of the prospectuses in which they were included, were often drawn up in great haste, above all in 1844–6. Naturally they contained errors – names wrongly spelt, addresses wrongly given. More serious, they sometimes claimed as supporters people who had never authorised them to do so. The Town Clerk of Norwich preserved four letters written in 1845 from people listed in the prospectus of the Wolverhampton Walsall Leicester Peterborough & Norwich Junction Railway as members of the Provisional Committee, some of whom stated roundly that they had never heard of it.[8] The intention here, on the part of the secretary or some other person responsible for drawing up the prospectus, may not have been to claim support that he knew the project did not enjoy. He may simply have made mistakes, through extreme haste, from carelessness or misunderstanding. Some members of Provisional Committees, regularly appointed, changed their minds and withdrew their names while the Bill was being considered: as Sir Henry Bunbury did, for example, in the case of the London & Norwich Railway in 1844–5; and Mr Benton of Daventry, who acted in this way towards the Burton-upon-Trent Stafford Shrewsbury & Newtown Railway in 1846.[9]

3. The lists of advisers and designated officials also vary greatly. Some represent hardly more than a statement of cheerful hopes. Should the project succeed in Parliament, it would then be time enough for the proprietors to secure directors and managers who would really drive the railway through. Meanwhile, these names would grace the prospectus as part of its advertisement. Every one of the men who figured in these lists (and had consented to do so) was a speculator, in the literal sense of that word and not necessarily in any discreditable one. Whoever he was – engineer, solicitor, secretary – he was linking himself with a scheme that might or might not come off. If it did, it would perhaps bring him work and money, adding to his reputation; if not, then he would have to look for those things elsewhere.

The plainest illustration of this is provided by the engineers. Robert Stephenson – generally agreed to be a man of high integrity – consented to report to the Midland Railway board on nine railway projects at once.[10] He went over the ground and laid out the line for the Nottingham & Lincoln Railway (33 miles long) in three days in February 1844, furnishing too an estimate of the charges that would arise from constructing it.[11] He was stated to be connected as engineer, either on his own or jointly or as consultant, with no less than 32 railway companies towards the close of the Mania in 1847. Locke was similarly connected then with 17, Brunel with 16.[12] These men were all highly successful. Other engineers sought desperately for engagements, in the end to little effect. W.S. Moorsom, for example: a man involved in numerous railway schemes promoted in 1844–5, who was actually engaged to build only two of them – one an Irish line on which his work seems to have done him no credit (see p.111). Strenuous efforts might be made to bribe the well-known leaders of the profession, in order to secure a lien on their services as witnesses before parliamentary committees. One morning in 1845, Robert Stephenson and G.P. Bidder received over £1,000 in cheques, coming to them for this purpose from the promoters of companies with which they had no connection whatever. Needless to say, the cheques were all returned.[13]

The other persons who figured in these lists were usually in less demand, or they could meet a large number of demands more easily. The secretaries engaged by the promoters seldom served more than one company, or perhaps a group of associated companies. Solicitors fell mainly into two classes: local firms in the provinces, which were drawn in by their connections with one or another of the leading promoters; and large London firms, able and willing to handle the business of a number of quite separate railway companies. As examples of the first kind we may take Nicholson Hett & Freer of Brigg, much involved through their acquaintance with Lord Yarborough in the promotion of railways in north Lincolnshire;[14] John Beedham of Kimbolton, Huntingdonshire, who handled a good deal of business for the South Midland Railway and the schemes that succeeded it in 1845–56;[15] and

Francis Mewburn, whose Darlington firm was handling the affairs of five railway companies in Co Durham in 1847.[16] Among the London firms the one that had the most widely-extended railway business at that time was W.O. & W. Hunt, of 10 Whitehall, who were also parliamentary agents. They had the affairs of at least twelve companies in their hands, including one in Scotland and two in Ireland. Burchell Kilgour & Parson were already established, and rising then (to win a most unsavoury reputation later). Baxter Rose & Norton had also emerged; by the late 1860s they were catering for nine railway companies, including such important ones as the Great Eastern, the London Brighton & South Coast, and the Metropolitan District.[18]

Similarly with bankers. During the Mania of the 1840s most of those involved in railway projects were local men, for the day of amalgamations to make national firms, with their headquarters in London and branches in the provinces, was only just dawning. Here too prospectuses disclose some alliances and affinities among them.

4. The statement of capital to be raised is perhaps the simplest of all these seven elements. It is to be taken at its face value as the sum that those responsible for the project conceived it would cost. That figure might be reached as a result of careful reckoning, in consultation with experienced engineers, land valuers, and builders (and in some cases supported by traffic censuses, specially taken),[19] or impressionistically, as a round figure arrived at by guesswork. Any discussion of the true cost of building an individual railway – a difficult sum to calculate at all accurately; few detailed efforts were ever made to reach one – will usually have to begin with the figure stated in the prospectus, if a copy of it can be found. That figure is not always the same as the one given by the projectors in their application to Parliament for powers to build the railway.

The actual cost of the task, when it was finished, usually exceeded the sum set down in the prospectus – quite often by a very large amount. The first prospectus of the Great Western, for example, issued in 1833, named £3 million as the sum necessary for building and equipping the line between London and Bristol. By the time it was completed in 1841, it had cost £6,282,000.[20] There was nothing surprising there. For one thing, the prospectus was an advertising document designed to tempt people to invest in the undertaking it described, and it was natural to set the forecast of expenditure low and of the likely revenue high. Prediction was often genuinely difficult, and some of the obstacles encountered in building the lines could not have been anticipated by their first promoters. The price that would actually have to be paid for the land a railway needed was impossible to forecast accurately, nor could any realistic precautions have been taken – in early days at least – against sudden, unexpected increases in the price of materials or the charges made by manufacturers. It is rare to find any large railway that was carried through at or within the original estimate of cost. Among the rarities may be mentioned the Bristol & Exeter,[21] the Lancaster & Carlisle,[22] and the Salisbury Yeovil & Exeter (which was built for less than two-thirds of the expense forecast);[23] but in each of those cases the company undertook only the construction of its line, making arrangements before it was opened with another one, already established, to work it, thus saving the capital required for the purchase of rolling stock and a good deal of other equipment.

5. The general statements made in these documents about the route of the line, and the nature and quantity of the traffic expected from it, usually occupy a large part of their space. Here the character of prospectuses as advertisements is particularly obvious. Sometimes they were compiled very simply indeed, the route derived from a glance at a small-scale map and the traffic stated accordingly in a way that an intelligent reader could have arrived at from a pipe-dream in his armchair. The first Oxford & Cambridge Railway (several bearing that title appeared in succession; this one was launched in 1836) was in fact for a line to run from Tring on the London & Birmingham, then being built, to Cambridge; continuing another, put forward at the same time, which was to approach Tring from Cheltenham and Oxford. In the abundant fancy of the prospectus this amounted to promoting a route from Falmouth, Bath, Hereford, and Aylesbury not only to Cambridge and Bury St Edmunds but also to Gothenburg, Hamburg, Danzig, 'and other ports of the north of Europe', and it was to supply 'the immense population of Birmingham' with fish from the coast of East Anglia.[24] The literature of prospectuses abounds in vague claims of this sort.

Not all of these estimates should be condemned, however, as flimsy or frivolous. Some were based on surveys that had been very carefully prepared; how many we cannot say for certain now, since no more than a few of that sort have survived. Among those that can still be studied perhaps the most remarkable is the one worked out in great detail by the engineer J.U. Rastrick in 1831 for the Birmingham & Liverpool Railway, which emerged as the Grand Junction two years later – the first trunk railway in Europe.[25]

6. Nothing need be said about the form of application for shares except that it sometimes reveals, in the space allotted to the date, the year to which the project belongs.

7. The historical value of these prospectuses often depends in part, sometimes largely, on the dating of them. This is rarely given any prominence in the document itself. The date is sometimes stated in an obscure place, and it is often omitted altogether; not for any sinister reason but because all these prospectuses had a very short life – usually of nine months or less, from their

issue in the autumn to the decision of Parliament on the scheme in the following spring or summer. If the proposal was thrown out, it might be renewed in a subsequent session, but that would call for a fresh prospectus. Those to whom prospectuses were addressed treated them as we treat advertisements sent to us now through the post, throwing them away at once or considering them carefully or putting them aside for examination later. But they were never in any doubt that a prospectus related to a plan that, if it reached Parliament at all, would be pronounced on during the current session. The prospectus was always an urgent application for immediate support and therefore had no insistent reason for declaring the year in which it was issued.

There are various ways in which a student of these documents may succeed in supplying one. Confronted with a prospectus of a railway one has never heard of, one should turn first to the *Index of Local and Personal Acts* (1949). That ought to reveal whether or not the project received parliamentary sanction, under the title given in the prospectus. If it did, the *Index* should also record any subsequent absorption of the railway into a larger company. If the project was not sanctioned, the indexes of parliamentary Bills for a likely series of sessions should be searched. These were issued annually and can be found with sets of the *Parliamentary Papers* at the British Library and the copyright libraries in Oxford, Cambridge, Edinburgh, and Dublin.

Reference may happen to be made in the prospectus itself to the existence of railways already built, with which the projected line was intended to link up. If a map is provided, it may show them quite clearly. It is usually possible to discover when a line was opened, though critical students have repeatedly warned us that all dates of openings, given at the time or in books written since, need careful checking. If the dates of opening of the lines on the map, which were already at work, can be established, the one described in the prospectus may be supposed to have been launched later.

Other aids may be sought for too. Sometimes the prospectus refers to a recent event or a new economic enterprise in the locality the railway is intended to serve: the opening of new iron works, the extension of a coalfield, the building of new docks. A development of this kind may be the chief cause of the promotion of the railway, and its date can usually be established from a local history or a newspaper. Sometimes the list of leading promoters may afford clues. One of them may be singled out, and the student can ask about him. If he was a prominent public man, when did he die, or move into the district or out of it? Local directories may be helpful, though they have to be used cautiously, for the information they print is often out of date, carried over unchanged from one edition to the next.[26]

2

Composed of the elements that have just been enumerated, compiled in a great hurry, for the direct purpose of financial gain, what use are these documents to the student of railway history, and how can they best be read critically?

A prospectus offers him a bone to worry at. It is the first formal printed statement of the thinking that lay behind the promotion of a railway. It does not represent the very beginning of that process. Discussion had always preceded it, and the record of that may have to be sought in correspondence (if it is preserved) or in the accounts of public meetings given in newspapers. But no railway could be built without the expenditure of a large sum of money, and the prospectus embodied the first attempt made by the projectors to raise that capital from the public. It was therefore one of the founding documents of a railway, joined later by its Bill and its Act of Parliament, and by the title-deeds of the property it acquired. The prospectus differed from Acts and title-deeds, however, in the strength of its binding force. Theirs was absolute, part of the law under which all railway companies must operate. The force of the prospectus was much weaker, or nothing at all. Even the legal meaning of a company prospectus was not statutorily defined until 1900.[27] Moreover, it was not a criminal offence to publish an untrue statement in a prospectus. The only trouble that might arise for the directors or promoters of a company doing that would be a civil prosecution by someone who claimed to have incurred loss or damage through acting on the statement.[28]

But even though these documents could carry no weight in a court of law, in tracing the history of what became an important railway company it is always desirable to follow back the first statements of its intentions to their sources in its prospectuses (for one reason or another there were often several) if copies of them can be found. This can be done quite simply, for instance, for the London & South Western (the London & Southampton of 1831),[29] the Great Western (four successive revisions, 1833–4),[30] and the Caledonian (1844).[31] Here and there one comes on a prospectus of an enterprise concerned not with the building of any kind of railway but with some attempt to launch one for the general benefit of railwaymen: like the Railway Institute of 1836, intended to be a scientific body 'with all the advantages...of the best modern clubs'.[32] It must however be remembered that most of the great British railway companies were created by some form of amalgamation, an arrangement that did not call for the issuing of any prospectus. None was ever produced for the London & North Western, for example, which was set up in 1846 as an amalgamation of three existing companies, the London & Birmingham, the Manchester & Birmingham, and the Grand Junction (the last of those three having already absorbed four smaller ones, the Liverpool & Manchester, Bolton & Leigh, Warrington & Newton, and Chester & Crewe, each of which may be supposed to have issued a prospectus of its own). Nine of the other principal pre-1923 companies were amalgamations too: the Glasgow & South Western, Great Central, Great Eastern, Highland, Lancashire & Yorkshire, London Brighton &

South Coast, Midland, North Eastern, and South Eastern & Chatham. There were never prospectuses for any of them.

What were the main kinds of false statements that the framers of these prospectuses practised? Two have already been referred to: the inclusion in the list of promoters of people who had not consented to support the scheme, and of estimates of potential traffic that might be valueless or deliberately misleading. Others were more difficult to detect, except by those who knew the country that the railway was to traverse. The route to be taken by the proposed line might be described in what were really false terms, by minimising the physical difficulties it had to overcome in its construction and ignoring altogether those that would arise when it came to be worked. For example, the prospectus of the Plymouth Devonport & Exeter Railway (later known as the South Devon), issued in 1843, describes the line with the blandest inattention to the way in which it was obliged to run to the west of Newton Abbot, going no further than to observe that it 'passes across a ridge at the village of Dainton'. When built, it had to rise and fall on either side of that village on gradients as steep as 1 in 36–41, and to ascend from Plymouth eastwards for over 2½ miles continuously at 1 in 41–7. Such climbing as that was then unknown on any trunk railway in Britain, except the 1 in 41 ascent from Glasgow on the line to Edinburgh, and there trains were hauled by locomotive and cable together – a cumbersome mode of traction, and costly too, for it called for two separate sources of steam power. The prospectus of the Plymouth company confined itself to stating that the work proposed by the company involved 'less engineering difficulties than are found to exist on either of the other lines which have been projected'.[33] Similarly, the Newtown & Machynlleth Railway stated in its prospectus, on its engineers' authority, that the line would require no gradient steeper than 1 in 60, whereas in the event it turned out that the eastward climb up to the watershed it had to cross at Talerddig included 2½ miles at 1 in 52.[34]

3

Where are these prospectuses to be found?

The largest quantity of those relating to railways that has been brought together in Britain is in the Public Record Office at Kew. Those that are kept there fall into three main groups. First, there are two very extensive collections of prospectuses that were assembled by railway companies themselves,[35] together with a much smaller number in a general collection of papers relating to railways made by Francis Mewburn, the methodical solicitor of the Stockton & Darlington company.[36] Secondly, there are those scattered through the whole collection of the companies' records, preserved by them individually. Anyone searching for the prospectus of a particular English or Welsh company, and failing to find it in the collections just mentioned, will do best to look at the earliest of its records surviving at Kew, to see if there is a copy in the company's group there. To give a few examples from different parts of the country, prospectuses are to be found among the records of the Staines & West Drayton Railway,[37] the Ware Hadham & Buntingford,[38] the Charnwood Forest,[39] the North Staffordshire,[40] the York & North Midland,[41] the Leeds & Thirsk,[42] and the Wear Valley,[43] the last of these containing a statement of the traffic it hoped to secure that is more interesting and probable than many other such estimates put forward in 1845.

In the two greatest English libraries there are large collections of prospectuses, which include a good many of those issued by railway undertakings. At the British Museum indeed (now the British Library) the principal librarian, Sir Henry Ellis, set himself deliberately to collect railway prospectuses for it in October 1845, rightly considering them to form a branch of historical literature that would be of lasting interest. The chief collections in that library are two, the one that he formed and another mainly due to a lawyer named Langdale, who seems to have been an investor himself.[44] Langdale's range over the whole of the British Isles, including a useful group of a dozen prospectuses for Irish railways in 1845, followed by another nine for lines in Scotland. This collection is also valuable in displaying to us something of the extent to which British railway investors and engineers were involved in the promotion of railways on the mainland of Europe in 1845–6: in all of what became the great French private companies except the Est, in several Belgian railways, in the Dutch Hanoverian, the Madrid & Valencia, and the Royal Northern of Spain.[45]

The prospectuses at the Bodleian Library, Oxford, are particularly valuable because they form part of a very large collection extending to companies of many different kinds, including manufacturing industries, many of which were closely involved with the making of the equipment and goods that railways wanted:[46] carriage and wagon builders, for example, at Preston and at Newnham, Gloucestershire;[47] makers of fog-signalling apparatus and station indicators.[49] The railway appears here as an element in the growth of general manufacturing industry.

The National Library of Wales at Aberystwyth has some prospectuses of important Welsh railway companies: the Denbigh Ruthin & Corwen, for example,[50] and the Rhondda & Swansea Bay;[51] besides several put out by the companies that attempted unsuccessfully to construct lines stretching right across the country, including the England & Ireland Union,[52] and the Llanidloes & South Wales.[53]

The collection of prospectuses at the Scottish Record Office is very small. The main file comprises no more than eighteen of them. Prospectuses are included, as in England and Wales, among the records of many of the individual companies themselves.[54] Some of these documents reflect the importance of one business that was growing steadily in Scotland at the time when mechanically-operated railways carrying passengers got to work: they make play, in their appeal to prospective investors, with the value of the tourist traffic that could be hoped for. The Caledonian stressed it prominently in 1844.[55] Twenty years later the projectors of the Callander & Oban line asserted in their prospectus that the visitors to Oban in the summer were 'not equalled in number by those of any other provincial town in the Kingdom'.[56] Even if 'the Kingdom' is to be read as confined to 'the Kingdom of Scotland', that is a startling claim. Could it be substantiated, it would be a remarkable demonstration of what the horse-drawn coach and the steamer were still able to do in the mid-1860s, where they put their backs into it, in a territory not yet penetrated by railways.

There are also a good many railway prospectuses to be discovered in local record offices. They may have to be searched for with patient persistence, for they are seldom itemised in the catalogues and lists. In looking for one, it is perhaps best to begin by ascertaining the names of the landowners whose estates the railway proposed to cross. Those names will appear on the deposited plans of the line that had to be lodged with the clerk of the peace for the county concerned, and his records – at least for the earlier part of the Victorian age – are likely now to be in the county record office. If they are not, and no copies of the plans are to be found locally, the plans are best sought for at the House of Lords Record Office in London. Among the names of the landowners that emerge in this connection there will probably be some whose family papers have now been deposited in a county record office (not necessarily that of the county concerned, if he was a large landowner with estates in several counties). If those papers can be traced, it may be found that the landowner involved was sent a copy of the prospectus by the railway company, with a view to enlisting his support, or at least appeasing his opposition; and he may have preserved it. A number of such documents are in the Hothfield papers at Maidstone, for example, relating to railways in Kent, including one for a 'Direct Kentish Railway without a Tunnel from London to the Port of Sandwich'.[57] Sir John Chichester of Arlington Court in North Devon seems to have taken a considerable interest in railway promotion in the 1840s, and three bundles of railway prospectuses are now to be found in his papers.[58] Nearly all of them relate to railways that were never built. Did he keep them so carefully on that account, one wonders, as curiosities, or are they memorials of investments made by him that unhappily failed?

Among single prospectuses surviving in such collections of papers as those I may instance, simply by way of illustration from different parts of the country, one of the Dartmouth & Torbay Railway in the Somerset Record Office;[59] others from Southampton Corporation – often much engaged in considering new routes to serve the town, by breaking the monopoly of the London & South Western company;[60] the prospectus of the Bolton & Leigh Railway (Hulton Estate, Lancashire Record Office),[61] and the Solway Junction, among the Senhouse papers in the Cumbria Record Office at Carlisle.[62]

Another valuable source of prospectuses that are now in county record offices is formed by the collections of papers that have come in from local solicitors. As those offices multiplied from the 1940s onwards, such firms often found it convenient to deposit with them some of the older records they held, accumulations that were crowding up their own premises. They too naturally included a good many papers relating to railways, and prospectuses figure among them: for example, those of the Cheltenham & Oxford, Buckinghamshire, and Aylesbury & Buckingham companies deposited in the Buckinghamshire Record Office at Aylesbury by Messrs Tindal & Baines.[63]

If one is interested in these documents it is always worth while to inquire after them in one of these offices or in a large public library. There are a dozen of them, for instance, in the Fairbank Collection at Sheffield Central Library, which was made by members of the Fairbank family of civil engineers: one for the Sheffield & Humber Railway, for instance, an unsuccessful early project of 1836; another for the partially-realised Manchester Buxton Matlock & Midlands Junction Railway, with which Joseph Paxton was energetically concerned in 1845.[64]

A last word. Particularly at times of intense railway promotion, at home or abroad, when prospectuses were flying through the post around the country every day, often landing up on the breakfast tables of people who had no intention of making any investments of the kind at all, the temptation to guy the absurdly extravagant language in which the projects might be described – indeed to guy the projects themselves – became strong. They positively invited parody, and parodists were forthcoming. *Punch* produced a good facetious one, relating to an imaginary Indian railway, in October 1845.[65] The British Library possesses some documents of this kind. To them we may perhaps add one at Kew: a cheerful spoof prospectus for a Donkey Express Co Ltd, designed to afford an improvement on the seemingly poor service provided by the London & South Western Railway over its Hounslow loop line. 'Steam having proved a total failure, the company proposes to set on carriages drawn by four donkeys, driven by an experienced costermonger, which, it is confidently expected, will accomplish the journey in about half the time now occupied by the railway'.[66]

NOTES

1. Lincolnshire RO, Stubbs 7/13.

2. Birmingham Public Library, Jewel Baillie 310/30.

3. Hereford & Worcester RO, BA 6234.

4. Both in Devon RO (Exeter), 50/11.

5. North Yorkshire RO, ZOP. Some projects were launched under vague and pretentious titles, and then re-announced in later prospectuses, cut down to their real extent. So the Hull Great Grimsby & Southampton Railway shrank to the Lincoln & Northampton, as the prospectus of that company itself (Copy in BL, 1881 B.23) explains.

6. Hertfordshire RO, 53936.

7. BL, Maps 18c.1; R1075/89, No. 51. See the excellent discussion of these matters in relation to Scottish companies in C.J.A. Robertson, *Origins of the Scottish Railway System* (1983), 292.

8. Norfolk RO: Norwich City Records, case 23, bundle A.i.n.

9. Suffolk RO (Bury St Edmunds), E18/760/1; Elton Engineering Books, Hammersmith, London: catalogue (1992), item 22.

10. R490/5, mins. 1264, 1270–1.

11. R491/12, min. 567.

12. *Post Office Railway Directory for 1847*, 351, 302, 230–1.

13. J.C. Jeaffreson, *Life of Robert Stephenson* (1804), i. 287.

14. Lincolnshire RO, Stubbs 1/7; REW, 309–10.

15. Bedfordshire RO, WG 2774–2802.

16. *Post Office Railway Directory for 1847*, Nos. 109–13.

17. *Ibid.*, Nos. 40, 53, 55–6, 73–4, 110, 138, 173–4, 191–2.

18. *Bradshaw's Railway Shareholder's Manual*, 1869. This firm had played a large part in the development of the Great Northern Railway, down to 1853, when it lost that company's business.

19. Peter Lecount in his *Practical Treatise on Railways* (1839), 4–15, discusses the taking of censuses of this kind. For examples of them see R113/51 (Chester & Holyhead, 1848); R69/25–9 (Bridport Railway, 1854–5): and R299/2 (Helston Railway, 1879). A careful estimate of the traffic to be expected on the East Anglian Railway in 1841 is in Norfolk RO: Norwich City Records, case 23, bundle A.i.a.

20. MacDermot, i. 4, 82. A copy of the first prospectus, with the carefully-worded covering letter written by the company's Bristol secretary, W. Tothill, is in R1075/89.

21. MacDermot, ii. 75.

22. B. Reed, *Crewe to Carlisle* (1969), 144–5.

23. L.H. Ruegg, *Salisbury & Yeovil Railway* (1878), 28, 65.

24. Prospectus in Bodleian Library, Oxford: Eng. rlwys. 8.2b.87.

25. Rastrick's survey is now in the Goldsmiths' Library, University of London. See also N.W. Webster, *Britain's first Trunk Line* (1972), 23–5.

26. Among general works of reference that may be useful here, three stand out: the *Dictionary of National Biography*; F. Boase, *Modern English Biography* (1892–1921: reprinted 1965), for people who died in 1851–1900; and G.E.C., *The Complete Peerage*, ed. V. Gibbs and others (1910–40; reprinted 1987), a most accurate and comprehensive work.

27. In the Companies Act, 1900: PGA 63 & 64 Vict., cap. 48, sect. 30.

28. *Halsbury's Statutes of England and Wales*, 4th ed., vii (1985), 183.

29. See copies of early Southampton & London Railway prospectuses in BL. 1890 i.6.

30. R1075/89.

31. SRO, BR/PROS(S)/1/1.

32. Birmingham PL, MS. 177408, p.5.

33. Copy in Devon RO (Exeter), 316 M/53; MacDermot, ii. 105. The atmospheric haulage that was later to be adopted by the South Devon Railway was not envisaged when this prospectus was issued.

34. R1110/55. It is perhaps worth noting that the prospectus of this railway was printed both in English and in Welsh; so was that for the Ffestiniog & Blaenau company in 1866: R1075/89, no. 23.

35. R1075, 1076.

36. R1016/5.

37. R659/16.

38. R709/1–2.

39. R108/1.

40. R532/3.

41. R770/13.

42. R357/9.

43. R718/19.

44. BL, Maps 18c.1; 1881 b.23, 1890 c.6.

45. Documents relating to all these companies are in 1881 b.23, vols. 4 and 5.

46. See *A Checklist of Company Prospectuses, 1873–1911* (Bodleian Library), with an admirably clear introductory note by Alison M. Gee. The prospectuses connected with railways are listed on pp. 178–87.

47. Shelfmark 232865 b. 3/14; 232865 b. 7/76.

48. 23286 b. 3/19.

49. 232865 b. 7/2.

50. Caer, p. 82.

51. Picton, p. 310. This collection is quite extensive, varying in time from 1824 to 1906; see the index in the Library.

52. Dav. LT(1149).

53. Mayb. I. 463.

54. It is in BR/PROS(S)/1.

55. BR/PROS(S)/1/1.

56. BR/COB/4/16.

57. Kent RO, A/G 118.

58. Devon RO (Exeter), 50/11.

59. Luttrell papers: DD/L2/80/106.

60. Southampton RO: South Midland Railway, SC 19 (DNS) 4; Swindon Southampton &

New Forest Railway, SC19, Box 26/1.

61. Lancashire RO, DD/HU.

62. Cumbria RO (Carlisle), D/Sen. Rlwys 40.

63. D/TL/B/1–7.

64. Sheffield Central Library. CP 18 (152 and 41).

65. *Punch*, 9 (1845) 153.

66. R1075/112. The prospectus is undated, but its typography suggests that it was printed about 1860. It may perhaps have been influenced by G.W. Ancell's delightful squibs about Hoy's Donkey, directed against the Eastern Counties Railway in 1856. For them see VRY, 211.

12
BRADSHAW

What commercial man has ever made himself widely known throughout Great Britain by his surname, as a single word, without the aid of powerful advertising campaigns like those which have stamped Lyons and Haig and Guinness on our minds? And if there is one, can he be said to figure – as a 'household word' requiring no special emphasis or explanation – in English literature? Possibly 'McIntosh', as an observant friend suggests to me; but the garment he invented cuts no figure in literary works. Only one such man, I believe, meets these conditions fully: Bradshaw.

He began to issue timetables of railway services in 1838. They became a monthly *Guide* in January 1842 and went on appearing as that, enlarged and revised but essentially unchanged, until May 1961. 'Bradshaw' began to be a household word in the 1850s and continued so for over 100 years. Even when publication ceased the name of the book did not die. It still figured in dictionaries, revised or newly published – the *Concise Oxford*, for example, down to its seventh edition (1982)[1], and *Chambers' English Dictionary* of 1988.

Its history was first treated by Percy Fitzgerald in 1890.[2] It was the subject of a paper read to the Bibliographical Society in 1921. Since then it has been worked over by Canon R.B. Fellows,[3] G. Royde Smith,[4] and Charles E. Lee.[5] It need not therefore be rehearsed in much detail here.

I shall begin with brief accounts of Bradshaw himself, and of the main stages by which his famous book advanced to its final form. Next I shall illustrate the impact it has made on the minds of those who used it. And then I wish to suggest some of the ways in which this highly technical publication can be of value to students of history.

I

George Bradshaw was born at Pendleton, Lancashire, on 29 July 1801, went to school at Overton, near Lancaster, and was apprenticed to an engraver, either J. Beale or Thomas Tonbridge, both of Manchester.[6] He became specially interested in the engraving of maps and produced *Bradshaw's Maps of Canals, Navigable Rivers, Railways, etc.* in 1830. He took an apprentice of his own at that time, W.T. Blacklock (born in 1817), who presently became a partner with him. Bradshaw soon turned his attention to railways and brought out a map of those in Britain in 1839.

He had by this time joined the Society of Friends. His nephew, an architect, tells us that 'on a "first day" (Sunday) morning, whilst walking together from meeting (the religious gathering of the Friends), Mr Bradshaw remarked that he thought it would be a good thing to publish a table of times at which trains would run between Liverpool, Manchester, Bolton, and one or two other places connected by railways. The idea was voted a good one, and the first number of 'Bradshaw's Railway Time Tables' was given to the world during the year in which the conversation I have mentioned took place, namely in 1839'.[7]

It usually happens, when a new commodity of any kind is produced and at once makes the producer's name famous, that other people claim to have devised it first, or that a similar claim is made on their behalf. Several such 'inventors' were spoken of, at one time or another, in connection with Bradshaw's timetables – James Drake, James Cropper, G.F. Mandley, John Gadsby, for example;[8] R.D. Kay (1811–97), who was a letterpress printer, taken on by Bradshaw when he decided to extend his business from engraving into printing, about 1838. It was he who composed the type for the first issue of what became the famous *Guide*, and he presently went on to be its editor. He seems to have been a sound and honest craftsman, but nothing more.[9] The story just quoted, even though it was published nearly 60 years later, carries the stamp of clear recollection on its face, of truth without embellishment.

It does however contain one mistake. The first timetables Bradshaw produced came out in 1838, not 1839.[10] Thereafter they were for a time issued at irregular intervals. Soon Bradshaw was trying out another idea, a *Railway Companion* containing little maps, still giving the times of trains but now with a text that afforded some other information too. He might have gone on experimenting in this way – and so perhaps have lost the advantage of his original notion to somebody else – if it had not been for his London agent, William James Adams,[11] who appears to have seized upon the idea represented by the timetables promptly. It is said to have been he who urged Bradshaw to publish his timetables every month. That practice was proclaimed in January 1842; 'January' figuring on the title-page in the Quaker form '1st mo.', as it continued to do on all subsequent issues down to 1927.

This was an important change. Bradshaw now bound himself to produce his work on a fixed date 12 times a year, which imposed two duties on him: dependable regular publication and an ability to keep up with the starting of new railway services, as well as with changes in the times of those already existing. The first of these requirements was largely under Bradshaw's own control, depending on his printing presses in Manchester. The second called for the prompt supply of information from all parts of the country, and chiefly from the railway companies themselves.

The railway system was at that moment growing faster than it ever had before. In 1840, 528 miles of new line had been brought into use for passenger traffic, almost as many again as in the three preceding years put together; a further 278 miles were added in 1841.[12] How could Bradshaw keep himself informed of all these changes? He was then in too small a way of business to employ an agent in every large railway centre. His arrangement with Adams in London must have cost him a good deal of money in commission. That seems to have been well earned, however. It was already clear that London was going to be the centre of the national railway system, and Bradshaw's risk, at this critical moment in the expansion of his business, lay in the emergence of an imitator there, in close touch with the managers of the leading companies. Adams was alert, and well placed in Fleet Street to act as watchdog.

If the *Guide* remained the only source of information about railway services throughout the United Kingdom, then it would be worth while for every company, except perhaps the very small ones that were of local importance only, to supply correct particulars of those it ran, and to see that they were kept up to date. The responsibility Bradshaw took was limited to the accurate printing of matter sent in to him by the companies and to publishing it punctually on the first day of every month. If a traveller arrived at a station expecting to find a train shown in his *Guide*, only to learn that its time had been altered, or that it had been taken off, he would naturally blame Bradshaw for misleading him. Nevertheless, if the traveller was well-to-do and simply hired a post-chaise instead, the company would lose his money: so Bradshaw and the companies had a common interest in seeing that the published times were right.

We seem to know almost nothing of Bradshaw's relations with the companies. In June 1850 he asked Adams to send for a time-bill from the South Wales Railway, and to forward it to him at once.[13] Many more such requests must have had to be made to the companies, but I have come upon no correspondence passing between him and any of them.

Competing publications sprang up quickly. At least five appeared in 1840–3, in various forms; another – published at Derby and dedicated to George Hudson – in 1848.[14] These failed and vanished, leaving the field to Bradshaw. Some local timetables were established in these years however, setting out the railway services of quite large districts, and a few of these enjoyed very long lives. The most distinguished was the work that came to be known as *Murray's Time Tables*, published in Glasgow and giving the railway, coach, and steamer services for the whole of Scotland. Its production was always superior to that of Bradshaw's *Guide*. The paper used was of a higher quality, and the text much easier to read: better printed, with its notes less awkwardly laid out. It was issued monthly, under various titles, from 1843 to 1966.[15]

Bradshaw had to confront another, more dangerous rival, with a publication appearing in London monthly from 1853; successful, and continuing today. This was the *ABC Railway Guide*, arranged on a quite different principle from Bradshaw's, to give the service between London and every station in the country, set out in alphabetical order. It related only to journeys beginning or ending in London – doing nothing, for example, to help a prospective traveller by the various routes from Manchester to Hull. From the outset it had one valuable feature: it gave not only the times of the trains but also the fares, by each class, for the journey. Bradshaw tried to publish fares too, side by side with the times of trains, but he did not always manage to do so and gradually abandoned the attempt, sometimes doubtless because the companies failed to list their fares for him. How much did it cost to travel between London and, for example, Lincoln in 1875? The *ABC* alone gives this information conveniently. It may be of value to some students of Victorian history, or of inflation since 1914. These two national railway guides could coexist comfortably, for they were different, not strongly competitive with each other.

The *Guide* became Bradshaw's chief publication. But he undertook others as well, two of which grew, and remained, important.

The intense railway speculation of the 1840s prompted several efforts to produce guides for investors, summarising the purposes of the projects and listing the names of their promoters and officers, together with addresses. The most successful of these was Henry Tuck's *Railway Shareholder's Manual*, which went through nine editions in 1845–8, increasing in size from 112 pages to 491.[16] This was designed chiefly as a speculator's handbook, and the demand for it ceased when the investing mania of these years died down. But there was a continuing need for some of the information that Tuck had supplied – lists of the companies' directors and officers, for example – to help all those who had any kind of business with railways. Although Bradshaw was no financial speculator himself, he set out to provide such a handbook in 1847, when the frenzy of investment was already drawing to a close, and kept it going as an annual publication thereafter. It started as *Bradshaw's Railway Almanack etc.*, and went forward under various titles until it settled down as *Bradshaw's Railway Manual, Shareholders' Guide, and Official Directory*. It continued to be published every year until 1923, when the amalgamation of the British railways into four large units removed most of the demand for it.

The other large publication that Bradshaw undertook also dates from 1847. He had shown an interest in the railway services that were being provided on the mainland of Europe by including some of them in his *Guide* in 1845. Now he was determined to make a separate book of them. In each Continental country, as its system of railways extended, a timetable was produced, collecting all their services together. In France that had begun in 1846 with the *Livret-Chaix*, taking its title as Bradshaw's did from its publisher, Napoléon Chaix. But Bradshaw now went further, to assemble as many timetables as he could from the whole European mainland. He must have worked here through correspondents, putting their contributions together and using all his experience of editing this kind of information, to form a guide as helpful as possible to the British traveller. The effort succeeded, and continued to succeed even when it was confronted with a rival, in the *Continental Timetables* produced by the firm of Thomas Cook from 1873 onwards. Here the competition must have been direct, though the books were by no means identical. There was evidently room for them both, however. Bradshaw's *Continental Guide* was not published during the first World War, and it succumbed finally in 1939. Cook's remains in the field, eventually extended to cover the whole world.

So there were then three main works, all published from the offices of Bradshaw

& Blacklock in Albert Square, Manchester, in association with W.J. Adams at 59 Fleet Street, London. They produced other small books too – *Bradshaw's Descriptive Guides* to the London & Brighton and London & South Western Railways, for example, written by E.L.L. Blanchard (1844–5); but these were of no lasting importance. Bradshaw also went into the field of magazine publishing for a short time, with *Bradshaw's Journal* (1841–4) and *Bradshaw's Little Magazine of Useful and Entertaining Knowledge* (1842–3); the *Journal* a very respectable piece of printing, enriched with steel engravings well above the average of such publications.

He was now very firmly settled in Manchester. He had married Martha Darbyshire, a Lancashire woman, in 1839, and they had two sons and three daughters.[17] They lived for a time on Cheetham Hill, but moved to Eccles Road, Salford, in the early 1850s. His attention remained entirely concentrated on Manchester, though in 1842 he did become an Associate of the Institution of Civil Engineers in London. He led his life in the context not only of his business but also of his religious community. Part of his time was given to the establishment of schools for the poor. He actively supported Cobden and Sturge in their efforts to further international peace, and the American Elihu Burritt in his unceasing advocacy of a universal penny postage.[18] Indeed he himself produced an envelope that depicted a steamship with its sail inscribed 'The World's Want and Should Be Britain's Boon – an Ocean Penny Postage'.[19] The strain of all this work, especially of his own business in the cramped and unhealthy centre of Manchester, had begun to tell on Bradshaw by 1850. He was ill early in that year, and he was growing deaf.[20] This may perhaps have been why he moved to Salford, which then enjoyed a purer air. In August 1853 he went to Norway to transact some business and visit English friends working at Christiania (now Oslo). There he caught cholera and died in six hours, on 6 September, at the age of 52. He is said to have been buried in the graveyard of the cathedral.[21]

2

What sort of man was George Bradshaw? We have an agreeable drawing of him that carries some conviction with it, reproduced in his nephew's reminiscences, and an engraved portrait,[22] both made towards the end of his life, together with a really good portrait of him in oils by Richard Evans, painted in 1841 and now in the National Portrait Gallery. His face there is neither complacent nor unctuous; the broad mouth and widely-spaced eyes give a clear hint that he could smile. He does not seem to have been involved in controversies about mis-statements, or to have infringed anyone else's copyright; and there were rarely any serious complaints about his *Guide*, with a single exception, which we shall come to shortly.

Two things about him, however, appear a little puzzling? The serial numbers of two of his publications were altered. No 40 of the *Guide*, published in March 1845, was followed in April by No 141. This could well have been due to a printer's error, but if it was it would surely have been noticed and silently corrected in subsequent issues. It was not altered, and Canon Fellows – a well-qualified judge, moved by no animus against Bradshaw – considered it was a deliberate fake, designed to make the *Guide* appear to be older-established than it was in truth. He pointed out that something similar occurred in another of Bradshaw's publications, his *Threepenny Guide to all the Railways of England, Wales, and Scotland.* Here it seems that what should have been No 40 came out as No 171. Bradshaw must have known of these oddities, even if he did not think them up himself. It is difficult to look on them as anything but sharp practice.[23]

It may also seem a little strange, at first sight, that the title of each of his publications, without exception, should have opened with his own name: it is *Bradshaw's Map, Bradshaw's Railway Companion, Bradshaw's Guide, Bradshaw's Railway Manual.* What made him force his name on the public with such persistence? It is not necessary to say that he was a quiet little man with a secret passion for self-advertisement. Other people had published maps of canals and railways before he did. The best way in which he could differentiate his product from theirs was by the use of his own name. Though it is true that his timetables were the first of their kind, he must have known that they would soon be imitated. When he turned to producing a shareholders' guide, Tuck's was already established and well known. For success in the market, Bradshaw's had to be distinguished from its predecessors. He seldom advertised, beyond drawing attention occasionally to one of his own publications in some space that stood empty in another of them. There was no need for that. His name had itself become a hallmark.

Unfortunately it soon embodied a different standard too: not of the excellent but of the incomprehensible. The information offered in the *Guide* might be commendably correct, but many people found it very hard to understand.

The earliest hint of criticism of Bradshaw's timetables that I have come across is a passing remark in *Punch* in 1850, suggesting that the *Guide* formed a suitably difficult puzzle to exercise children's wits on at school.[24] In the following year the novelist Surtees was more explicit. 'Do not buy a Bradshaw', he wrote, 'unless you want a headache'.[25] He was soon joined by Dickens, with his 'Narrative of Extraordinary Suffering', which depicts an innocent tradesman trying to get from London to Worcester by the light of Bradshaw's *Guide*, making his way there through Scotland and the Isle of Man and ending up at the Euston hotel, his starting-place; 'now a ruin', able to utter nothing but the word 'BRADSHAW'[26]. 'No one knows what he means' are Dickens's last words. Yet his piece would have been pointless if most of its readers had not recognised immediately what that one name stood for.

Next year a Frenchman made the same complaint. In the introduction to his guidebook to Scotland, Adolphe Joanne, a seasoned and expert traveller, observed that 'in Britain it is absolutely necessary...to be provided with a *Bradshaw*, a little guide more useful than convenient, a kind of sphinx whose riddles tourists do not always manage to guess. Until someone publishes more methodical and less confused timetables, one is compelled, at the risk of giving oneself violent headaches, to use this one.'[27] Joanne courteously refrained from observing, as he might have done very fairly, that his own country's *Livret-Chaix* was laid out and printed with an elegance beyond Bradshaw's scope. But then Bradshaw's task was far more complicated and difficult because he had to deal with a system that was bigger than the French one and carried a much heavier traffic, the times of the trains always being liable to be changed at short notice, and more and more frequently as the pressure of competition grew stronger.

Trollope first refers to the timetables in a neutral way in *Barchester Towers*. In the fifth chapter (written in 1855), the Evangelical clergyman Mr Slope observes that 'on looking at the "Bradshaw", I see that there are three trains in and three out [of Barchester] every Sabbath'. But by 1869 Trollope was making the frequently-heard complaint too: 'At what hour I shall get to Glasgow I cannot learn without an amount of continued study of Bradshaw for which I have neither strength nor mental ability'.[28] By this time he finds no need to put Bradshaw into inverted commas. To him the book has become part of the vocabulary of ordinary life.

The wry jokes continued. Henry James treated Bradshaw as one of the mysteries of its country, unintelligible to any foreigners, except perhaps Americans.[29] Arnold Bennett made fun of its intricacies in 1911,[30] joined in the same year by Max Beerbohm – 'We always repulse, at first, anyone who intervenes between us and Bradshaw. We always end by accepting the intervention. We never have any confidence in the intervener. Nor is the intervener, when it comes to the point, sanguine'.[31]

There were however other people who looked into Bradshaw's publications, not in urgent search for the times of trains needed for journeys they had to make, but treating them in a quite different way, as an intellectual diversion. Here is one of them, under amused and attentive scrutiny: 'I lent that entertaining work [*Bradshaw's Continental Guide*] to an American friend, and found the utmost difficulty in recovering it from him. It was duly restored, indeed, on the morning of my departure, and I found that my friend had sat up all night, "just to see how it ended", he said.'[32]

Another writer remarked of the British *Guide* that 'the different threads of its plot [are interwoven] like the patterns in the products of the Jacquard loom'.[33]

All timetables, other than those showing the simplest out-and-back journeys, necessarily demand a little patience. 'It has long been agreed on all hands that nobody can understand a railway timetable', *Punch* remarked in 1854.[34] Nothing had changed in that matter 100 years later. L.T.C. Rolt considered that 'the average traveller seems totally incapable of deciphering even the simplest of timetables, or if he can he refuses to believe what he reads'.[35] But Bradshaw's *Guide* did labour under one defect that might have been remedied. The size of the page changed scarcely at all. The book grew enormously thick: by 1939 each issue comprised over 1,100 pages. The small square format set problems to the printers – striving to accommodate the lists of stations, the times of the trains, and the necessary notes – that were not soluble satisfactorily under these conditions. In most countries on the mainland of Europe and in the United States the pages of the national railway timetables were made larger, which considerably eased this task. No such change occurred in Britain until after the railways had been nationalised. The new management then arranged to amalgamate some of its regional timetables with Bradshaw's, as the former Southern Railway had done from its formation in 1923. This produced a curious new Bradshaw. It was taller than the old one, but scarcely any broader; and that was still a most troublesome restriction, requiring much matter to be set sideways. The last issue, of May 1961, is a sorry spectacle of mixed typography, through the printing of some of the text in accordance with the railways' own specification, interwoven with Bradshaw's. Turned out in this way, it was discreditable to everyone. Plainly it must be abandoned in favour of a new timetable, planned and laid out as such. That was duly produced at last, in a well-considered form, by the British Railways Board in 1974. It was a pity that this sensible conclusion had to be reached so slowly, and by such a disorderly route.

3

What can a modern student, armed with patience, industry, and sound eyesight, learn from Bradshaw's *Guide*?[36]

It became, for certain purposes, something like a handbook to the United Kingdom. Here are some illustrations of its value in that way. We often find it surprisingly difficult now to discover the distance between one town or village and another in Great Britain, except those between London and the larger cities, for which tables are available in some road atlases. We usually have to reckon it up by the tedious process of adding together short lengths of road given in those atlases, and yet sometimes capriciously omitted there. Bradshaw made the task a great deal simpler for the Victorians. If the two places had railway stations that stood on the same line, the distance could usually be read off in a moment from the list of stations given at the beginning of the table that set out the service provided between them: Ilford to Diss, for example, 86¾ miles; Menai Bridge to Flint, 48¾. For journeys involving changes of train the route had to be established and the lengths of each section of it added together: eg Dunbar–Huntly, 201 miles (Dunbar–Edinburgh, 29¼; Edinburgh–Aberdeen, 130½; Aberdeen–Huntly, 40¾). That convenient service offered by Bradshaw to its Victorian users may still sometimes help us today, where both places have retained their stations.

The *Guide* throws a great deal of light on times and habits of work. The intensive service of commuter trains into London from the suburbs (excluding the special trains for workmen, which all ran very early)[37] did not then begin to arrive until after 8 o' clock. Those who travelled up to London from towns within a radius of 120 miles or more – there came to be a good many of these people before 1914 – all had to start their day's work there, to our way of thinking, late. Bradshaw shows us that the first train up from Birmingham reached its terminal station in London in 1887 at 10.05, from Bristol at 10.45, from Manchester (three trains, by competing routes) not until mid-day. It would have been quite easy to provide trains running at no more than average express speed to arrive on each of these journeys an hour or more sooner, without requiring a start so early as to be unacceptable; but there was evidently no strong demand for that. A business man might go up to London for one main engagement and then return home the same evening. If he had much more work than that to do, he must stay the night. In 1914 there were services from Leeds and Bradford that allowed a fairly long spell of work in London (just under 200 miles away), with a return the same evening. By 1939 the radius had extended, though not by very much. Bradshaw shows us that the trip could then be made comfortably from Plymouth (226 miles) and that it could *just* be made, allowing four hours in London, from Newcastle (269 miles).

Bradshaw summarises for us the whole growth of the practice of daily commuting from the suburbs into London and the chief provincial cities by railway: a fairly steady process from the 1860s onwards until about 1900, when in most districts it came to be much slowed down through the arrival of electric trams, successfully competing for much of the trains' business. Some railway companies then turned to electrification themselves and, when it had been completed, put on services that recovered for them a good deal of the traffic they had lost. All these changes are recorded for us very clearly in the *Guide*. The number of weekday trains on the London & South Western Railway from Isleworth to Waterloo, for example, increased in 1887–1914 only from 28 a day to 32; the introduction of electric trams there in 1901 put a stop for a time to the growth of railway services. But those services jumped up after the electric trains began running in 1916. By 1922 the number of them provided was 44. On the north bank of the Tyne this development was very striking. The circular route from Newcastle, by Tynemouth and Monkseaton and then back to Newcastle, carried twelve trains a day in 1887. Much traffic was lost over the southern part of this route to electric trams after they had been introduced there in 1902. The North Eastern Railway responded promptly by electrifying the whole of its circle. That work was completed by July 1904. In 1908–13 the number of passenger bookings at the suburban stations had increased by over twenty percent compared with those in the 1890s (the trams also continuing to run in full force).[38] The financial gain to the company was however a good deal less than appears at first sight, for the new service brought an almost fourfold increase in the number of trains run, entailing a much heavier expenditure on the provision and maintenance of rolling stock and track, as well as a higher bill for the wages of the additional staff that was required.

Bradshaw also displays to us the growth of the Saturday holiday. Let us observe it in Manchester, where the practice of closing banks, warehouses, and offices on Saturday afternoons first emerged as a recognisable policy in the 1840s and 1850s.[39] In 1887 the *Guide* shows us that there were seven trains on the Lancashire & Yorkshire Railway running out of Manchester and Salford on Saturdays only, during the middle hours of the day. By 1914 that number had increased to 29. But Saturday was gaining acceptance as a *half*-day holiday, no more. The early morning services into Manchester (and into London) were in 1914 the same as on Mondays to Fridays. So the commuters were evidently travelling up to their work as usual, though a fair number of them were returning home earlier; in other words, they were working a $5^1/_2$-day week. By the time Bradshaw ceased publication in 1961 the Saturday timetable had grown so different that for some important services, over long and short distances alike, they required tables of their own.[40] The five-day week had arrived, and it was extending fast.

The *Guide* has much to show us about Sunday services too. I have examined those that were run in Great Britain during the Victorian age elsewhere.[41] In England and Wales nearly a quarter of the railway system was closed down completely on Sundays in 1914, in Scotland some sixty percent of it. There are hardly any traces of this practice to be found anywhere on the European mainland.

However, as Bradshaw shows us, these matters were differently arranged in some parts of Ireland. The suburban services maintained on Sundays into and out of Dublin and Cork were remarkably abundant. Forty-two trains ran from Dublin to Bray on weekdays in 1914, and as many as 35 on Sundays. From Cork to Aghada, Crosshaven, and Youghal the numbers of trains running on weekdays and Sundays were the same. To Blarney the Cork & Muskerry Railway offered a Sunday service of eleven trains, compared with six on weekdays. In London, though by English standards the Great Eastern provided a liberal Sunday service on the Chingford line, it still amounted to no more than sixty percent of that which ran on Mondays–Saturdays.

Here we can see, mirrored in Bradshaw's columns, two wholly different attitudes towards Sunday recreation: benevolent in Catholic districts, restrictive and grudging wherever Protestantism prevailed. No practices like those just spoken of at Dublin and Cork appear in Northern Ireland, in and around Belfast.

Most of what has been considered here relates primarily to large towns and industrial districts. But Bradshaw has something to tell us about other communities too. We can, for instance, discover from its index the name of nearly every place that claimed to have a market throughout the United Kingdom, with the day or days of the week on which it was held. The number of them had been gradually declining during the nineteenth century.[42] But, reckoning by the *Guide*, it added up to the surprising total of about 960 in 1887, which had increased by 1914 to 1,100: sixty-four percent of them in England, seven percent in Wales, nine percent in Scotland; and twenty percent in Ireland, where the rural nature of the economy called for them insistently. To them should be added, in Ireland again, the number of Fair Days for which additional trains were run: thirteen of them are named in the *Guide* in 1887, 28 in 1914. Here we can see the market business – an essential part of rural commerce – continuing right down to the end of the railway age. After 1918 the carriage of most of this traffic passed to petrol-driven vehicles on the roads. The number of Irish Fair Days figuring in the *Guide* in 1939 was no more than eight.

As with the train services, the statements about markets and fairs were added, altered, or removed according to information received in Bradshaw's offices. But the list was not carried over there from issue to issue, unrevised for years on end. Deletions and additions were made, as well as changes in the days on which these marts were held.[43] From 1756 onwards the work known as *Owen's Book of Fairs* had provided this information about them and about markets, in a series of successive editions. It was compiled first by William Owen and later by J. Donaldson; but the last edition seems to have been issued in 1859, and after that no comprehensive lists of markets and fairs were available until the publication of those in the reports of the Royal Commission on Market Rights and Tolls (1888).[44] The numbers that were given there were sometimes criticised as being too low. Those in Bradshaw may be too high; they certainly include a number of markets that were falling into disuse. But new ones were added, and the list is worth consideration by anybody interested in this element of agricultural trade. The student of railways will find it valuable in helping to explain the provision of additional services in rural districts on one or two days in the week. Most of these were primarily trains for market folk.

Knowledge of all these things was of course to be had elsewhere: in county directories, for example, and the national gazetteers. But those were large and expensive volumes, and not many of them were revised frequently for new editions. Down to 1916 Bradshaw's *Guide* cost only sixpence; and it always came out every month. Its indexes form at least a very useful checklist of this information.

There is another important way in which the *Guide* furnished a handbook to the United Kingdom. Within the British Isles the railways could provide transport only on land or by means of under-water tunnels – except on the Firths of Forth and Tay, where ferries carrying railway vehicles operated, until the waters were bridged in 1878–90. Communication with the islands had to be made partly by sea; and the *Guide* set it all out.

Regular services were provided from at least ten ports in Great Britain to Douglas and Ramsey in the Isle of Man and to Ireland. Only half of these are to be found today. Among those that have gone, Bradshaw mentions one or two curiosities: the services from Silloth in Cumberland to Belfast, Dublin, and Douglas, run in conjunction with the North British Railway; and that from Aberdovey (on Cardigan Bay) to Waterford, which lasted from 1883 to 1889, supported by the Cambrian Railways until the London & North Western, with its interests concentrated further up the Welsh coast at Holyhead, decided to snuff it out.[45] There were no railways in the Hebrides, but all shipping services made connections with railways on the mainland, at Strome Ferry and Kyle of Lochalsh, at Mallaig, at Oban and the Clyde ports. Travellers to Orkney and Shetland usually changed from train to steamer at Aberdeen, Wick, or Thurso. Those complicated services were crammed into one of Bradshaw's most tightly-crowded pages.[46]

The *Guide* gave the railway and steamer services to and from the mainland of Europe a good deal more prominence. Those across the Narrow Seas were intensely competitive, their advertisements shouting one another down. Some of the cheapest fares quoted in them in April 1910 are interesting: third-class return tickets from London to Paris (available for one month) via Havre £2 0s 8d (second class, no third provided), via Dieppe £2 7s 1d, via Calais or Boulogne £3 9s 10d; but the last of these routes also allured the English traveller by the offer of a week-end ticket from London to Paris and back for £1 10s.[47]

The information about shipping services is given mainly in the section of advertisements appended to the *Guide*, over 200 pages of them in each issue by 1910. Advertisements form a valuable element in the book; it is deplorable to cut them out when a copy is rebound. Most of them relate to hotels and boarding houses. The publishers were not answerable for the quality of the accommodation described. The main value of these advertisements for us now is that they showed the facilities that the proprietors thought would attract middle-class custom to them.

Consider some of the information the *Guide* had to give about hotels and boarding houses in August 1887. The provision of lifts, even in tall hotel buildings, is still very sparse. These advertisements mention them in twelve hotels, together with three hydros,[48] in the provinces, and only one hotel in London; a number of other London hotels had in fact had these appliances for some years, and by this time it may not have been thought worthwhile to refer to them specially. Another twelve provincial hotels (and one boarding house) announce that they have the telephone; in London no more than three. That was, however, a newer device, which had been available for less than eight years.

The miscellaneous information these advertisements afford is sometimes curious: for example, at the Rumbling Bridge Hotel, near Stirling, 'the grounds are open on Sabbath only to those living in the hotel'; the Castle at Taunton claims that it is 'the only hotel between Paddington and the Land's End which is lit by the electric light'. At some much-frequented tourist centres there was evidently a good deal of competitive jostling between the agents of the various hotels, who went to meet travellers off incoming services. The Castle Mona Hotel, near Douglas (Isle of Man), had its own bus to meet every steamer, 'which visitors will please inquire for on landing, and not allow themselves to be misled by the statements of parties made to recommend inferior houses'. There was perennial discontent at Killarney with the Great Southern & Western Railway, which admitted the servants of its own hotel on to the station platform: as 'Touters for their Hotel', the other establishments complained, whose representatives had to be searched for outside the station doors.

The advertisements of some hotels came to be worded with a comic exactitude. The Queen's at Southport declared that it was 'the only hotel in Southport in immediate front of which the tide regularly ebbs and flows'.

The boarding houses' advertisements in the *Guide* are fewer, and less informative. Many of their proprietors were reluctant to throw their establishments open to casual customers in this way, and those who restrained themselves looked down on their rivals, who were not so discriminating as they were. Dickens's Mrs Lirriper spoke for them in 1863:

'My dear. You never have found Number Eighty-one Norfolk Street Strand advertised in Bradshaw's *Railway Guide*, and with the blessing of Heaven you never will or shall so find it. Some there are who do not think it lowering themselves to make their names that cheap, and even going the lengths of a portrait of the house not like it with a blot in every window and a coach and four at the door, but what will suit Wozenham's lower down on the other side of the way will not suit me, Miss Wozenham having her opinions and me having mine'.[49]

The whole of this business was much played on by snobbery, an influence that is always worth notice, in its infinitely various manifestations.

The number of these establishments advertising in the *Guide* in 1887 was about 25. By 1910 it had risen to nearly 90, though it was in truth a good deal larger than that, for a fair number of boarding houses had by then turned themselves (without making any essential changes) into 'private hotels'. In 1939 only three boarding establishments advertised in the *Guide*; in 1961 none at all.

4

Bradshaw's *Guide* has much to show us of Victorian class-distinctions. It was not part of its business to comment on them in any way. All it had to do was to set out the arrangements that the railway companies imposed. The book is a strictly neutral witness in a debate that sometimes grew hotly contentious.

Its usual practice in earlier days was to state the classes of accommodation included in each passenger train, first, second, and third. To these, three more were soon added: on some lines fourth class[50] and express, on all lines Parliamentary – that is, the trains provided in accordance with the Regulation Act of 1844, running at a minimum speed of 12mph, the 'Parliamentary' passengers conveyed in closed-in vehicles provided with seats, and paying fares of not more than a penny a mile. So by 1845 as many as six different fares were being charged on some British railways. A seventh was added from 1864, the specially-low workmen's fares offered for travelling by a limited number of trains in and out of London and some provincial cities. After the passing of the Cheap Trains Act in 1883 the Parliamentary train soon began to disappear. On most lines the service purchased by the ordinary third-class passenger was now the same as the one that the Parliamentary ticket had offered him.

By that time the number of passenger classes on the British railways was beginning to be reduced through the discontinuance of second class. One of the more important companies, the Great North of Scotland, had never provided it. The Midland withdrew it from the beginning of 1875; but its example was not followed by any other leading company until the 1890s. By 1914 second class had disappeared (except in certain suburban services and in Continental boat trains) from all of them but the London & South Western and the South Eastern & Chatham.[51]

At the upper end of the scale the entry 'exp.' in the *Guide* at first indicated an express train, for travelling in which a supplementary charge was made (of some unstated amount, varying from one company to another: see p.28). By 1882 the levying of that charge had been discontinued by every British company except the three in the south-eastern corner of England. The term is still found in the *Guide* here and there, however, now merely indicating a train booked to run somewhat faster than the rest. By this time Bradshaw's timetables had become, in the eyes of the railways, a useful advertiser of superior facilities of all sorts, such as Pullman, sleeping, and dining cars.

The *Guide* also recorded certain facilities that can never have been used by more than a very few people. A number of express trains could be stopped at certain named stations at the special request of passengers, who usually had to be travelling first-class. In July 1914 seven of these stations were listed in Bradshaw: Badminton, Bawtry, Chelsfield, Evershot, Glynde, Hampden Park, and Little Bytham, nearly all of them lying on or near large rural estates whose owners had negotiated this arrangement, usually at the time when the railway was built. Not all those who desired the privilege had secured it. Even so great a magnate as the Duke of Rutland, who had acted benevolently towards the Great Northern and London & North Western companies by agreeing to sell land they needed for their Newark-Market Harborough line at little more than its agricultural value, was refused the right to stop trains at Bottesford and at Redmile in east Leicestershire (close to his Belvoir estate) when he asked for it in 1876.[52] He might perhaps have secured it if the Great Northern company had not been a party to the negotiation. But it had been intensely irritated for more than twenty years past by the tenth Earl of Lindsey, who relentlessly exercised a right he had to stop trains at Tallington on its main line, and it may well have decided that it would not expose itself to any more such arrangements. It bought out the privilege from his successor for £1,000 in 1887.[53] There were also at least 60 stations on the British railway system that private persons had been allowed to erect for their own use, some of which – though by no means all – appear in Bradshaw too.[54]

But in general the *Guide* is a witness much less to the continuance of social privilege than to the progress of democratisation. When it was first published, it was a record of privilege everywhere. The quicker trains and the more comfortable – even, for a time, the safer – ones were reserved for first and second-class passengers. By 1914 privilege among railway travellers in Britain was limited only to a few agreeable inessentials – more quiet, greater leg-room, and a few other luxuries. Third-class passengers enjoyed on almost all railways (except in suburban travel) something more than a minimum of comfort that was perfectly acceptable; they might travel at the highest scheduled speed and take meals, if they chose, in dining-cars *en route*.[55] But then surely that was no more than fair: for of the journeys made on the railways of Great Britain in 1913, ninety-six percent were in the third class.

5

A good many changes in service that Bradshaw records arose from the competition between railway companies that was established over most of the island, not to be seen working to anything like the same extent anywhere on the Continent. The competitive principle became so strong that – at least in passenger business – if one company decided to quicken a service or lower a fare its competitors might feel they had to do the same (see p.28). Bradshaw is one of the prime sources for our observation and understanding of this principle at work.

The *Guide* displays to us some of the artful arrangements of competitive services. For example, the weaker of the two competitors – weaker through having a longer route or one that was physically more difficult to work than its rivals – might attract some business by a careful choice of the times at which its trains were appointed to run. Between London and Leeds the Great Northern had a shorter and very much easier route than the Midland, and the average time taken by its best trains in 1914 was accordingly a little less. On the other hand, the number of these trains run by the Midland was seven against the Great Northern's five, and whereas the last Great Northern train down in the evening left London at 5.45, the Midland provided one at 6 o'clock and another at 7.15. The 5.45 was the last Great Northern train for Bradford too; and here the Great Central evidently hoped to pick up some crumbs, for it put on a good express leaving Marylebone at 6.20.

The total convenience of each rival route would be assessed by experienced travellers in their own ways, some of which Bradshaw could not show. Among all the trunk lines running northwards the Midland was widely known, for a great many years, as the most unpunctual: what it claimed to be going to do, it frequently did not perform.[56] The siting of termini might be an important consideration. Paddington and Waterloo lay nearly four miles apart, in entirely different quarters of London. Which would be more convenient to someone travelling from London to Exeter? And at the other end of that journey, did he know that the train from Waterloo would deliver him close to the centre of the city, whereas the Great Western's St David's station was a mile and a sharp climb away from it?

Before 1914 it had come to be accepted by most British railway managers that the rivalry in the provision of passenger services had been taken too far and was costing too much. That was reflected in the many train-working and pooling agreements entered into by the competitors from 1899 onwards. These began with the 'working union' of the South Eastern and London Chatham & Dover companies – the rowdiest and most ridiculous squabblers of them all. The London & North Western and the Lancashire & Yorkshire reached a pooling agreement in respect of certain kinds of traffic in 1904, presently joined by the Midland; the Caledonian and Glasgow & South Western companies did something to regulate their wild rivalry on the Clyde coast in 1910; and in that year also the Great Western and South Western companies concluded a pooling agreement applied to services between London and the West of England. Bradshaw records some of the practical consequences of these arrangements.

The multiplicity of competitive services must astonish us now. A brief summary, with a few examples, may give an idea of their number and variety, as Bradshaw unfolds them before us in the summer of 1914. Let us look first at two of these services where the competitive principle prevailed, uncontrolled by any inter-company agreements.

There were 25 trains making the journey up and down between London and Sheffield every weekday at about 50mph or more, running over four routes owned by three companies. Here is a summary of them:

TABLE 6

EXPRESS SERVICES BETWEEN LONDON AND SHEFFIELD, 1914

1	2	3	4	5	6	7	8
Company	Route via	Miles	Number of trains (up and down added together)	Average time	Average Speed mph	Fastest train	Speed of of trains in col.7 mph
Great Central	Nottingham	165	7	3hr 20min	49.5	2hr 57min	55.9
Great Northern	Retford	163	5	3hr 15min	50.2	2hr 58min	54.9
Midland	Derby	158	7	3hr 10min	49.9	3hr 2min	52.1
Midland	Nottingham	169	6	3hr 19min	51.0	3hr 0min	56.3

Source: Bradshaw's Guide, July 1914

Between London and Birmingham there were 38 trains of the same sort in 1914, run by two companies. Their competition had become fully effective only in July 1910. Before that time the Great Western's route was sixteen miles longer than that of its rival the London & North Western: so they did not compete on equal terms. Now, with the completion of the Great Western's route through Bicester, the terms *were* equal, and the two services added together constituted the most lavish provision of express trains between two great cities in Europe over a distance of more than 100 miles.

TABLE 7

EXPRESS SERVICES BETWEEN LONDON AND BIRMINGHAM, 1910 AND 1914

1	2	3	4	5	6	7
Company	Miles	Number of trains (up and down added together) 1910	Average time	Average Speed mph	Fastest train mph	Speed of trains in col.6 mph
Great Western	129	9	2hr 36min	49.6	2hr 20min	55.3
London & North Western	113	17	2hr 15min	50.6	2hr 0min	56.5

1	2	3	4	5	6	7
Company	Miles	Number of trains (up and down added together) 1914	Average time	Average Speed mph	Fastest train mph	Speed of trains in col.6 mph
Great Western	111	17	2hr 3min	54.1	2hr 0min	55.5
London & North Western	113	21	2hr 7min	53.4	2hr 0min	56.5

Source: Bradshaw's Guide, April 1910, July 1914

Still faster trains ran between Paddington and Bristol, the fastest of them all at 59.3mph: but the Great Western company had that business to itself, and the total number of 50-mph trains provided there in 1914 was no more than twelve.

The fastest services of this kind to be found on the European mainland in 1914 were those between Paris and Lille and between Berlin and Hamburg. For these we can turn to Bradshaw's *Continental Guide*. Both were non-competitive, like those between London and Bristol. They were fixed to run as follows:

TABLE 8

EXPRESS SERVICES, PARIS–LILLE AND BERLIN–HAMBURG, 1914

1	2	3	4	5	6	7
	Miles	Number of trains (up and down added together)	Average time	Average Speed	Fastest train	Speed of trains in col. 5 mph
Paris–Lille	154	8	2hr 58min	51.9	2hr 53min	53.4
Berlin–Hamburg	178	15	3hr 36min	49.4	3hr 14min	55.1

Source: Bradshaw's Continental Guide, August 1914

Although the British services were more numerous and a little faster, as they had always been, the margin of those differences had by this time been narrowed. One very sharp contrast still remained, however. No third-class passengers were admitted to any of the trains between Paris and Lille that are shown in Table 8; they were excluded from four of the fifteen between Berlin and Hamburg. Between London and Sheffield, Birmingham, and Bristol they were conveyed by every train, including the fastest.

Still, it must not be supposed that the British competitive system automatically produced a liberal and convenient service. Between London and Portsmouth the South Western and Brighton companies simply arrived at an understanding that they would not compete with each other. The South Western had the shorter route, via Guildford. Bradshaw shows us that its quicker trains ran at an average speed of 36mph in 1914; not one of them reached 40mph, to qualify by the then-accepted standard as an express. And this to and from a place with 230,000 people, the tenth provincial town in England. Portsmouth could indeed be said to have come under a 'railway monopoly'; but here the monopoly was exercised by two companies, acting in a silent unpublished collusion, not by one.

6

So there is Bradshaw's *Guide*: an indispensable key to our understanding of the movement of people by public transport throughout the British Isles between 1842 and 1961. Many other railway operations lay outside its scope. No freight trains ever figured in it at all; none of the workings of empty rolling stock and light engines without which the Victorian railway system could never have functioned. Some attention is given to services and workings of that kind in the study that follows this one. There are oddities that occur here and there in the *Guide*: strange statements put out by the companies themselves and dutifully passed on by the publishers to the users of the book. Here are two examples, both occurring on the North Staffordshire Railway. In the August 1887 issue (p. 242) we come upon a 6.25pm 'express' from Crewe to Derby, which makes the journey of 50¼ miles at 24.2mph. In whatever sense can that have been an express? On the next page there is a train booked to leave Stoke-on-Trent for Crewe at 10.50pm. This note is appended: 'Conveys first-class passengers only on signing a form indemnifying the company from all liability in case of accident to the train, etc'. What special dangers can have attended travelling by this particular train? And what sinister meaning may lurk in that final 'etc'?

Although, on any fair test that it can be subjected to now, the *Guide* stands as a remarkably accurate piece of printing, it does of course contain mistakes. Most of these probably originated in the copy supplied to the publishers by the railway companies. Nevertheless, for certain sorts of errors the printers in Manchester must be held responsible. One kind needs special mention, for it is very tiresome to users of the book: the inclusion of a single letter printed among the times of the trains, referring to a note that does not occur in the rubric elsewhere on the page. In April 1910, for instance (p. 297), the 9.10pm train from Liverpool Street to Cambridge is shown as stopping at three stations, all marked 'p', indicating some special condition that is not specified. In the same issue there are two notes (p. 727 'r' and 'y') evidently applying to Staddlethorpe station between Selby and Hull, no explanation of which is given either here or on p. 721, where these trains ought also to have figured. In July 1914 (p. 76) the 8.45am Fishguard boat-train from Paddington is shown as detaching a slip carriage at Carmarthen, with a connection for Aberystwyth; but that carriage makes no appearance in the account of the express on p. 56, where the train is shown as merely passing Carmarthen by without serving it.

Nevertheless, the final reflection of anyone who has occasion to use Bradshaw's

Guide in quest of the many kinds of knowledge it has to offer must surely be one of gratitude and respect: gratitude for the care and good sense with which, on the whole, the information was conveyed, respect for the printers who set up all this great quantity of complicated matter (by hand, of course, throughout the Victorian age) and for those who directed and supervised their work; respect above all for the competent, quietly busy man who established and moulded it, stage by stage, into a convenient form in Manchester, aided by his lively and intelligent associate in London.

NOTES

1. It has been dropped, however, in the eighth edition of 1990.

2. *The Story of Bradshaw's Guide* (1890).

3. RM 76 (1935) 391–2.

4. *The History of Bradshaw* (1939). This was an official centenary publication, undertaken for the firm of Henry Blacklock & Co Ltd (by then the publishers of the *Guide*), and evidently based on its records.

5. *The Centenary of 'Bradshaw'* (1940).

6. Smith, 11–12.

7. A. Darbyshire, *An Architect's Experiences* (1897), 10–12.

8. Smith, 17–18, 31–2.

9. Lee, 7–9.

10. Fellows demonstrated that conclusively.

11. For him see Boase, i.20.

12. H.G. Lewin, *Early British Railways* [1925], 186.

13. See Smith, 21.

14. Ottley, 7909–11, 7913, 7918.

15. Long runs of these timetables, though not a complete set, are in the Mitchell Library, Glasgow. I am grateful to Murdoch Nicolson for showing them to me there and discussing them with me. See J. House, *The Romance of Murray* [1952].

16. Ottley, 5258.

17. These particulars come from Bradshaw's will, at the PRO (Chancery Lane, London).

18. H. Robinson, *Carrying British Mails Overseas* (1964), 254.

19. Burritt wrote an extensive obituary of Bradshaw, quoted from in Smith, 24–6.

20. *Ibid.*, 20–1.

21. I have been unsuccessful in my attempts to secure any confirmation of this statement from Oslo.

22. Reproduced in Smith, 10.

23. In summarising Fellows's arguments, Lee appears to endorse them (17, 27).

24. *Punch*, 18 (1850) 167.

25. R.S. Surtees, *Town and Country Papers*, ed. E.D. Cuming (1929), 234.

26. First published in *Household Words*, 12 July 1851. Reprinted in Dickens, *Miscellaneous Papers*, ed. B.W. Matz (1914), 317–22.

27. A. Joanne, *Itinéraire descriptif de l'Ecosse* (1852), xliii. He is referring here to Bradshaw as the indispensable guide to the railways of the whole of Great Britain; on p. xxxix he recommends Murray's timetables cordially, as a guide to services within Scotland.

28. *Letters*, ed. B.A. Booth (1951), 435.

29. *The Golden Bowl* (Penguin ed.), 271.

30. *Hilda Lessways* (1911), 338–40.

31. *Zuleika Dobson* (1947 ed.), 133–4.

32. E. OE. Somerville and M. Ross, *Some Irish Yesterdays* (Nelson ed., n.d.), 227–8.

33. RM 22 (1908) 327.

34. *Punch*, 27 (1854) 238.

35. *Railway Adventure* (Pan ed., 1971), 133–4.

36. No quite complete set of the *Guide* is to be found in any one place. The fullest is in the British Library, though it is available to readers there only on microfilm. The set in the Bodleian Library at Oxford is almost as extensive. There is a useful collection, complete from 1864 to 1927, otherwise irregular, in R903. The issues of the *Guide* for August 1987, April 1910, and July 1922 were reprinted by David & Charles. Since copies of them are more widely available than the rest, I have made use of these here as frequently as possible.

37. See for example those from Croydon and Norwood into London: *Guide*, August 1887, 81–2.

38. See RTC, 116–17 and 384 (note 85).

39. *Ibid.*, 133–4.

40. See *Guide*, May 1961, 7a–8, 357–69, 632, 807–15.

41. VRY, 282–9.

42. See RTC, 326.

43. Take a sample, from the entries for the letter H. In August 1887, 59 stations are shown as serving places with specified market days. In August 1914, the number is the same. The additions are offset by some deletions. Harwich, Haslemere, Hatfield, and Hythe (Kent) evidently lost their markets in these years. The *Guide* seems to have been mistaken in attributing markets to Harlech and Hemyock in 1887. The days for the holding of markets change at Hanley and Haywards Heath.

44. pp. 1888, liii; 1890–1, xxxviii.

45. R. Christiansen and R.W. Miller, *The Cambrian Railways* (1967 and n.d.), i. 96, ii. 16.

46. *Guide*, August 1887, 418.

47. *Guide*, April 1910, 972–4.

48. The rise and decline of hydropathic treatment (see above, pp. 44–5) is reflected plainly here. In August 1887 the number of hydros advertising in the *Guide* is 24. By April 1910 it is down to 20; by June 1939 to six; by May 1961 (when the total quantity of advertising had been much reduced) there is only one – the Bowdon Hydro, south of Manchester.

49. *Christmas Stories* (Oxford Illustrated ed.), 369–70.

50. Fourth class was provided in early days by more than a dozen railway companies in Great Britain. It is scarcely heard of there after 1855, except on the North British Railway, where fourth-class accommodation (so described) was offered into the 1870s, though it seems likely that this was what was elsewhere described as 'Parliamentary'. See SRO, BR/TT(S)/52/13, Newcastle–Riccarton service.

51. For the dates of its withdrawal see C.E. Lee, *Passenger Class Distinctions* (1946), 68.

52. R234/1, min. 182.

53. Wrottesley GNR, i.78. There is a file of papers concerning this business in R1006.

54. See G. Croughton and others, *Private and Untimetabled Railway Stations* (1982).

55. Third-class sleeping accommodation was not provided on any British railway, however, until 1928.

56. See J. Simmons, *St Pancras Station* (1968), 71–5.

13
WORKING TIMETABLES

Working timetables, with the appendixes and special notices that go with them, have received very little attention from those who have written about the history of railways. They are not always easy to use, nor are they wholly satisfactory as historical evidence. But their deficiencies do not account for – still less justify – the neglect of them.

That neglect springs to a large extent, I believe, from the tendency of most of those who have written about the history of railways in Britain to interest themselves in their business as carriers of passengers more than as carriers of freight. The documentation of passenger traffic is simpler to understand, fuller, and a good deal more complete. Commentators – politicians, journalists, observers of every kind – spoke and wrote much more about services affecting passengers than they did about the handling of coal or fish or general merchandise. I am quite fairly entitled to point to this imbalance of treatment because most of my own work too has dealt primarily with the railways' movement of human beings.

But the human beings could seldom be moved without reference to the movement of freight. Throughout the Victorian age, and far into the twentieth century, passenger trains travelled on the main lines of the British railways very much faster than the great majority of freight trains. The system had to accommodate both sorts, moving at different speeds, except on a few urban railways that handled no freight at all. The public timetables – Bradshaw's *Guide* by far the most important of them – give scarcely a hint of the problems that arose in this way, for they refer wholly to passenger services. Freight services are shown only in the companies' working timetables.

But more than that. Many other movements were involved in the operation of a railway. Empty rolling stock, passenger carriages and goods wagons alike, had often to be conveyed along the lines, either to stand still in sidings for hours, or even days, or to be used at some distant place. Engines had constantly to travel on their own ('light'), to their running sheds or to some fresh assignment. For an example see Table 5, p.101. And finally, many goods trains, in the Victorian age and in the first half of the twentieth century, were appointed to stop at all or most of the stations on their way to deliver or receive goods or minerals. How long did that business take, and how were these operations fitted in with the rest of the traffic?

These were all important elements in the running of a railway, inconspicuous but indispensable. They can be observed and analysed, and calculations made from them, only by recourse to the working timetables.

I

The railways produced two sorts of timetables, quite different: public, and working (or 'service', as they were called by some companies). Their public timetables were put on sale at a nominal charge, but working timetables remained private, with 'for the use of the company's servants only', or some such phrase, printed at the front of them.

The companies' public timetables are seldom of great value to students now. The information they afford about passenger services was also sent in to the publishers of Bradshaw's *Guide*, and it can be found there, for most purposes, more conveniently. They are not negligible, however, because they sometimes address their passengers on matters other than the times of trains. They often go into detail, valuable to us, about facilities and fares. The Lancashire & Yorkshire penny timetable of April 1850[1], for example, tells us about the week-end return tickets at reduced rates that the company was already offering, from Saturdays to Tuesdays, from Manchester to Lytham, Blackpool, and Fleetwood. Again, it has been usual to say that the revenue from season tickets did not become important to the railway companies until the 1870s. But the Board of Trade had concerned itself about them as early as 1853, when it started to inquire into the contribution they made to the companies' receipts. By June 1875 the Lancashire & Yorkshire Railway was informing the public in its timetables of the season-ticket rates charged from every station on the whole of its complicated system.[2]

Occasionally one of these timetables will address the public to explain or defend one of the company's own practices. The South Eastern timetable of October 1858, for example[3], in setting out the services between London Bridge and Southborough Road, includes this note: 'the Sunday trains, marked with an asterisk, at Lower Sydenham and Beckenham, are prevented from stopping at those stations owing to restrictions imposed upon the Mid-Kent company by Mr Cator of Beckenham', a landowner who was a strong Sabbatarian.

As in Bradshaw's *Guide* (see p.184) so here in these official public timetables, the advertisements often repay attention. Nothing is too improbable to win a place in them. Who could expect to find a Titian (or at least a picture that was asserted to be his work) offered for sale in one of those timetables? Yet here is a 'Marriage of St. Catherine', formerly in the collection at Fonthill, offered at 700 guineas, together with a portrait of King James V of Scotland, at 25 guineas. The advertisements are in the North British Railway's public timetable of July 1866.[4] They were put in by Hugh Paton, who printed these books for the company and had many other business interests too, among them the dealing in works of art.

The special interest of the advertising that appears in publications associated with railways is always the same: it arises from the infinitely varied nature of the business they handled, of the advertisers and of the readers themselves.

Some general accounts of working timetables have occasionally been written. The earliest I know of was the work of F.S. Williams; the most intelligent expositor of railways to the lay public in Britain in the late nineteenth century, Acworth alone excepted – and *he* was a prince among such writers. When Williams revised his book *Our Iron Roads* for its later editions he included two pages in it about all this literature of operation, drawn from a working timetable issued by the Midland Railway.[5] This was followed presently by several more extended accounts of these timetables. One of them refers to those of the London & North Western, written by J. Mallinson, a member of the staff of its timetable department;[6] another, published in 1915, was based on the Great Central's.[7] The editor of the *Railway Magazine*, G.A. Sekon, began a series of articles there on the working timetables of various companies in 1907, promising 'an analytical article' comparing their different practices at its conclusion. But that never appeared, the series being broken off when he left the paper in 1910.

The small attention that seems to have been paid to this assemblage of evidence by even the best historians of railway companies is regrettable.[8] But it must be recognised that there are serious impediments to the satisfactory use of them.

The greatest of these is fundamental, and now irremovable. The number of working timetables that have survived is, by comparison with the total number issued, unhappily small. That is not surprising, for they were books that had a limited period of currency, at the end of which new ones were issued to the companies' servants, entirely supplanting the old ones. Some companies indeed specifically told their employees that old copies of working timetables must be thrown away as soon as they had been thus replaced. The instruction 'Last month's tables to be destroyed' appears on some of the earliest copies of these timetables that have survived in the national collections, those for the Edinburgh & Glasgow and Caledonian Railways of 1853.[9] (Even so far back as that, when train-working was relatively simple, we must notice these Scottish companies stating that they produced new working timetables *every month*.) At the end of the nineteenth century the economically-minded Highland Railway gave a somewhat different direction on this point: 'When new copies of the timetables are being supplied to the members of staff the old timetables must be collected and torn up for lavatory use'.[10]

The earliest of these timetables are in the National Railway Museum at York. The first is not a working timetable in the full sense of the term, but it is a table of goods trains produced by the London & Birmingham Railway in 1846. The other, which shows goods and passenger trains in one book, though in separate tables, comes from the Lancashire & Yorkshire Railway and dates from 1852. Then there are several for 1853–4, from the London Brighton & South Coast and the Eastern Counties in the Public Record Office at Kew and from others at Edinburgh, two of which have just been mentioned. The survival of copies of these timetables continues to be quite haphazard and irregular. At Kew those for the Midland Railway form an almost complete series from 1855 onwards; the same is true for those of the North Eastern from 1856, the London & South Western from 1860, and the Great Western from 1862. At Edinburgh there are similarly long runs of these timetables, of the Great North of Scotland company from 1856 and of the North British from 1865. On the other hand, for the great London & North Western there are very few indeed for the years 1857–1922 – none of them in any continuous series stretching over several years. There are also eight at York.

After 1922 things grow easier. At Kew and Edinburgh there are nearly complete sets of these timetables from the four big companies, issued in 1923–47, and the series has been carried on (though it continues to show some gaps) since nationalisation.

2

Let us now look at three of these timetables, to pick up some examples of what they have to offer us, beginning with one of the earliest of all: that for the Lancashire & Yorkshire dated June 1852, now at York. It is printed, one notices, by Bradshaw & Blacklock (see p.173); the company turned to the firm most experienced in the production of timetables, which happened to be on its doorstep in Manchester. It is a well-organised pamphlet, divided into two sections. The first shows the passenger services. Although this little book is declared to be for the use of the company's servants only, there is nothing concerning those services that needs to be addressed to them alone, and it may well be that this first section was also put on sale separately as the company's public timetable. The second section, however, lays down the running of freight trains, and since they were of no concern to passengers the company kept the information about them to itself. These freight services show no unusual features, except that on pp. 23–4 we find the names of the collieries whose coal each train was to carry – one presumes by special, exclusive arrangement: Balcarres, Mackay, Kirkless Hall, and Blundell's.

The other two timetables to be examined here are both from the London & South Western Railway: one of August 1857, the other of June 1909. I choose them because they exist in far more copies than any other such books, both having been photographically reprinted and put on sale to the public in recent years.[11] So some readers of this study will have copies of them in their possession, in which they can follow what is to be said here, without the need to leave home in search of them.

The 1857 timetable is a very simple affair of 54 small pages, clearly printed and easy to read. The company's system then comprised a main line 140 miles long from London to Dorchester, throwing off seven branches, together with a cluster of short suburban lines at the London end; a little more than 300 miles in all. No very fast travelling was attempted. The expresses between London and Southampton (78 miles) ran at an average speed, including stops, of 34.2 mph. The suburban service was good. Richmond was favoured with 22 trains in each direction to and from London on weekdays, the fastest at a fraction under 30 mph; brisk running for a journey as short as 9¾ miles. There was only one service at all out of the ordinary:

the daily Necropolis train from Waterloo to the cemetery's station at Brookwood, down at 11.20 and returning from the funerals at 2.30.[12]

On the main line the passenger and freight trains are shown in separate tables, though on the other lines they appear together. Five freight trains run through to Southampton in the evening and night time, besides two by day. On Sundays none go down the line, but there is one up, taking nearly eight hours to get from Southampton to London. Four trains are reserved for the conveyance of coal to various destinations, and there are some additional trains taking cattle and sheep. Five goods and coal trains travel from Willesden to the South Western company's system at Brentford on weekdays, and return; that link with the London & North Western trunk line from the north was already important.

The little book closes with a series of miscellaneous notices to the staff, enjoining the proper use of distant signals for example, and setting out procedures to be observed in shunting. 'The disgraceful practice of making drawings and writing on the walls of water closets and other places must be prevented'; daily inspection by stationmasters is ordered, and they must 'cause to be removed or obliterated immediately, everything of the kind'.

By 1909 the company's system has become nearly three times as long as it was in 1857, and the timetables and notices occupy 572 pages about twice as large as those of the earlier book, with its 54. The whole is divided into three parts: the main lines of the system as far west as Salisbury and Dorchester; the suburban lines into London; and the Western District, stretching down into Devon and Cornwall.[13] Here are a few, widely diverse examples of what the book has to show us, nearly all drawn from freight traffic, the expected quantity and the management of which are set out in detail.

Two tables display the magnitude of the business that was now passing between the northern systems and the London & South Western, by two routes, through Willesden and Brentford[14] and through Ludgate Hill and Clapham Junction.[15] The first of these routes carried the North London Railway's passenger trains running from Broad Street to Richmond, as well as the freight trains from the North Western and the Midland lines to the South Western, of which there were about a dozen on weekdays in each direction. The second line was used by a large variety of local passenger trains, but in the night time it might take as many as eight from the Great Northern system carrying minerals and goods according to requirements.

Coal was the most important single commodity handled by these trains. It was the fuel consumed then, almost exclusively, in factories, in business premises, and in dwellings of all kinds; and every lump that was used in and around London had to be brought up there over great distances, for scarcely any was mined less than 100 miles away. The north-eastern suburbs could still draw most of their stocks easily enough from cargoes carried down from the Tyne, the Wear, and the Tees by sea. Some of that coal was also taken up the Thames. But most of the supply called for in the London & South Western company's territory came by rail over these two cross-London routes.[16]

The sorting of the freight traffic, wagon by wagon, converging on London from other companies' systems as well as its own, presented difficulties. It was carried out chiefly at Nine Elms, the company's main base at Battersea. That however grew more and more congested, in spite of the purchase of additional land and the removal of some divisions of the company's business to distant places. Carriage-building went to Eastleigh in Hampshire in 1891, and locomotive-building was to follow it in 1910. The space available at Brentford was limited too. Plans were presently laid for a wholly new sorting yard for goods traffic on a large empty site further west near Feltham, but they were not realised until after the first war. In 1909 almost all the London & South Western's own long-distance freight traffic, not intended for transmission to any other railway, had to be handled at Nine Elms.

Much of it was conveyed in competition with the Great Western, and the phrase 'competitive traffic' appears in these timetables repeatedly – even 'important competitive traffic' for which (when it was waiting) one of the chief night trains had to be stopped by signal at Basingstoke.[17] The speeds at which some of this long-distance traffic moved were high. The 'Plymouth fast goods' went from London to Exeter at 31.2 mph. Though this may not appear at first sight remarkable, the wagons composing this train were still not controlled by automatic brakes, which meant that great caution had to be exercised in negotiating the banks, on gradients as steep as 1 in 80–100; two in Wiltshire and Dorset, and then two more in Devon that were each about thirteen miles long. The only traffic of this sort that was conveyed in trains fitted with continuous brakes was that in fish; milk and mails also went over long distances in trains so equipped, but they were handled as passenger traffic. Two schedules are required to show the times of the fish trains from Plymouth to London, one for those fitted with continuous brakes, the other for those that lacked them. The whole journey from Exeter eastwards was an hour quicker by the first kind than by the second.[18] The provision of these two separate timings makes it plain that the supply of vehicles fitted with the new brakes was limited and that the older type might still have to be used.

A simple illustration of the speed maintained by some of the South Western company's freight trains is offered in Table 9, distinguishing between the times spent on whole journeys including stops ('overall time') and the 'running time' made when the trains were in motion. The Plymouth fast goods heads it, accompanied by the schedules of four other trains, running much more slowly over shorter distances. Their running times stand in strong contrast with the overall times, which represent the actual speed at which goods were transmitted to the consignee, lowered by the long stops that had to be made for shunting wagons in sidings and yards on the way. At overall speeds of no more than 6–7½ mph, these trains were not moving so very much faster than horse-drawn wagons and carriers' carts. But they had other superiorities over the older means of road transport. The timetables show that they usually offered a service at least twice a day, whereas most carriers' carts ran only once or twice a week. The loads they could handle were far greater, and the objects they transported could be much bulkier, than any conveyed by the horse-drawn vehicles. So it can be seen that the railways afforded a much better total service than that provided on the roads, even if it was not always a great deal quicker.

TABLE 9

THE SPEED OF SOME GOODS TRAINS: LONDON & SOUTH WESTERN RAILWAY, JUNE 1909

Train	Distance miles	Speed overall mph	Speed running mph
10.35 pm London (Nine Elms)–Exeter ('Plymouth fast goods')	172	31.2	32.7
2.22 pm Yeovil Jct.–Exeter	49	7.5	19.3
11.1 am Exeter–Barnstaple	40	6.6	19.6
7.37 am Eastleigh–Salisbury	24	7.3	19.5
12.20 pm Milford (Salisbury)–Southampton (Bevois Park) via Eastleigh	27	6.1	20.8

Source: Working Timetable, June 1909, III, 6; II, 54; I, 190, 192.

This book also displays, or at least hints at, the extraordinary varieties of traffic the railway carried. One extensive branch of it was in cattle, in and around Tavistock and Crediton for example.[19] Others, at special places, include beer for Bentley in Hampshire (presumably for the soldiers in the camp at Bordon)[20], gunpowder from Hounslow,[21] flowers from Chertsey,[22] pottery carried (why? and where from?) to Addlestone.[23] At 8.20 am, when necessary, a 'Bank Note Paper Train' would run from Overton – that is, from Portal's mills, which manufactured it – to Basingstoke, its specially valuable cargo to be taken on from there in another train.[24] Such loads as these must all have been substantial, or of particular economic importance, to require individual mention here. The railways' working timetables can offer a useful tool to general historians of agriculture and trade.

And finally, the timetable has a little to show us of the provision the company afforded for the convenience and comfort of its own men and their families. Wherever signal-boxes stood in isolated places away from stations, stores were dropped off at them from trains appointed to stop specially for the purpose – and stores must have meant pre-eminently coal, for the boxes cannot then have been allowed any other form of heating. On Saturday mornings a train stopped at

Alderbury box to take up the signalmen's wives for Salisbury market, and another set them down again in the afternoon.[25] A similar service was afforded at Maddaford Moor box to take the women to Okehampton[26]. Perhaps the most comforting provision of all, however, was that of 'Engine and Van with Paymaster, Sats. only', running out from Waterloo to Nine Elms.[27]

3

There then is a choice from the many things this London & South Western book has to tell us, none of which are to be found in any document issued to the public. Let us now change the method of examining all this great mass of information, to look at certain practices as they are exemplified in working timetables, not of one company alone but of railway companies, large and small, throughout Great Britain. The selection must be very limited, but it should suffice to indicate the range and value of what is to be found there.

These timetables – particularly where we have a long continuous sequence of them – allow us to observe closely the effects of the quadrupling of tracks[28] and the introduction of more powerful locomotives. Obviously those improvements enabled the traffic to move faster. But also (no less important) the big new engines could handle the freight traffic, which went on increasing steadily after 1900, in a smaller number of trains, each one a larger unit: so the density of occupation of the lines was lessened, and the speed of movement increased accordingly, for freight and passenger trains alike. The North Eastern company was among the leaders in this achievement, which had far-reaching effects in reducing the running costs of its main lines.[29] Off those main lines, however, most things continued much as they had been in an almost immemorial past. At the very end of its independent life in 1922, a North Eastern stopping goods train was booked to leave Hexham at 9.25 am and arrive at Carlisle (39 miles away), after stopping and shunting at most of the stations *en route*, at 8.13 pm, so travelling at an overall average of 3.7 mph, only a little above a good smart walking pace. Nevertheless one ought to note that in 1829 the time taken on this journey by the ordinary goods wagon, horse-hauled on the road, had been not eleven hours but two days.[30]

The South Eastern company's working timetable of July 1857 (there is a copy at York) contains a good deal of useful information, some of it of uncommon sorts. It is one of the earliest we now have that shows light-engine workings and the times allotted for the movement of trains of empty carriages. It also sets out the hours of duty of each individual guard and brakesman, by name. 'General orders and notices for the month' are appended at the end of the book.

A number of peculiarities of British railway working, well known to students of the subject but not yet referred to here, can be profitably investigated in working timetables.

It has generally been believed that, after the very early days, the railway companies never allowed trains to run on their lines hauled by their customers' locomotives.[31] Even the great breweries at Burton-on-Trent, which had their private railway systems, 40 miles long by 1900 and worked by a fleet of their own engines, were never permitted to put one of them on to any track belonging to the main-line companies, although they and the breweries worked closely together in the distribution of the beer, to find its way all over the world.[32] Exceptions to this rule can be found, however. The North Staffordshire Railway's working timetable for July 1914 shows us five industrial firms hauling *passenger* trains with their own engines over the railway company's system, three of them conveying their work-people.[33] Was that practice then unique in Britain? A careful examination of the working timetables of other companies that served heavily-industrialised districts like that one might perhaps show more exceptions to a rule that has generally been thought of as absolute.

Or again, the carrying of goods and passengers together, in 'mixed trains'. This had been a practice common enough on most railways in early days, in Britain and everywhere else. To combine the two sorts of traffic, at least for the slower services, offered an obvious economy in the provision of motive power and rolling stock. This method was also employed sometimes as a temporary measure, when lines of railway had to be opened in a hurry over imperfectly-consolidated earthworks, and all fast trains were on that account prohibited. The westward extension of the London & South Western Railway was opened on 1 May 1857 from Andover to Milford, east of Salisbury. The working timetable shows us that at first passengers were not carried on this line in trains reserved for them only; all four that were offered to them carried goods too, and they proceeded over the last three miles at no more than 13 mph.[34]

As the system grew, however, and the larger companies had more engines and passenger carriages at their disposal, mixed trains gradually became fewer. By the 1860s the Board of Trade inspectors were beginning to criticise them as dangerous to the passengers conveyed,[35] especially where their carriages were marshalled behind the goods wagons. That arrangement was obviously convenient in working, when the engine of the train might have to shunt wagons at every station on the way; but it was a practice that placed the carriages containing the passengers, and their brake van, as far from the engine as possible. As the use of continuous brakes increased, it became more dangerous still, since the wagons used on these trains lacked them, and that broke the continuity between the carriages and the engine.

The Regulation Act of 1889[36] required all trains carrying passengers to be fitted with continuous brakes, and it was widely assumed that this made it obligatory for the carriages in mixed trains to be marshalled next to the engine. The Board of Trade was then authorised to enforce this decision, though the curious wording of the first section of the Act appeared to allow it some power of dispensation. Relying on that, the Highland company continued the old practice, to which it remained stubbornly addicted. The company fought a long delaying battle against the Board until at last it capitulated after a really dangerous accident to one of its trains, marshalled in the illegal way, in 1897.[37]

Mixed trains were not an expedient used by the poorer companies only. In 1886 one of those that were well-to-do was publicly reproached by an inspecting officer on this account: 'on a line occupying the position of the London & South Western', he wrote, 'they should be unknown'.[38] But the company continued to run them, listing in its working timetables nearly 30 regular services maintained in this way in 1909, besides others running on certain days only (all of them worked according to the rules laid down in the 1889 Act). Other big companies still ran a few mixed trains: the Midland on its Keighley–Oxenhope branch for instance in 1912.[39] The Cambrian, smaller and much less wealthy, came to dispense with them on its main lines, while allowing them to continue on five of its branches. On the Mawddwy Railway – closed entirely from 1908 to 1911 and then worked (though not owned) by the Cambrian – all the trains were still mixed in 1920.[40]

Some Continental railways continued to provide mixed trains when their use was declining in Britain. In 1888 it was stated that the average running speed maintained by mixed trains in France was 15.6 mph, a good deal higher than the usual British one. That speed would have been lower if the French railways had not seen to it that, as far as possible, goods sent by these trains were for transmission solely between their terminal points, which cut out the need for shunting by the way – a task that had then come to be performed in France, as a rule, by goods trains only.[41]

4

One other group of services must be considered here also: trains that ran at high speeds, exactly like express passenger trains, but figured in no public timetable, for they carried no passengers. They were intended solely for three sorts of traffic: mails, newspapers, and perishable goods.

Most of the mails and newspapers went by trains that also conveyed passengers, however few of them there might be in the darkest hours of the night. The Great Western company put on a train from London to Bristol by a special arrangement made with the Post Office in 1855, to carry mail alone. It lasted in that form, however, only until 1869, when the Post Office consented that one first-class carriage – and never more than one – should be included in it.[42] That turned it, in the railways' technical parlance, into a 'limited mail train' ('limited' because the number of seats in it was firmly restricted), which put it into the public timetables and into Bradshaw. The train that carried nothing but mail did not reappear anywhere in Britain until 1885, when the London & North Western company accepted a proposal from the Post Office that one should be introduced to travel overnight from London to Carlisle, and so on to Aberdeen. This train conveyed mail alone for the first 400 miles of its journey, admitting passengers only from Holytown Junction northwards;[43] and presently it appears that even they were excluded from it. This train provided a service of first-rate importance to all the districts it traversed, comparable in every way with expresses (like them, it was fitted with continuous brakes), but it is traceable only in the working timetables. In 1902 the Great Western company reintroduced a mail train like the original one of 1855, but extended over the whole main line from London to Penzance. It ran much more slowly than the one from Euston. For the rest, the mail travelled in special vehicles, equipped for sorting letters *en route*, that were included in publicly-advertised passenger trains.

So did almost all the newspapers, sent out from London and the large provincial cities in the small hours of the morning. But this business was a purely commercial arrangement between the newspapers and the railways, which were quite willing to run trains to carry the papers only, supposing the consignments brought on to them justified it. Once, for a short time in exceptional circumstances, that was done at the instance of a single paper – the *Daily Mail*, anxious to get itself from London to Manchester every weekday at the highest possible speed, with the earliest news of the South African War in 1900.[44] Or this special provision could take humbler forms than that. There came to be, as we find from the working timetables, two trains leaving London at 3 am that were entirely reserved for the conveyance of newspapers. One went from Waterloo to Portsmouth; the other ran out from Euston, and this train included separate vans for a variety of destinations – Birmingham, Liverpool, Carlisle, together with one to be slipped for Northampton at Blisworth.[45] But small country towns, served by branch lines, might get their early morning newspapers only by goods train, as we find that Braintree did for example in 1897.[46]

Special arrangements were adopted by the railway companies from an early date for the carriage of perishable goods of all kinds.[47] Here the speed of transit that they could offer – much higher than any attainable by road or water – had a direct market value (see pp 63–4). Such goods could be conveyed, in moderate quantities, by passenger train, paid for at a higher rate than if taken by goods train. As this business developed, however, some of it outgrew the accommodation that could be provided in that way, and it then called for special trains, travelling at speeds as high as those of passenger trains, reserved entirely for this class of traffic. There were also some other kinds of services that had to be made available frequently, many of them at hours that could not be predicted with any exactitude: those with passengers and urgent goods taken off ships and to be conveyed over long distances, for example.

The traffic to and from the liners serving the United States by way of Southampton had grown very substantial indeed by the beginning of the twentieth century. On the outward journey from London the quantity of it was variable, but it could be controlled or at least it could be assessed in advance, where passengers and their baggage were concerned, without much difficulty, by the numbers of seat reservations that were made. Wednesdays and Saturdays were the busiest sailing days, for the White Star and American Line ships respectively. Up to six special trains were provided in 1909 to accommodate passengers leaving Waterloo between 7.30 and 10 am on Wednesdays, with four on Saturdays between 10 am and 2.10 pm.[48] That is to say, paths were set down for these trains in the working timetables, occupied according to the numbers of passengers who decided to travel and the number of boat-trains required in consequence.

But the arrival times of the inward services at Southampton were another matter. They depended on the weather in the Atlantic, though some advance warning of the ships' progress could usually be given as they passed up the coast from Cornwall eastwards. The task of the enginemen taking the boat trains up to London, running to times that could not be fixed beforehand, and also of the signalmen, was eased by including in the working timetables an outline schedule of the times allowed for passing or stopping at intermediate stations, starting from '00 00 hours'.

The Great Eastern company provided sets of such timings even for some special freight services that were travelling overland and originating within its own territory; particularly important owing to its large carriage of perishable agricultural produce. In addition, in 1912 it ran up to three special express trains every weekday from Harwich to London 'when required', for perishable traffic from the Continent, which was conveyed in passenger-train vehicles: that is, in vans fitted with continuous brakes. They made one stop only (at Witham, roughly half-way, for watering the engines), and when they were running all ordinary goods trains had to be shunted off the line in front of them. Paths were allocated for as many as sixteen trains, to bring up more ordinary goods, from Harwich to London on weekdays.[49]

5

It is now time to turn to the appendixes. Again the number of those that survive is, in relation to the total that were issued, very small.

For many years it was possible for the working timetables to include standard instructions, applicable over a long period of time, addressed to the staff responsible for running the whole of the companies' systems, or large sections of them. Gradually however, as the systems grew bigger and their working more complicated, the timetables governing them became bulkier and more complicated too. This arrangement was then seen to be less satisfactory, and most of the large companies split off the general instructions, to form a separate pamphlet or book, known as the appendix to the working timetables.

The earliest of these appendixes now extant in the national collections seems to be one of 1877 for the North Eastern Railway at York; followed by two at Kew, for the North Eastern (1879) and the London Brighton & South Coast (1882). The Scottish Record Office has something that is unique among the holdings of all three national collections: a complete set of the appendixes issued by the Highland Railway from the first it ever issued, in 1897, to its demise as an independent corporation in 1922.

The practices of the companies in the production of these appendixes varied very much. They were not, as a rule, issued at regular intervals, but only when the changes were numerous and important enough to call for them, largely in accordance with the complexity of their systems. If we may judge from the survival of copies of these books, few of the smaller railways took to issuing them until after 1890.

The appendixes were intended to include all the general instructions that governed the running of trains, imposed either permanently or over long periods of time. Collected thus, they did not have to be repeated in each issue of the timetables, and that produced an economy in printing. No less important perhaps was the psychological effect of separating them from the timetables, to make them a set of regulations for the running of trains over the whole system, which every railwayman in any of the operating departments had to study and carry in his head, along with those in the company's rule-book. That was an entirely distinct publication, applying to all its servants everywhere.

Many of these instructions help to show us in detail how certain operating practices were performed: the arrangements for the working of snow-ploughs, for example;[50] the operation of special kinds of bridges, such as Deptford, Ford, and Langston on the London Brighton & South Coast Railway, which all had to be opened at times to let ships pass through.[51]

Or there was the Seven-Mile Bank on the Brecon & Merthyr Railway between Torpantau and Talybont, almost the whole of it laid out on a continuous gradient of 1 in 38. This was the scene of many dangerous 'wild runs', as the northbound trains descended on it, heavily laden with coal and equipped with brake power that was either inadequate or inadequately applied. A fearful accident occurred here in 1878 to a train worked by three engines, which plunged down the incline at more than double the speed called for in the timetable and was derailed, killing four of the six enginemen. The regulations were later tightened up, as we can see from the appendix of 1905, and apparently enforced.[52]

The appendixes offer much detailed information on other aspects of working too, and some of it was occasionally pertinent to the communities that the railway served. Here may be found tables listing all the companies' signal boxes, with their distances from one another and the hours of the day and night when each of them was manned, noting also the electrical equipment with which every box was fitted. That included telephones (unknown before 1880 and rare in all country districts for a long time after that), which might be made available at any time in case of a big fire in a town or village, or some other large public emergency.

And finally, from this miscellany of information, we can extract a knowledge of a good many things that have nothing to do with operation at all. Anyone could hire a special train for his own exclusive use, either at short notice in an emergency or as a matter of simple convenience, to be arranged in advance. But – it is natural to be curious – what did the hirer have to pay for this service? The London &

North Western company seems at one time almost to have encouraged the practice, which could easily be afforded by some of the wealthy men who travelled on it. At all events it allowed a summary of the rates it charged for the facility to be published in 1902: 5s. a mile for a single journey, 7s. 6d. for a return journey, on top of the ordinary fares, with a minimum charge of £3.[53] Not long afterwards, it quietly abandoned the public announcement of these charges. One wonders why.

6

In the offices of some superintendents of the line it appears to have been a rule to retain a file copy of each issue of these timetables, and their appendixes, but the limits of shelf-space doubtless discouraged that practice, and the salvage drives of the two wars must have been fatal to a good many such collections. The notices of special workings were more ephemeral still, most of them referring only to a single week in the year, or to some other very short period of time – and few railwaymen can ever have wished to keep any of them as souvenirs of bank holidays, periods of hard and often particularly disagreeable work. Still, long-continued files of these notices were maintained at the chief offices of at least some companies, partly no doubt to show what special arrangements had been made in the past for the handling of certain sorts of traffic that followed recurring patterns year after year. I believe the longest file of any such now extant for any English company is that for the Midland at York, which runs from 1886 to 1922; but it has, from the point of view of the student interested in the general history of railways, the serious limitation that it relates only to engineering works, to 'signal alterations and other arrangements'. The notices of special provisions to be made for the conduct of the Midland company's traffic in a broader sense formed a separate series, which does not seem to have survived anywhere. There are apparently no lengthy, complete sets of the notices for any of the large English railway companies at Kew. But at Edinburgh there are good and uninterrupted series, for the Great North of Scotland and the North British Railways, extending from 1888 and 1889 respectively down to 1922.

The notices were issued to the companies' servants either as pamphlets, at regular intervals, each covering a week or a month, or as leaflets when they related to some unexpected interruption in the timetabled service or to some special addition to it. The Victorian railways were run on the assumption that the services they offered to the public must be provided in the terms in which they had been announced or, if some unforeseeable difficulty had arisen, in some other form as close as possible to the one they had promised. The traveller did not then arrive at a station to be curtly informed that his train had been 'cancelled', as he is always liable to do on the British railway system today.

As far as possible, changes in the timetabled service had to be communicated to the staff in writing, which meant then that they must be printed. These notices were the instrument used for this purpose. They were themselves by their very nature throw-aways. but that did not mean they were unimportant. They can perhaps be described best as the lubricating oil of the whole timetable system.

They set out, for example, the interruption of services that might be necessary on account of engineering works – the rebuilding of a bridge, the installation of a large crossover from one set of tracks to another. Above all, they served to explain the arrangements that had to be adopted in case of some sudden emergency that could not have been foreseen: the washing-away of a bridge in a storm, for example, or the unsettling of the foundations of earthworks, or an accident blocking the line. These notices also supplied details of any additional trains to be run on special occasions, or – every year – at holiday times, when the number of them often became very large.

In reading the notices we come perhaps as near as we ever can to appreciating the extraordinary range of the work that railway companies might be called on to perform, as public carriers in the widest and most general sense of the phrase, handling passengers who wished to travel for every conceivable reason (or none) and carrying commodities of all sizes and sorts, from jewels to elephants.

Let us look first at a company in southern England, the London Brighton & South Coast, whose notices of this kind have been preserved, in a single volume covering the whole of the year 1874, now at York. It shows us the railways very clearly as instruments of political and social life. Numerous transfers of soldiers have to be made, for example, down its line to Portsmouth, *en route* for service overseas; the numbers of the regiments are noted, together with the numbers of men and women for whom accommodation has to be provided in each train. The notices throw a good deal of light on the business of the Crystal Palace. It is well known that gradually, after its removal to Sydenham in 1854, the success it met with was very uneven. The railway lists the events there week by week, and the numbers of additional trains (if any) required to service them. Through most of the year the programme presents a regular round of pantomimes and concerts and billiards matches, but they are interspersed occasionally with special events – a visit of Bullock's Marionettes for instance, performances of *Macbeth*, a balloon ascent, 'Great Foundations and Cat Show'. Plainly the management had to cast about for any possible means of increasing its revenue. That is a single volume, not standing in a series. It is therefore impossible to see the events to which these notices relate in any sequence or to make comparisons of the magnitude of the operations involved in one year with those of another. For that we do best to go to Edinburgh, to the records of the Scottish companies, and particularly those of the two that have been mentioned.

The North British served a large tract of central Scotland from Aberdeen and Perth southwards; economically and socially very diverse, including the Fife coal-field, the industrial Forth-Clyde basin, and the big urban communities of Edinburgh and Glasgow, as well as some very remote and sparsely-peopled districts, up the west coast to Fort William and Mallaig and through the southern hills to the

English border. The Great North of Scotland, based on Aberdeen (where it came to provide a brisk suburban service), fanned out along the coast to Peterhead and Fraserburgh, and north-westwards to Elgin and Speyside. It had a rich rural empire, famous especially for whisky and fish.

The demands made on the North British for additional and special services are very numerous.[54] Anybody interested in the history of Sunday schools ought to pay attention to them – indeed any student of Victorian religion, for the information they afford about excursions connected with churches and chapels, charitable bodies, lodges of freemasons, and others. They open out before us a very wide panorama of secular life also. Here, for instance, in June 1890 we come on a special train to convey 'Mr Carnegie's Establishment' from Edinburgh to Perth, on its way to Newtonmore on the Highland company's main line. On the next day another special train is called for to run from South Leith to Glasgow, carrying Wilmot's Galloping Horses.[55] So here is the railway transporting a millionaire's household and one of the most spectacular components of a circus, in large trains over substantial distances. But any special journey of this kind might be of just the opposite character: intimately private. In the previous year the Great North of Scotland company notified its servants of a special train to be run from Aberdeen to Ballater, consisting only of one first-class carriage and a van, for the funeral of Col. Farquharson of Invercauld.[56] The railway is here seen fulfilling part of the duties of an undertaker.

These notices form something like a running commentary on the incidence of sporting events. As early as 1853 we can observe the anxiety of the Edinburgh & Glasgow company to encourage the traffic to the 'Royal Curling Club Station' outside Perth, where all trains from Edinburgh and Glasgow are to stop 'when the ice is good'; first and second-class day return tickets being issued at the single rates.[57] The hunting traffic was evidently profitable. The North British company provided for it with special trains all through the season from Edinburgh to Linlithgow, Upper Bathgate, Haddington, Dunbar, and Kelso;[58] the Glasgow & South Western from Kilwinning to Ayr and Cassilis, 'and back if required'.[59] Much larger crowds to be conveyed to football matches – which became a common task for almost all British railways throughout the winter – and to race-meetings.[60] The Glasgow & South Western's 'General Notices for Bogside Races' (near Irvine) display to us a complete set of the workings required for one not very large event of that sort.[61]

7

The whole of the literature of operations that has been reviewed in this study comprises a set of orders, as terse and as seldom explained as military commands. On first acquaintance, these orders make very dry reading. But, taken all together and read with care, they show us how railways were *made to work*, in normal service, as no other documents can. They give us the sole complete view of the ceaseless motion on which the social and economic life of Victorian Britain largely depended. The task of interpreting them, knitting them together, trying to form some estimate of what the running of these trains may have cost – in capital expenditure and wages and maintenance, set against receipts – is a complicated and challenging one, but it can bring its own rewards. As for the dryness, it is after all (or it certainly ought to be) one of the main purposes of historical inquiry to make dry bones live.

NOTES

1 R942/1.

2 R942/3.

3 R951/455.

4 SRO, BT/TT(S)/53/23, p. 72.

5 1888 ed., 384–7.

6 RM, 10 (1902) 12–22.

7 C. Travis, D.R. Lamb, and J.A. Jenkinson, *Practical Railway Working* (1915), 78–83.

8 R.J. Irving, for example, in his admirable economic history of the North Eastern Railway does not seem to have consulted these timetables when discussing freight traffic and line occupation (241–3).

9 SRO, BT/TT (S)/59/14; TT(S)/54/64.

10 SRO, BR/TT(S)/60/17.

11 The 1857 book by Turntable Publications, Sheffield, in 1981; the 1909 one by Ian Allan (n.d.).

12 M. Clarke, *The Brookwood Necropolis Railway* (1983).

13 They are referred to in these notes as I, II, and III respectively.

14 II. 146, 182.

15 II. 150.

16 See RTC, 43–5.

17 I. 44.

18 III. 50, 26; I. 130.

19 III. 43–50.

20 I. 39.

21 II. 24. For the powder mills see M Robbins, *Middlesex* (1953), 224, 301.

22 II. 182.

23 II. 185.

24 I. 130.

25 I. 136–7.

26 III. 162–3.

27 I. 22.

28 This process can be profitably traced in minute detail in J.V. Gough, *The Midland Railway: a Chronology* (1989).

29 See VRY, 92–3.

30 R968/79.

31 An example of such a service permitted in the 1850s is cited in M. Robbins, *North London Railway* (4th ed., 1953), 3.

32 See I. Peaty, *Brewery Railways* (1985), 89–91.

33 R970/15, p. 52.

34 Working timetable, August 1857, 26.

35 Acc. Drem, North British Railway, 12 November 1866: PP 1867, lxii. 80.

36 PGA 52–3 Vict., cap. 57, sect. 1.

37 H.A. Vallance, *Highland Railway* (4th ed., 1985), 111.

38 PP 1886, lviii. 362.

39 R963/100.

40 Working timetable, October 1920: R923/47.

41 P. Lefèvre and R. Cerbelaud, *Les chemins de fer* (1888), 225, 235–6.

42 MacDermot, i. 344–5.

43 G.P. Neele, *Railway Reminiscences* (1904). 305–6.

44 See VRY, 241.

45 Working timetable: marshalling circular. October 1912. p. 3: R946/19.

46 Working timetable, 1897: R933.

47 See RTC, 45–52, 128–9.

48 Working timetable, London & South Western Railway, June 1909, I. 15–27.

49 Working timetable, July 1912, pp. 169, 172–3, 177 (Leicester University Library, AJ 281).

50 SRO/TT(S)/15, pp. 55.

51 Appendix, 1882: R1136/63, pp. 37–9.

52 R1116/3.

53 *Railway Year Book*, 1902, 117.

54 For a sample of those run in 1913 see VRY, 307–8.

55 SRO, BR/NBR/30/2, 17 June 1890.

56 SRO, BR/GNS/30/1, no. 1249.

57 SRO, BR/TT(S)/53/1, p. 11.

58 SRO, BR/NBR/30/1.

59 SRO, BR/GSW/30/2, 28 February 1910.

60 See VRY, 301–3.

61 As in note 59, 29 October 1910.

14

ACCIDENT REPORTS, 1840–90

I

The reports of railway accidents, made at the time when they occurred, fall broadly into three classes.

Some were produced by journalists at once, to form part of the current news of the day. They might be valuable where they included statements of eye-witnesses or of people travelling in the trains concerned. But the journalist himself was dealing with testimony at second hand, and he had to be the judge of what that was worth. He naturally tended to emphasise the most striking elements in what he was told: horrifying, pathetic, occasionally miraculous. It is never possible to take a newspaper report, compiled in these circumstances, as a trustworthy account of what had really happened in an accident, still less of what had caused it. But the report may reflect local opinion usefully, for example on the alleged danger presented by a level crossing at which an accident occurred.

The second kind of report was contained in the accounts of the coroner's inquests that had to be held if anybody died in consequence of the accident. The verdict of the jury – which might be of manslaughter against an engine-driver, for instance, or a signalman – was recorded officially; the rest of the proceedings were not, though they were often reproduced from shorthand notes in the local newspapers. One thing gave them a special value. The proceedings at inquests were, in the legal phrase, 'absolutely privileged'. No lawsuit for defamation could be founded on any document produced at the inquest or on any statement made at it verbally when the actions of individuals or their responsibility came under discussion. It should also be observed that verdicts returned at inquests were sometimes serviceable to the companies, as one of the Board of Trade inspectors remarked, 'in concealing the mismanagement of the company from the public'[1] or by placing the blame for an accident wholly on one of its servants.

The third class of these reports must carry much the heaviest weight with us now, and it is the one that is chiefly to be discussed here. Under the Regulation Act of 1840 the Board of Trade was authorised to appoint 'any proper person or persons to inspect any railway, ... [who should] be allowed to enter upon and examine the line, its working, engines, and vehicles', and the companies were required to notify the Board of any accident to their trains involving personal injury.[2] Two years later their obligation to notify was restricted to 'accidents attended with serious personal injury to the public'. But they were now to be reported within 48 hours of their occurrence, and the companies were told to list all accidents of every kind, whether they injured anyone or not, making returns of them to the Board of Trade at whatever times it should fix.[3] Neither of these statutes laid it down that the Board's inspectors should investigate or report on accidents, but the companies evidently accepted that this was implicit in the inspectors' powers to 'examine' the working of the railway, and its equipment. None of them seems ever to have refused to allow an inspector to inquire into an accident. The first of all those reported on by any of them had occurred, indeed, before the Act of 1840 had gone into force.

This may appear odd. The companies resented government interference with their business. Why then should they have permitted these investigations to be made – even quite frequently assisting them – when no law compelled them to do so? There are two answers to that question, and they should be taken together.

H.W. Parris has pointed out that the inspectors' reports – like the verdicts at inquests – were sometimes helpful to the companies, by ascribing the blame for accidents to mistakes made by their servants rather than to defects in their own arrangements for working the lines, and that the inspectors' careful inquiries might allay public alarm about the state of their structures or machines.[4] Moreover, the shrewder managers of the companies must have realised that if they obstructed the inspectors' investigations they would be likely to force the government to secure compulsory powers in the matter that might be unpleasantly comprehensive. On its side, the government was not anxious to assume such powers, for that would involve it in some responsibility for the working of the railways, which it had no desire to incur. It was only in 1871 that the Board of Trade was statutorily authorised to send inspectors to look into accidents, not merely those involving members of the public but any 'attended with loss of life or personal injury to any person whomsoever'. That is to say, the investigations were now to extend to accidents producing death or injury to the companies' own servants.[5]

The inspectors had a multitude of tasks to perform. Perhaps the most important of them at the beginning, when the railway system was growing at its fastest, was that of examining lines and structures before they were brought into use. Here they had well-defined powers, written into the Regulation Act of 1842. No railway might be opened to public traffic unless it had been inspected by one of these men, and passed by him. Should a line be opened without an inspector's certificate, the company made itself liable to a penalty of £20 for every day on which the line carried traffic.[6] Perhaps the most outrageous breach of this rule was committed by the Midland company, which operated a very short but important section of line at Leeds for eight years, uninspected, until an accident occurred there in 1880; whereupon the Board pointed out that the company had laid itself open to a fine that by then amounted to £60,000. It did not press the matter any further when the inspection had at last taken place and the company had admitted it was in the wrong.[7] In general the regulation was obeyed, and the inspector's objections were met or – very rarely –over-ruled (see p.220).

The inspectors were also called upon sometimes to act as mediators in conflicts between companies, or between companies and their customers: gradually resolving a serious dispute between the Grand Junction and the Manchester &

Birmingham Railways that emerged in 1842,[8] quietening the anxieties felt by some people at Guildford about the arrangements made by the London & South Western for the accommodation of coaches meeting trains at Woking.[9]

2

Who were these inspectors? The Board of Trade was authorised to appoint any 'proper person' it chose to inspect a railway on its behalf; but, with a single exception, every man who acted in this capacity was an officer of the Royal Engineers. The first of them was Sir Frederic Smith, an Engineer then currently engaged under the Treasury as one of the Commissioners reporting on the rival routes proposed for railway communication between England and Scotland. He was charged with the whole task of inspection, but he had assistants for a short time in 1840, Lt. Col. R. Thomson and Capt. S.C. Melhuish, and two inspections were undertaken for him by a civilian, Peter Barlow, professor of mathematics at the Royal Military Academy, Woolwich. Smith was succeeded at the Board of Trade by a distinguished man, Charles Pasley, who served from 1842 to 1846. During his first two years he made all the investigations of accidents himself, until in 1844 he was joined by a second inspector, Joshua Coddington, who went on to become secretary of the Caledonian Railway in 1847. The normal complement of inspectors was now increased to three, and it stood at that figure for the rest of the nineteenth century except in 1867–76, when there were four. That their number was larger in those years was entirely due to the heavy burden of their work in reporting on accidents, which were more numerous then than ever before or since. There were altogether fifteen of these soldiers who served as inspectors between 1840 and 1891, Henry Tyler and William Yolland being employed in the work for 24 and 31 years respectively.[10]

Pasley is know to us better than all the rest of them, for he kept an extensive diary.[11] He was a soldier with some of the instincts and talents of a literary man. Much earlier in his life he had produced a little book on military policy that caught the eye – most improbably – of Jane Austen, who thought he wrote 'with extraordinary force and spirit'.[12] More recently, he had published an important book on the use and manufacture of cement and concrete in building works, which brought him into widespread notice on the Continent as well as in his own country.[13] To a greater extent than any other of these inspectors he was an intellectual, with a lively, wide-ranging mind; a student of languages, for example, including Welsh and Irish. Though he was over 60 when he first turned away from military and civil engineering to the mechanical working of railways, he was still in full vigour, and that comes over in his published reports and his private diary.

The other inspectors include one who took a very broad view of railway management. This was Tyler, who in later years became a director of the Grand Trunk Railway of Canada and subsequently its president, as well as chairman of the board of the British division of the Westinghouse Brake Company. Of the rest,

Yolland was perhaps the most entirely devoted to his single task, becoming the archetypal *inspector* of them all. He went further than any of his colleagues in advocating the extension of the government's direct power over railways. He was the only one of these men who died (in 1885) while still in office, encouraged perhaps in his last years when he saw that the cautious Board of Trade itself was beginning to support the policy he favoured most.

3

The formal procedure arising from a railway accident quickly became stereotyped. The company on whose line it had occurred reported it to the Board of Trade, which would – if it appeared sufficiently important – appoint one of the inspectors to investigate it. He communicated his findings to the Board, and it might send a copy of what he had said to the company, together with any questions it wished to ask arising from what had happened, or such admonitions as it thought necessary. Sometimes the company would reply, protesting against what the inspector had said and trying to controvert it, and that might elicit a rejoinder from the Board of Trade. In due course the report, together with any additional documents it had given rise to, was printed and laid before Parliament. At first the reports were, in theory at least, confidential,[14] but in 1854 they began to be furnished to the press, and from 1860 onwards they were put on sale to the public.[15] No considerable attention seems to have been paid to them in the country at large. 'The official reports go to the Board of Trade', said one commentator, 'and so into Blue Books and oblivion.'[16] However that may have been, the doings of the companies and their servants, scrutinised with care by the inspectors, were now no longer kept secret. From 1871 onwards it became the practice for the Board to issue a general report on all the accidents that had occurred in the previous year, analysing their causes and surveying them as a whole.

In making their reports the inspectors had to pick their way carefully, in order to antagonise the companies no more than was necessary, while at the same time doing justice to the men. And they had to use another kind of caution too, which became more and more pressing in the 1870s and 1880s. They constantly noticed the introduction of new appliances and new methods of working. But they had to beware of taking any responsibility for recommending individual devices – even more, of seeming to advocate one for some commercial reason. That became especially important when various types of continuous brake were under discussion, marketed by competing firms. The Westinghouse company's representatives sometimes pushed its products by means that were clearly improper. Yolland exposed an attempt by one of them, for instance, to suborn a railwayman who was involved in an accident at Blackburn in 1881.[17]

All this necessarily came to raise a broader question: how far did the inspectors' responsibilities extend? If one of them recommended a particular type of appliance in working and a railway company adopted it, would that exonerate the company from blame in the event of its failure? The same issue arose in another part of the inspectors' duties. When one of them had examined a bridge and passed it as suitable for opening, did that then make him answerable for its safety? This question first appeared prominently when the failure of the Dee river bridge at Chester was under investigation in 1847. The Railway Commissioners then produced a minute that set out a very sensible view of their inspectors' duty in such matters:

> 'With respect to retaining walls, bridges, viaducts, and tunnels, he [the inspector] can see only the surface of each work... But the responsibility for the execution of the works, the material parts of which are not exposed to view, must rest with the company and their engineer. As to such portions of the structure no one can form a satisfactory opinion who has not been present during the actual execution of the works, or constantly inspected them in their progress'.[18]

The inspecting officer, G.S. Hutchinson, was the target of a good deal of criticism in 1879–80 for having tested the first Tay bridge insufficiently, when he examined it in February 1878, before its opening. There were plenty of people – among them the designer and builders of the bridge, and the North British Railway – who would have been glad to persuade the public that this most responsible task had been ill performed, and that part of the blame for its collapse must therefore rest on him. But they did not succeed.

These reports provide a commentary on many aspects of engineering, operation, and management, and it is primarily in those terms that they have been treated by railway historians since. Accidents have been recounted and analysed in a number of books, the best of them L.T.C. Rolt's *Red for Danger*, and monographs have been written on several of the most celebrated of them individually.[19] But the reports are not interesting solely for the contributions they offer to the study of technology. It is part of my purpose here to enlarge the view that may be taken of railway accidents, to present them more broadly as records of sudden interruptions of the normal course of life, attending to their causes and consequences and to their effect on public opinion. For this is one of the cases (they are not very common, in spite of all the din made by the manipulators of the media today) in which public opinion was, broadly speaking, right, and the opinions of many of the experts wrong. As Acworth said truly, it provided 'a remarkable testimony to the irresistible force exerted by public opinion even in matters of which it can only pretend to understand the barest outline'.[20] That public opinion had been much influenced – to a large extent it had been moulded – by the inspectors' comments on accidents. It is those that are examined here from 1840 to 1889 when, under the force of the shock administered by the fearful accident at Armagh in Ireland, the British government at last obliged the companies to adopt much more stringent measures for securing the safe operation of their lines.

4

The inspectors' reports begin tentatively; Sir Frederic Smith was feeling his way into railway engineering. His work at the Board of Trade extended over less than eighteen months. The Board included extracts from his reports in its own report to Parliament in 1841. In the very first accident he investigated, on the Hull & Selby Railway, there was no doubt whatever about the cause. An iron casting had been insufficiently secured on a wagon at the front of the train; it dropped off, derailing the carriages behind it, and five people were killed. Smith wasted no words. 'It was quite clear,' he wrote, 'that there was unpardonable neglect in the parties whose business it was to attend to such matters at Selby.'[21]

The first accident of real importance, leading to large consequences, occurred on Christmas Eve 1841. This was the derailment in the Sonning cutting of the Great Western Railway, which killed eight passengers and injured seventeen more. They were all travelling third-class, in open vehicles that lacked spring buffers and had low sides: so when the locomotive was suddenly derailed and stopped, the passengers were pitched out of the train, and there was no barrier to break their fall. Smith's investigation was made instantly, and he wrote his report on Christmas Day. The company admitted that it had been wrong to carry passengers in these conditions. It had already decided, before the accident, to build new vehicles for this purpose, with higher sides and equipped with spring buffers, and promised to expedite the work on them.[22] The accident drew attention to the conditions under which many – indeed most – of these third-class passengers were then being carried. The Board began at once to inquire into the provision made for this kind of travel on all British railways, and it worked steadily towards securing the legislation embodied in Gladstone's Act of 1844.

Smith's work set good precedents. He was not only conscientious, he displayed humanity. When the York & North Midland Railway conveyed men on a flat carriage truck attached to a passenger train from Castleford, and its secretary was questioned about this dangerous practice, he replied that they were not passengers but 'workmen on the line'. Smith's rejoinder was prompt: 'the workmen of the company should not be subjected to the risk to which such a mode of conveyance would expose them in trains moving at high velocities'.[23]

Pasley, who succeeded him, was a different sort of man; outgoing, positive, less cautiously restrained than Smith had usually been in expressing opinions. His forthrightness was put to what might have been an awkward test almost as soon as he took up office, a special inspection of an embankment just north of Swindon that was denounced to the Board of Trade by a private person as unsafe. The risk he now faced was of a collision with the engineer, Brunel, who held all government officials in a high contempt that he never concealed. However, the alarm turned out to be exaggerated, and effective measures had already been taken to repair what had become unsafe owing to a long continuance of exceptionally heavy rain. Pasley noted that Brunel's reports on the matter to the Great Western Railway board were 'strictly accurate, and nothing unfavourable diminished or palliated'.[24] That was not soft soap, but a well-justified comment on Brunel's normal practice.

Many of these early accidents were due to enginemen's carelessness or inexperience, or to defects in the track; and the inspectors considered that a good deal of traffic was being worked at excessively high speeds. Two of them, however, were of very unusual kinds. One was a collision between a mail train and a stage-coach at Bridgwater, fully described in the evidence given to the inspector (Barlow).[25] The other occurred at Barnsley in 1842 and arose from the decision of the North Midland Railway's board to reduce the wages of its enginemen (see further, p.220). Pasley's report includes a lengthy statement covering the careers of the individual men concerned, and its tone is clearly, though quietly, sympathetic to their grievances against the company.[26]

The policy of the Board of Trade in the publication of these reports soon underwent changes. Though it continued to issue the returns of accidents made to it by the companies, those became for a time a bare record of occurrences, only a small number of the inspectors' reports and comments on them being printed. The remainder of those that survive from the 1840s (very few) are to be found only in manuscript at the Public Record Office. Unfortunately the files were drastically 'weeded' at the Board long ago.[27]

A large number of the accidents on which the inspectors reported turn out to be due, as one might expect, principally to errors of judgement and to dereliction of duty. But they very often had to inquire how it was that a man concerned had been led to act as he did. Ought not some superior official to have corrected his fault? Was the delinquent transgressing one of the company's rules? In that case, was the rule worded ambiguously? Was it indeed a sensible one? The inspectors often had to be prepared to investigate and speak about the management of the companies themselves.

Sometimes an official of one of them showed himself to be a fool: George Richardson of the Eastern Counties Railway, for instance, in 1851. He had been responsible for framing regulations that were quite impracticable to carry out, and – worse still – made no proper effort to defend a driver who tried to obey his rules and found himself brought in by a coroner's jury as guilty of manslaughter.[28]

In grappling with the managers and boards of directors of railway companies the inspectors confronted a difficult task. The working men whose actions they inquired into seldom found any effective defenders for 30 years and more – except sometimes the inspectors themselves. A Tamworth signalman, called on to give evidence to the inspector concerning an accident to the Irish Mail that occurred there in 1870, refused to do so except in the presence of a solicitor. His demand was met.[29] He was sounding a note that was heard more clearly towards the end of the century, when the growing trade unions began to look after the interests of some of their members in such situations. The first occasion I have noted on which a union man (in this case from the Amalgamated Society of Railway Servants) was present at one of the inspectors' inquiries and put questions in the course of it was in 1888.[30]

For the companies it was quite a different matter. They had money at their backs. They might consider that the inspector's findings had been unjust, and say so in an official letter to the Board of Trade. Sometimes they would go further, if they thought they could play to a gallery. Hudson's North Midland Railway was doing just that when it embarked on a dispute with the Board in 1842–3, concerned with the effects brought about by a general reduction of wages and the consequent widespread disturbance of the company's staff, leading to the accident that has been mentioned at Barnsley. The North Midland company had not been alone in adopting this practice, at a time of general economic difficulty, and its board was now coming forward to defend the interests of the companies in general. It would probably have done better to keep quiet.[31] On the other hand, in 1849–50, the Manchester Sheffield & Lincolnshire Railway, under pressure from its highly combative engineer John Fowler, demanded that the Railway Commissioners should rescind the decision of their inspector to refuse permission for the opening to public traffic of the Torksey bridge over the Trent. They agreed, and the company won a substantial victory.[32]

5

The most obvious value of these reports lies in their recording and discussion of the technology and management of railways. Those are the matters that have chiefly occupied the attention of the writers of the best books on the subject, the general surveys that have already been referred to and a few specialist studies such as C.H. Hewitson's *Locomotive Boiler Explosions* (1983). But the inspectors' reports also supply much evidence of the conditions in which railwaymen were employed: particularly of the hours of work that were required from them, sometimes for low rates of pay.

These managerial practices began to come under close examination very early: for the first time on the London & South Western Railway in 1843.[33] In 1853 they were being noticed in letters to *The Times*.[34] Next year the criticism was sufficiently familiar for *Punch* to take a hand in it, commenting on an assertion that a London & North Western driver had been worked for 30 hours at a stretch.[35] Two years later the same company's management came in for repeated disapproval from the inspectors; and one of them, Charles Wynne, gave evidence to a parliamentary committee in 1858 on the dangers to passengers arising from this cause.[36] In 1862 the *Lancet* joined in, with statements in the same sense.[37] By the late 1860s both the inspectors and the press were in full cry against the companies, as bad employers in this respect.[38] Certain newspapers sympathetic to the men were printing allegations made by them themselves. Some of those that appeared in *Reynolds's Newspaper* found their way into the first volume of Karl Marx's *Capital*, published in 1867.[39] The first large-scale railway strikes in Britain had occurred almost simultaneously on the Brighton and North Eastern companies' lines in the spring of that year. Both boards of directors stood firm (impelled strongly to do so by their difficulties at a time of financial crisis), and both strikes were crushed. But the men's grievances had now come right out into the open, and the inspectors kept them there from this time onwards: not of course by way of agitation, or of any attempt to interfere in the companies' unquestionable right to manage their own finances, but as the appointed protectors of public safety.

The growth of traffic, both passenger and freight, on the Victorian railways is obvious from the published figures. Those figures do not become reliable until the mid-1850s, but in 1856–89 the numbers of passenger journeys made annually in the United Kingdom (excluding those of season-ticket holders) may be seen to have multiplied six times over, the tonnage of freight that was carried by 4½, and the number of miles travelled by passenger and freight trains by 4¾. The railway system carrying all this traffic increased in length during these years by no more than a factor of 2½, however.[40] The intensity of use of each mile of track had therefore been doubled. As the system came to be more heavily occupied, the dangers arising from all movements on it increased.

The inspectors commented on this growth, and its implications, with increasing frequency after 1870. They urged the importance of providing more ample siding accommodation, partly in order to allow the freight work at stations to be carried on entirely clear of the through lines and also for the purpose of receiving slow trains, shunted into them to let quicker ones pass.[41] That kind of movement, however, was itself a source of danger, particularly when the train to be shunted was a long and crowded excursion.[42]

Such risks as these could be reduced by the improvement of points and signals. New systems, promising well, were evolved with the aid of the telegraph and of other electrically-operated machinery. Our present business is not with this technology itself but with the reception accorded to it by the inspectors, keeping watch on accidents that new devices might have prevented, and by the railway companies, faced with the expenditure required for installing them.

Each new invention had first to prove itself: so the inspectors needed to be cautious in recommending even those that seemed most hopeful. They had, for example, reported very often on accidents in which the desirability of affording some means of communication between passengers, guards, and drivers while the train was moving had been clearly demonstrated, and they had considered many appliances that were designed to offer that communication. Public alarm at the want of it mounted from 1863 onwards, in consequence of a series of horrifying outrages that occurred in the compartments of railway carriages, and in 1868 Disraeli's government included in its Regulation of Railways Bill a requirement that every passenger train running more than twenty miles without stopping should be equipped with 'such efficient means of communication between the passengers and servants of the company in charge of the trains as the Board of Trade may approve'. But that clause showed the blandest disregard of the technical difficulties involved in devising any 'efficient means' – quite inexcusable, for they had been set out very plainly by Tyler in a paper laid before Parliament in 1864.[43] This clause was no more than a politicians' cynical device to quieten clamour. The railway companies reiterated their opinion that no system yet produced was suitable for general introduction. One that found some favour had been invented by T.E. Harrison, chief engineer of the North Eastern Railway, using a cord and pulley, but the inspectors refused to recommend it, or any other system either. The Board itself and the government went against their advice, and the Act laid it down that satisfactory equipment must be fitted by 1 April 1869.[44] The general managers of the companies then felt obliged to recommend the Board to accept Harrison's system. It was widely installed, and quickly found unreliable; so unreliable (as accident reports repeatedly demonstrated) that the Board was compelled to withdraw the approval given to it.

The inspectors alone came out of this sorry business well. They had never trusted Harrison's system, and in that they had been proved right. The long farce that then followed – the companies being required to install a system approved by the Board, and the Board now declining to approve any[45] – does not concern us here. It was brought to an end only after 1900.[46]

Among the other technical problems the inspectors discussed most frequently after 1860 one is of particular interest, in showing that they were not always urging the companies to take up new practices, that they sometimes felt that innovations had been adopted before they had fully proved themselves. The use of steel in railway work provides some examples.

The first rails made wholly of that material were laid down at Derby in 1857 and at Crewe four years later;[47] steel axles and boilers were tried out on British locomotives in the early 1860s.[48] But the inspectors were long held back by doubts of the dependability of the new material. In 1879 Hutchinson put it in this way, writing of an accident caused by the breakage of a steel rail: 'the great difficulty in the use of steel [is] that it is almost impossible to secure a uniformity of quality, at any rate without paying prices that would render its employment practically impossible'.[49] That caution must surely have been a little over-stated, for even a company so conservative and economically-minded as the Great Western had already, when those words were written, relaid four-fifths of its main line with steel rails and virtually discontinued the use of iron for this purpose altogether.[50] And yet – on Hutchinson's side – steel did not come to be generally regarded as reliable in British locomotive building until the 1890s. Beyer Peacock was the first railway firm in the country engaged in this work to install its own steel foundry at Manchester, and that was not done until 1899.[51]

What the inspectors could sometimes do very usefully, however, was to state a demand that became evident to them in the course of their work, for a new mechanical appliance that might help to meet a danger, or even remove it. In the late 1880s they repeatedly urged the need for one that should ease the safe working of trains in fog: some form of audible signal, to be heard by an engine driver in his cab, set off automatically by mechanical means from the track.[52] If a mechanical aid of this sort could be adopted, it would then be possible to dispense with the dangerous labour of the companies' men undertaken in laying down fog signals, when the need arose. Here was a direct challenge thrown down to the signalling companies; an authoritative statement of the urgent need for a new device. Again and again in the history of railways challenges of that kind have served to stimulate the wits of commercial men, of inventive engineers, sometimes of the companies' own servants. But there were very considerable difficulties to be overcome here and it was not until 1906 that this demand began to be satisfactorily met, by means of the apparatus laid down first in that year on the Great Western branch lines to Henley and Fairford.[53]

The inspectors came to assume, in the forthright manner of their time, that every accident had a discoverable cause. They could not believe that at the outset, when they had to learn as one might say the grammar of their task; but within the next twenty years they built up a sufficient body of experience and knowledge in these matters to allow them to feel that they ought to be able to find an explanation – probable, if not certain – for every accident they investigated. In reports of the 1860s, 1870s, and 1880s I have found only a single clear case in which the inspector spoke of an accident as a matter of chance that could be accounted for in no way whatever. Having investigated one at Eastleigh in 1889, when the evidence 'was given in a remarkably clear and straightforward manner', the inspector (Marindin) concluded that 'this slight collision was due to a pure accident of an uncommon character… I am unable to explain how the coupling came loose'.[54]

The inspectors' verdicts were sometimes contested at the time of their publication, and a number of them have been criticised since.[55] But any unprejudiced reader who will work through a series of these reports, as they come, must surely be struck by the patience the inspectors display in their investigations, as well as by their intelligence and fairness in reaching their conclusions and apportioning responsibilities between the men involved and their employers. Let us look at a few of those from a single year by way of a sample: the year 1873, in which the number of inspectors' inquiries into railway accidents in the United Kingdom reached its peak, at 247.

6

The story opens in Ireland, on the Cork & Bandon Railway, with a great storm of rain on the night of 15 January, which washed away the track at the approach to Bandon, derailing a locomotive hauling a passenger train. The company was very poor, its rails and rolling stock both unsatisfactory. Its resident engineer was mortally ill and died on the day of the inquiry. By a further piece of bad luck for the railway, the train involved in the accident happened to be carrying the magistrates, lawyers, and journalists to Bandon quarter sessions. They were naturally 'irate', and later in the same year some influential persons in the district memorialised the Board of Trade on the condition of the railway. The same inspector (Rich) went to investigate the complaints, and thought they were substantiated. The rails were flimsy, the engines worn out (only four of the eight that the company owned were able to work), and many of the carriages ancient. The company stated that no fatality had occurred on the railway since it was opened in 1849. Rich's dry comment was that this must have been due to 'the great care exercised by the engine drivers in conducting the trains, and to the attention of the men in charge of the permanent way'.[56]

A more shocking carelessness of its passengers' lives was shown by a very different sort of company, at Mansion House underground station in London a month or two later. The lines there had been opened in two instalments, as it appeared without the Board's sanction. The Metropolitan District company stated untruthfully that they were worked on the absolute block system, the safest principle then known. 'The circumstances connected with the opening of the line... are, to say the least, very peculiar', wrote Yolland, 'and if anyone had been killed in this collision or may thereafter be killed at the same spot, a liability might attach to persons who do not expect it'. Did the company's board and senior officers pay any attention to that steely hint? Others of the same kind were thrown out at several companies in later years.[57]

There were further signs in 1873 that the inspectors were feeling they must make their warnings to the companies louder and clearer; not only to small companies, but to the largest too. Believing that an accident on the London & North Western Railway at Birmingham could have been averted if adequate brakes had been in use, Yolland observed: 'there is very little prospect of these trains being so fitted until the railway companies are compelled to do so'.[58] At the public court of inquiry into the disaster at Wigan on the same railway, where much was said about the high speed at which trains were then being run owing to the competition between the two main lines to Scotland, Tyler took occasion to remark that in coaching days, when drivers raced and a fatal accident occurred, *both* were liable to prosecution for manslaughter, going on to ask whether the same principle might not be held applicable to railway companies.[59]

The conditions under which the companies employed their servants went on attracting the inspectors' vigilant attention. They were always on the alert to note cases in which men were on duty for excessively long hours. A notable one occurred during this year on the North Staffordshire Railway in which a guard did not apply his brake, at the cost of his own life. His failure, said Yolland, 'was probably due to over-fatigue or weariness, as he had at the time been nineteen hours on duty'. One of the drivers involved had been at work for 32 hours, and his fireman was asleep. It has to be said that there was an exceptional blockage of traffic at the time on this and all lines leading into Crewe (on the London & North Western system); but the inspector was right to say that nothing could justify arrangements like these.[60]

The railways' traffic was increasing particularly fast at this moment. In 1871–5 the mileage of trains run in the United Kingdom (passenger and freight together) grew by 15.6%, over a system that grew in length by no more than 8.3%.[61] The overcrowding of some lines, not on special occasions but as a matter of daily occurrence, was becoming notorious. At Temple Meads station in Bristol, for instance, two accidents had to be investigated within six weeks in 1873. Tyler then reported that the enlargement of the station and the improvement of its complicated junctions was gradually going ahead, but that recommendations for these most necessary changes had been made again and again over the past ten years.[62] The state of things at Bolton was even worse. A very small rebuilding of the Lancashire & Yorkshire company's passenger station there had taken place in 1871, but that had done nothing towards meeting the demands of traffic on the move. Some trains were so timed as to leave within three minutes of each other or less, in flat disregard of the regulation that there should be at least five minutes' interval between one train and the next. The company laid down that regulation, and was discharging some of its servants for failing to obey it. Tyler said that those men could not possibly be blamed with any justice in these circumstances, and added: 'it is useless to recommend any detailed improvements for the working of such traffic under such conditions'.[63] The Lancashire & Yorkshire company was perhaps worse directed at that time than any other large one in England. Though the dividends on its Ordinary shares had been good ever since 1864 – in 1870–2 they had averaged 7³/₄% – it treated its customers and its men as if it had been handicapped by poverty. Presently, after 1880, its management grew much better. Yet it is to be noted that the changes at Bolton called for by Tyler in 1873 were not carried through to their completion until 1906.[64]

The inspectors did not hesitate to assign the responsibility for accidents wherever they found that established beyond doubt: 'the collision was entirely due to the misconduct of the Greenfield signalman in sending the Oldham train forward';[65] 'the occurrence of this collision is attributable to a very gross neglect of duty on the part of the driver, Kelly, who approached Irvine station without exercising the most ordinary caution';[66] 'the whole blame in this case must, in my opinion, fall upon the stationmaster at Penistone'.[67] Such accidents as these were however a minority. More often the inspector found that several men were at fault, though he could not always confidently apportion the shares of responsibility between them. Sometimes one or more of the men concerned or of the witnesses brought forward to testify on their behalf must plainly have been lying like Ananias.[68]

By way of contrast, there was one occasion in this year 1873 when, having attributed a minor accident to the negligence of a driver and fireman, an inspector felt impelled to salute the normal conduct of traffic, at an exceedingly busy station, by the company and its servants alike. Yolland pointed out that 386 trains were worked daily into and out of Moorgate Street station, which was then the Metropolitan Railway's eastern terminus. 'When I state that every in and out train necessarily involves the passage of an empty engine in order to get to its siding or to hook on to its train, this total of 386 is just doubled; and I think it reflects great credit on the company's management, and speaks volumes in favour of the care and attention of the company's servants engaged in working the traffic, that so few mishaps have occurred at this terminal station'.[69] The underground railway had been at work for ten years then, and Londoners had come to take it very much for granted. It is to be hoped that a few of them paid attention to this resounding tribute, from a man who was uniquely well qualified to render it.[70]

7

The reports give us many incidental glimpses of the more general life of the country, in which the railways came to play so great a part.

They call attention to some dates in the calendar for example, now almost forgotten but familiar in the Victorian age, brought down from the immemorial past and still determining then for many people in the British Isles the customary rhythm of the year. Traffic was certain to be heavy on 'the day after Martinmas, when the servants in the neighbourhood travel who are changing places'. In 1869 this pressure helped to cause an accident at Filey in north Yorkshire.[71] Another movement of labour, on a much greater scale, took place annually out of Ireland towards midsummer: that of men travelling, particularly from the far western counties, to work in the English harvest. The handling of this traffic presented the Midland Great Western company with considerable difficulties, leading to two accidents at Ballyhaunis in Co. Mayo in the 1880s. After the second of them the inspector was furnished by the company with a very interesting set of exact figures of the volume of this travelling, which he included in his report.[72]

Those were general movements of rural labour. But the reports also disclose to us, again and again, the remarkable *immobility* of many railway servants. In 1878 George Wild, who had driven railway engines for 39 years, said to Hutchinson: 'I have been all my life on the Newcastle & Carlisle line'.[73] Next year, at Bishopstoke, one of the original servants of the London & Southampton Railway appears, also with 39 years' service, 33 of them at that station.[74] Or, turning form the elderly to the very young, we get some light from these reports on the minimum age of boys employed in railway service. Thirteen seems to have been the usual age at which they entered it (a lad of 13½ appears at Pontardulais in 1872 who has, to the inspector's evident disapproval, 'the responsible charge of facing points and level-crossing gates');[75] but in 1876 we come across a platelayer at Heeley, outside Sheffield, who had begun work on the Midland Railway at the age of eleven.[76]

The reports present us with a gallery of individual men and women going about their ordinary work or pitched into sudden misfortune. Sometimes a single figure catches one's eye strongly for a moment. Here is a poor woman living in a lock-keeper's cottage on the Leeds & Liverpool Canal who crosses the railway daily to carry a supply of horehound beer* to the thirsty workers at Kirkstall Forge, suddenly crushed between the buffers of two wagons on the line.[77] A Neath & Brecon

* A bitter drink made from the herb horehound, *marrubium vulgare*.

company's driver, with appalling injuries, implores his fireman 'to knock his brains out'.[78] A young woman, overcome with train-sickness, leans out of the window and strikes her head against two of the heavy pouches waiting at the lineside to be picked up by the next mail train, dying a few hours later in hospital at Carlisle.[79] Or – nothing tragic here – we come upon a cunning little passenger, spoken with by a guard after an accident at Stafford, 'who said he was slightly hurt and wished it was worse as a friend of his had made the company pay, and he would do the same'.[80] Sometimes the speech of the men giving their evidence is reported word for word, with a photographic precision. At one point we are confronted with five closely-packed pages of it from the Mid-Wales Railway, the fireman painfully anxious not to criticise his driver (who has died) for drinking on the journey.[81] On the Carnarvonshire Railway we hear of much junketing before it was opened, passenger trains being run illegally by the contractors until one of them meets with an accident, killing six people.[82] On the same line we observe the special traffic going to Penygroes for an Eisteddfod in 1872, and an accident arising from it at Chwilog.[83]. Other special events of many kinds figure here not infrequently, as mishaps befall trains run in conjunction with them: Henley Regatta, for example,[84] Doncaster Cup Day,[85] the big Volunteer reviews that had begun early in the 1860s.[86]

These reports are one of the prime sources for our knowledge of excursion traffic, in revealing the scale to which that business grew in the Early Victorian age; most valuable of all in that they deal with a perfectly random sample of it – with the small minority of excursion trains that happened to meet with accidents.[87] The numbers of passengers to be conveyed were sometimes very large; so that the crowds at the stations, both going out and coming back, might get beyond the control of the staff.[88] Those numbers often proved much greater than had been provided for. (Few companies restrained themselves so wisely as the North Eastern did,[89] by limiting the number of tickets issued to the extent of the accommodation in the carriages.) More vehicles would then be put on, making the trains unwieldy, or extra trains might have to be run, not foreseen. At Colne 2,453 tickets were issued for a trip to the Bellevue Gardens, Manchester, in September 1860, requiring three trains instead of one, and that led to a serious accident at Helmshore. In the course of his inquiry the alert inspector (Yolland) elicited some interesting information about the cost of running these trains and the revenue accruing from them. The conclusion arising from his report is quite clear. It is useless to try to restrict the growth of these excursions, more useless still to think of doing away with them on the grounds that they are frivolous or dangerous, as some railway chairmen and managers wished. They have come to stay. What matters now is to see that this large traffic is conveyed with care, in safety.[90]

8

That is an example of the thinking of the inspectors at its best and most effective. They came to take a wide view of railway working, of its rationale and of the consequences that arose from it, as well as of the demands that the companies had to meet from their customers, rich and poor. But they avoided economic and moral reflections on social conduct. They set themselves to demonstrate and explain practice, on the part of all those who might have been responsible for the ill consequences that they were investigating, from directors down to platelayers and signalboys. The practice they were looking at was, in nine cases out of ten, one that was meant to be suitable for application by men of average abilities to a highly responsible task.

Their work in reporting on accidents was always an inquiry either into misfortune, or, much more commonly, into error, occasionally carelessness or irresponsibility that amounted to criminal error. As performed by these inspectors it was exacting, and it must sometimes have been painfully wearisome. But there is little evidence that their tempers were frayed by it, and when that did happen it was nearly always the misdeeds of the companies that brought their irritation to the surface. Investigating a collision on the Great Northern Railway between Peterborough and Spalding in 1872, in which one of the guards was killed, the inspector found that block-working was suspended at night, no signals whatever being shown. To change that thrifty practice would have increased the cost of working a little, and that, as he observed sardonically, would be 'a serious consideration to a company which is about to pay 8¾% to its shareholders from the last half-year's receipts'.[91] On the other hand, when Moon, chairman of the London & North Western Railway, observed that the Board of Trade was 'as responsible for railway accidents as the railways were', Tyler picked a good occasion for his rejoinder to this outrageous nonsense and delivered it with admirable suavity.[92]

For all the protests and criticisms that the inspectors' activities called forth – most naturally from the people they themselves criticised – their words took on an authority that the whole railway world had to recognise. Yolland's concentrated attack on the loose management of the North Eastern Railway, shown up in a series of accidents that occurred in the autumn of 1870, undoubtedly helped to cause the dismissal of the general manager of that company (see pp.126–30). It was a striking illustration of the power these men had come to wield; not because they were greedy for it but because the collective work of them all enabled them to analyse clearly what they saw, to attribute blame and praise dispassionately, and to advise on the means of rectifying what had gone wrong.

9

It is perhaps fitting to take farewell of these Victorian inspectors with a tribute to Tyler, who did much to enhance the public regard for their work during his long service at the Board of Trade, and to draw attention to one aspect of his conduct that particularly characterised him. The reports on accidents made in these years were written by fifteen men (disregarding those whose work as inspectors extended over three years or less). Tyler's are distinguished again and again by the sympathy he shows for the railwaymen whose work he was called on to appraise. There is nothing in the least sentimental about it, and when he detects bad work he will condemn it plainly enough, even pungently. He does not hesitate to write off a signalman as 'an utterly unfit man for performing such duties',[93] and he always declares that where even the most sophisticated machinery is in use it is necessary that the men working it shall be kept under discipline, strictly enforced. 'An inferior system, under good discipline', he once wrote, 'tends to better results than a superior system without good discipline'.[94] But that does not relieve the companies from their duty to install better equipment as soon as its value has been clearly proved. He goes to the limits of what he can properly say in defence of a Caledonian Railway pointsman, awaiting his trial on a charge of culpable homicide. Here again he finds it is the refusal to supply satisfactory equipment for controlling the traffic on a heavily-used main line that is to blame for the accident, rather than a failure on the part of this man, or any other one of the company's servants.[95] His insistence that justice should be done to the men involved in the accidents that he reported on appears throughout the whole of his work as an inspector. It is to be seen as early as 1855, only two years after his appointment.[96] In his last long report on an accident, written in 1877, he makes his feeling for the driver of a Great Northern express train (who had died in the accident) perfectly clear: 'if any good system of continuous brakes had been at the disposal of the engine-driver, he could have pulled his train up in time'.[97] Other inspectors evinced sympathies of the same sort too.[98] But Tyler gave expression to his more freely and frequently than any of his colleagues. An attentive survey of his work shows him as a wise and humane judge.

As they struggled with their task, coming new to it in the 1840s and 1850s, the inspectors had to meet with a good many harsh observations, in particular from those responsible for the management of the companies, who were bound to dislike these licensed critics. But the inspectors were soldiers and they soldiered on, learning from their mistakes, building upon experience, attending steadily to the performance of duty. They have a secure place beside other groups of public servants, to whose work more general attention has been given by historians, such as the inspectors of factories and mines, and the medical officers of health; all honourable bodies of men to whom the Victorians came to be deeply indebted. We remain indebted to them and their successors still.

NOTES

1. L. James, *Law of the Railway* (1980), 364; acc. North Eastern Railway, Brockley Whins, 6 December 1870: PP 1871, lx. 311.

2. PGA, 3 & 4 Vict., cap. 97, sects. 3, 5.

3. PGA, 5 & 6 Vict., cap. 55, sects. 7, 8.

4. GR, 43.

5. PGA, 34 & 35 Vict., cap. 78, sect. 6.

6. PGA, 5 & 6 Vict., cap. 55, sects. 4–7.

7. Acc. Midland Railway, Leeds, 21 December 1880: PP 1881, lxxx. 279–85.

8. GR, 38–40.

9. PP 1843, xlvii. 223–34.

10. A list of them, prepared by Lt.-Col. A.H.L. Mount (not quite free from inaccuracies), is given in *Railway Inspection* (pub. *Railway Gazette*, 1946), 19. Further biographical particulars of most of the men discussed here will be found in GR, 232–4.

11. See H. Parris, 'A Civil Servant's Diary, 1841–6' (*Public Administration*, 38, 1960, 369–80) and 'Pasley's Diary: a Neglected Source of Railway History' (JTH 6, 1963–4, 14–23).

12. *Letters*, ed. R.W. Chapman (2nd ed., 1952), 292.

13. *Observations on Limes, Calcareous Cements, Mortars, Stuccos, and Concrete* (1838; 2nd ed., 1847).

14. See PP 1842, xli. 110; GR, 92, 145.

15. This new practice is disclosed by the printing of the sale price on the title-page.

16. *The Influence of Railway Travelling on Public Health* (pub. *The Lancet*, 1862), 125.

17. Acc. Lancashire & Yorkshire Railway, Blackburn, 3 August 1881: PP 1882, lx. 184, 191. See also VRY, 96.

18. PP 1847, lxiii. 266–7.

19. See Ottley, Supplement, nos. 11495–11501.

20. W.M. Acworth, *Railways of England* (5th ed., 1900), 351; see also 104, note.

21. PP 1841, xxv. 196.

22. PP 1842, xli. 113–16.

23. PP 1842, xli. 122.

24. PP 1842, xli. 127.

25. Acc. Bristol & Exeter Railway, Bridgwater, 11 September 1841: PP 1842, xli. 99–102, 365.

26. Acc. North Midland Railway, Barnsley, 12 January 1843: PP 1843, xlvii. 264–76.

27. They are in class MT6. See D.B. Wardle, 'Sources for the History of Railways at the Public Record Office': JTH 2(1955–6) 214–34; esp. 217, 219.

28. Acc. Eastern Counties Railway, Ponders End, 8 January 1851: PP 1852, xlviii. 144–5.

29. Acc. London & North Western Railway, Tamworth, 4 September 1870: PP 1871, lx. 231.

30. Acc. North Eastern Railway, Harrogate, 28 April 1888: PP 1888, lxxxviii. 364.

31. See note 26 and M. Robbins, *Points and Signals* (1967), 132–9.

32. The voluminous documents in this dispute are printed in PP 1850, xxxi. 100–19.

33. Acc. London & South Western Railway, Nine Elms, 22 May 1843: PP 1844, xli. 43.

34. *The Times*, 20, 27 October 1853.

35. *Punch*, 27 (1854) 63.

36. PP 1857–8, xiv. 577.

37. *Influence of Railway Travelling*, 130.

38. P.S. Bagwell, *The Railwaymen* (1963), 36–40; P.W. Kingsford, *Victorian Railwaymen* (1970), 115–19.

39. Everyman ed., 255–6. It is interesting to notice the rhetorical exaggeration in what Marx has to say on the matter. He refers to a London coroner's jury inquiring into 'a terrible railway accident, hurrying hundreds of passengers into the other world'. At the time when he wrote the largest number of deaths arising from any British railway accident had been, not hundreds but 28 (Clayton Tunnel, 1861).

40. B.R. Mitchell and P. Deane, *Abstract of British Historical Statistics* (1962) 225–9.

41. See for example accs. Glasgow & South Western Railway, Maxwelltown, 4 August 1871 (PP 1872, lii. 234); Lancashire & Yorkshire Railway, Todmorden, 11 January 1872, when 'the line in each direction was absolutely blocked with trains' (*ibid.*, 362); Great Western Railway, Kingsbridge Road, 8 June 1878 (PP 1878–9, lxii. 104).

42. Great Northern Railway, Biggleswade, 22 August 1871 (PP 1872, lii. 248–9); Midland Railway, Crosby Garrett, 12 July 1888 (PP 1888, lxxxviii. 460).

43. PP 1865, i. 17–29.

44. PGA 31 & 32 Vict., cap. 119, sect. 22.

45. Except those peculiar to the London & South Western, Brighton, and South Eastern Railways.

46. See VRY, 97.

47. See D. Brooke, 'The Advent of the Steel Rail, 1857–1914': JTH 7 (3rd series, 1986–7), 18–31.

48. For examples see E.L. Ahrons, *The British Steam Railway Locomotive* [1927], 165–6.

49. Acc. Midland Railway, Hendon, 29 August 1879: PP 1880, lxiii. 205.

50. MacDermot, ii. 266.

51. R.L. Hills and D. Patrick, *Beyer Peacock* (1982), 80.

52. See accs. Great Eastern Railway, Manor Park, 7 January 1886 (PP 1886, lviii. 259); Midland Railway, Leeds, 18 December 1888 (PP 1889, lxvii. 109).

53. MacDermot, ii. 261–2. Its success in service led to the launching of a Railway Audible Signal Co. Ltd. in 1908 (prospectus in R1075/89, no. 60).

54. Acc. London & South Western Railway, Eastleigh, 29 July 1889: PP 1890, lxv. 155–6.

55. Notably by Hewitson, who in his *Locomotive Boiler Explosions* comes near to writing down the inspectors as ignoramuses in everything to do with the design, construction, and working of

locomotive boilers. His comments are sometimes justifiable, but they are consistently ungenerous, and some of them are unhistorical, in failing to appreciate the general state of knowledge at the times when the reports were being written. From 1899 onwards a specialist in steam boilers at the Marine Department of the Board of Trade sat with the railway inspector in each inquiry into a locomotive boiler explosion (Hewitson, 105).

56. Acc. Cork & Bandon Railway, Bandon, 16 January 1873: PP 1873, lvii. 515–6; special report by Rich, PP 1874, lviii. 41.

57. Accs. Metropolitan District Railway, Mansion House, 1 March 1873 (PP 1873, lvii. 553); Midland Railway, Kilnhurst, 24 August 1875 (PP 1875, lxvi. 525–6); Severn & Wye Railway, Severn Bridge, 16 March 1882 (PP 1882, lx. 450–3).

58. Acc. London & North Western Railway, Birmingham, 20 Oct 1873: PP 1874, lviii. 229.

59. Acc. London & North Western Railway, Wigan, 2 August 1873: *ibid.*, 789.

60. Acc. North Staffordshire Railway, Lawton Junction, 26 September 1873: *ibid.*, 615–17.

61. See Mitchell and Deane, *British Historical Statistics*, 225–8.

62. Accs. Great Western Railway, Bristol, 20 September, 29 October 1873: PP 1874, lviii. 453–7.

63. Acc. Lancashire & Yorkshire Railway, Bolton, 19 December 1873: *ibid.*, 480–5.

64. See J. Marshall, *Lancashire & Yorkshire Railway* (1969–72), i. 118–19, 194–7; ii. 100–1.

65. Acc. London & North Western Railway, Grotton, 4 February 1873: PP 1873, lvii. 526.

66. Acc. Glasgow & South Western Railway, Irvine, 28 February 1873: *ibid.*, 540.

67. Acc. Manchester Sheffield & Lincolnshire Railway, Wortley, 20 September 1873: PP 1874, lviii. 531.

68. See for example acc. North British Railway, Maryhill, 4 October 1873: *ibid.*, 819.

69. Acc. Metropolitan Railway, Moorgate Street, 31 May 1873: PP 1873, lvii. 608. Moorgate Street was a 'terminal station' until 1875, when the Metropolitan line was extended eastwards to Liverpool Street.

70. Another inspector paid a similar tribute to the record of safety at Liverpool Street station in 1889 (acc. Great Eastern Railway, Liverpool Street, 9 August 1889: PP 1890, lxv. 68).

71. Acc. North Eastern Railway, Filey, 24 November 1869: PP 1870, lix. 206.

72. Accs. Midland Great Western Railway, Ballyhaunis, 11 June 1880 and 14 June 1889: PP 1881, lxxx. 225; 1890, lxv. 192.

73. Acc. Carlisle Joint Station, 5 July 1878: PP 1878–9, lxii. 72.

74. Acc. London & South Western Railway, Bishopstoke, 29 July 1879: PP 1880, lxiii. 162.

75. Acc. Swansea & Carmarthen Railway, Pontardulais, 29 August 1872; PP 1873, lvii. 507*.

76. Acc. Midland Railway, Heeley, 22 November 1876: PP 1877, lxxii. 163.

77. Acc. Midland Railway, Kirkstall Forge, 6 November 1879: PP 1880, lxiii. 209.

78. Acc. Neath & Brecon Railway, March Howel Colliery, 24 April 1868: PP 1867–8, lxii. 215.

79. Acc. Caledonian Railway, Floriston, 19 February 1889: PP 1889, lxvii. 206.

80. Acc. London & North Western Railway, Stafford, 6 December 1879: PP 1880, lxiii. 139.

81. Acc. Mid-Wales Railway, Three Cocks, 28 September 1877: PP (H.L.) 1878, xii. 793–8.

82. Acc. Carnarvonshire Railway, Brynkir, 4 October 1866: PP 1867, lxii. 160–1.

83. Acc. London & North Western Railway, Chwilog, 1 April 1872: PP 1872, lii. 406–7.

84. Acc. Great Western Railway, Henley, 20 June 1866: PP 1867, lxii. 168.

85. Acc. Manchester Sheffield & Lincolnshire Railway, Hexthorpe, 16 September 1887: PP 1888, lxxxviii. 156–75.

86. Acc. Cockermouth Keswick & Penrith Railway, Penruddock, 2 September 1870: PP 1871, lx. 188.

87. See VRY, 279–82.

88. See for instance acc. Great Western Railway, Briton Ferry Road, 7 April 1871: PP 1871, lx. 352–3.

89. See poster reproduced in *Reg. Hist.*, iv. 81.

90. Acc. Lancashire & Yorkshire Railway, Helmshore, 4 September 1860: PP 1861, lviii. 66.

91. Acc. Great Northern Railway, Littleworth, 28 January 1872: PP 1872, lii. 361. A similar comment, applied to the same company by the same inspector (Yolland), was made in the report on the accident at Sykes Junction, 26 September 1873: PP 1874, lviii. 455.

92. Acc. London & North Western Railway, Coventry, 18 October 1872: PP 1873, lvii. 420.

93. Acc. London Chatham & Dover Railway, Borough Road, 9 March 1874: PP 1874, lviii. 699.

94. Acc. Great Eastern Railway, Norwich (Thorpe), 10 September 1874: PP 1874, lxvii. 205.

95. Acc. Caledonian Railway, McAndrew's Siding, 30 September 1873: PP 1874, lviii. 814.

96. Acc. Great Western Railway, Reading, 16 September 1855: PP 1856, liv. 427.

97. Acc. Great Northern Railway, Arlesey, 23 December 1876: PP 1877, lxxii. 191.

98. Yolland, for example, acc. London & North Western Railway, Walton junction, 29 June 1867 (PP 1867, lxii. 245); Hutchinson, acc. Lancashire & Yorkshire Railway, Halifax, 5 September 1876 (PP 1877, lxxii. 85); Marindin, acc. Glasgow & Paisley Joint Railway, Penilee, 8 September 1880 (PP 1881, lxxx. 93).

INDEX